3rd Workshop on Natural Language Processing Techniques for Educational Applications (NLPTEA 2016)

Osaka, Japan
12 December 2016

ISBN: 978-1-5108-3329-6

Printed by Curran Associates, Inc. (2016)

For permission requests, please contact the Association for Computational Linguistics
at the address below.

Association for Computational Linguistics
209 N. Eighth Street
Stroudsburg, Pennsylvania 18360

Phone: 1-570-476-8006
Fax: 1-570-476-0860

acl@aclweb.org

Additional copies of this publication are available from:

Curran Associates, Inc.
57 Morehouse Lane
Red Hook, NY 12571 USA
Phone: 845-758-0400
Fax: 845-758-2633
Email: curran@proceedings.com
Web: www.proceedings.com

Preface

Welcome to the 3rd Workshop on Natural Language Processing Techniques for Educational Applications (NLPTEA 2016), with a Shared Task on Chinese Grammatical Error Diagnosis (CGED).

The development of Natural Language Processing (NLP) has advanced to a level that affects the research landscape of many academic domains and has practical applications in many industrial sectors. On the other hand, educational environment has also been improved to impact the world society, such as the emergence of MOOCs (Massive Open Online Courses). With these trends, this workshop focuses on the NLP techniques applied to the educational environment. Research issues in this direction have gained more and more attention, examples including the activities like the workshops on Innovative Use of NLP for Building Educational Applications since 2005 and educational data mining conferences since 2008.

This is the third workshop held in the Asian area, with the first one NLPTEA 2014 workshop being held in conjunction with the 22nd International Conference on Computer in Education (ICCE 2014) from Nov. 30 to Dec. 4, 2014 in Japan. The second edition NLPTEA 2015 workshop was held in conjunction with the 53rd Annual Meeting of the Association for Computational Linguistics and the 7th International Joint Conference on Natural Language Processing (ACL-IJCNLP 2015) from July 26-31 in Beijing, China. This year, we continue to promote this research line by holding the workshop in conjunction with the COLING 2016 conference and also holding the third shared task on Chinese Grammatical Error Diagnosis. We receive 14 valid submissions for research issues, each of which was reviewed by three experts, and have 15 teams participating in the shared task, with 9 of them submitting their testing results. In total, there are 10 oral papers and 10 posters accepted. We also organize a keynote speech in this workshop. The invited speaker Professor Glenn Stockwell is expected to deliver a great talk entitled as "Technology and the Changing Face of Language Education".

We would like to thank the program committee members for their hard work in completing the review tasks. Their collective efforts achieved quality reviews of the submissions within a few weeks. Great thanks should also go to the speaker, authors, and participants for the tremendous supports in making the workshop a success.

Welcome you to the Osaka city, and wish you enjoy the city as well as the workshop.

Workshop Chairs
Hsin-Hsi Chen, National Taiwan University
Yuen-Hsien Tseng, National Taiwan Normal University
Vincent Ng, The University of Texas at Dallas
Xiaofei Lu, The Pennsylvania State University

Organization

Workshop Organizers

Hsin-Hsi Chen, National Taiwan University

Yuen-Hsien Tseng, National Taiwan Normal University

Vincent Ng, The University of Texas at Dallas

Xiaofei Lu, The Pennsylvania State University

Shared Task Organizers

Lung-Hao Lee, National Taiwan Normal University

Gaoqi Rao, Beijing Language and Culture University

Liang-Chih Yu, Yuan Ze University

Endong Xun, Beijing Language and Culture University

Baolin Zhang, Beijing Language and Culture University

Li-Ping Chang, National Taiwan Normal University

Program Committee

Yuki Arase, Osaka University

Rafael E. Banchs, Institute of Infocomm Research

Chris Brockett, Microsoft Research

Tao Chen, National University of Singapore

Barbara Di Eugenio, University of Illinois at Chicago

Vidas Daudaravicius, VTex Solutions for Science Publishing

Mariano Felice, Cambridge University

Cyril Goutte, National Research Council Canada

Na-Rae Han, University of Pittsburgh

Trude Heift, Simon Fraser University

Mamoru Komachi, Tokyo Metropolitan University

John Lee, City University of Hong Kong

Chen Li, Microsoft

Chuan-Jie Lin, National Taiwan Ocean University

Shervin Malmasi, Harvard University

Tomoya Mizumoto, Tohoku University

Courtney Napoles, John Hopkins University

Arti Ramesh, University of Maryland

Alla Rozovskaya, Virginia Tech

Mathias Schulze, University of Waterloo

Yukio Tono, Tokyo University of Foreign Studies

Table of Contents

Workshop Program

December 12, 2016

09:00–09:10   **Opening Ceremony**

09:10–10:00   **Keynote Speech**

10:00–10:30   **Coffee Break**

10:30–12:00   **Regular Paper Session**

10:30–10:45   *Simplification of Example Sentences for Learners of Japanese Functional Expressions*
Jun Liu and Yuji Matsumoto

10:45–11:00   *Effectiveness of Linguistic and Learner Features to Listenability Measurement Using a Decision Tree Classifier*
Katsunori Kotani and Takehiko Yoshimi

11:00–11:20   *A Two-Phase Approach Towards Identifying Argument Structure in Natural Language*
Arkanath Pathak, Pawan Goyal and Plaban Bhowmick

11:20–11:40   *Distributed Vector Representations for Unsupervised Automatic Short Answer Grading*
Oliver Adams, Shourya Roy and Raghuram Krishnapuram

11:40–12:00   *A Comparison of Word Embeddings for English and Cross-Lingual Chinese Word Sense Disambiguation*
Hong Jin Kang, Tao Chen, Muthu Kumar Chandrasekaran and Min-Yen Kan

December 12, 2016 (continued)

12:00–14:00   Luch

14:00–15:15   **Shared Task Session**

14:00–14:15   *Overview of NLP-TEA 2016 Shared Task for Chinese Grammatical Error Diagnosis*
Lung-Hao Lee, Gaoqi RAO, Liang-Chih Yu, Endong XUN, Baolin Zhang and Li-Ping Chang

14:15–14:30   *Chinese Grammatical Error Diagnosis with Long Short-Term Memory Networks*
Bo Zheng, Wanxiang Che, Jiang Guo and Ting Liu

14:30–14:45   *Automatic Grammatical Error Detection for Chinese based on Conditional Random Field*
Yajun Liu, Yingjie Han, Liyan Zhuo and Hongying Zan

14:45–15:00   *CYUT-III System at Chinese Grammatical Error Diagnosis Task*
CHEN PO-LIN, Shih-Hung Wu, Liang-Pu Chen and ping-che yang

15:00–15:15   *Word Order Sensitive Embedding Features/Conditional Random Field-based Chinese Grammatical Error Detection*
Wei-Chieh Chou, Chin-Kui Lin, Yuan-Fu Liao and Yih-Ru Wang

15:15–15:50   **Coffee Break**

15:50–16:50   **Poster Session**

A Fluctuation Smoothing Approach for Unsupervised Automatic Short Answer Grading
Shourya Roy, Sandipan Dandapat and Y. Narahari

Japanese Lexical Simplification for Non-Native Speakers
Muhaimin Hading, Yuji Matsumoto and Maki Sakamoto

A Corpus-based Approach for Spanish-Chinese Language Learning
Shuyuan Cao, Iria da Cunha and Mikel Iruskieta

Syntactic Well-Formedness Diagnosis and Error-Based Coaching in Computer Assisted Language Learning using Machine Translation
Luís Morgado da Costa, Francis Bond and Xiaoling He

An Aligned French-Chinese corpus of 10K segments from university educational material
Ruslan Kalitvianski, Lingxiao Wang, Valérie Bellynck and Christian Boitet

Analysis of Foreign Language Teaching Methods: An Automatic Readability Approach
Nasser Zalmout, Hind Saddiki and Nizar Habash

Generating and Scoring Correction Candidates in Chinese Grammatical Error Diagnosis
Shao-Heng Chen, Yu-Lin Tsai and Chuan-Jie Lin

Grammatical Error Detection Based on Machine Learning for Mandarin as Second Language Learning
Jui-Feng Yeh, Tsung-Wei Hsu and Chan-Kun Yeh

Bi-LSTM Neural Networks for Chinese Grammatical Error Diagnosis
Shen Huang and Houfeng WANG

Chinese Grammatical Error Diagnosis Using Single Word Embedding
Jinnan Yang, Bo Peng, Jin Wang, Jixian Zhang and Xuejie Zhang

16:50–17:00　Closing Remarks

Simplification of Example Sentences for Learners of Japanese Functional Expressions

Jun Liu
Nara Institute of Science and Technology
8916-5 Takayama, Ikoma, Nara, Japan
`liu.jun.lc3@is.naist.jp`

Yuji Matsumoto
Nara Institute of Science and Technology
8916-5 Takayama, Ikoma, Nara, Japan
`matsu@is.naist.jp`

Abstract

Learning functional expressions is one of the difficulties for language learners, since functional expressions tend to have multiple meanings and complicated usages in various situations. In this paper, we report an experiment of simplifying example sentences of Japanese functional expressions especially for Chinese-speaking learners. For this purpose, we developed "Japanese Functional Expressions List" and "Simple Japanese Replacement List". To evaluate the method, we conduct a small-scale experiment with Chinese-speaking learners on the effectiveness of the simplified example sentences. The experimental results indicate that the simplified sentences are helpful in learning Japanese functional expressions.

1 Introduction

In Japanese grammar, there is a large number of functional expressions consisting of one or more words and behave like a single functional word, such as "たい (want to)、に対して(to)、なければ ならない (must)". Matsuyoshi et al. (2006) developed a Japanese functional expression lexicon consisting of 292 headwords and 13,958 different surface forms. It is crucial to develop a Japanese learning assistant system which supports Japanese language learners to learn such a large number of complicated functional expressions.

Recently, with the help of natural language processing technology, many Japanese learning assistant systems have been constructed. For example, Pereira and Matsumoto (2015) presents a Collocation Assistant for Japanese language learners, which flags possible collocation errors and suggests corrections with example sentences. Han and Song (2011), and Ohno et al. (2013) attempt to develop Japanese learning systems for learning and using Japanese sentence patterns with the use of illustrative examples extracted from the Web.

As mentioned above, some studies have paid attention to assist learners to learn Japanese functional expressions. However, none of the existing studies has aimed at simplifying difficult example sentences for the need of Chinese-speaking learners of Japanese language. In this paper, we describe our proposed method in Section 2. Section 3 explains the result and evaluation of a small-scale experiment for examining the effectiveness of the proposed method. Finally, we conclude in Section 4.

2 Proposed Method

In this section, we propose a method to simplify difficult Japanese sentences that contain Japanese functional expressions for Chinese-speaking learners of Japanese language.

2.1 Making Japanese Functional Expressions List

In order to identify Japanese functional expressions, Tsuchiya et al. (2006) developed an example

Proceedings of the 3rd Workshop on Natural Language Processing Techniques for Educational Applications,
pages 1–5, Osaka, Japan, December 12 2016.

database with 337 types of Japanese compound functional expressions. Shime et al. (2007) proposed an approach to detecting 59 types of Japanese functional expressions through a machine learning technique based on a chunking program. However, the major drawback of these studies is in the scale of Japanese functional expressions, which does not reach the need of the five levels (from N1 to N5) of the new Japanese-Language Proficiency Test (JLPT).

According to the requirements of the new JLPT, we manually constructed a list of Japanese functional expressions, which consists of about 680 headwords and 4,000 types of different surface forms. Here, we consider levels 3-5 as easy level, and levels 1-2 as difficult level, respectively. Table 1 shows some examples of Japanese functional expressions and their surface form variations.

Headword	Difficulty Level	Surface Forms
たあとで(after)	N5	たあとで、た後で、だあとで、だ後で
かもしれない(maybe)	N4	かもしれない、かもしれません、かもしれず...
にたいして(to)	N3	にたいして、に対して、にたいしては、に対しては...
ざるをえない(have to)	N2	ざるをえない、ざるを得ない、ざるをえず、ざるを得ず...
やいなや(as soon as)	N1	やいなや、や否や

Table 1: Examples of Japanese functional expressions and surface form variations

2.2 Creating Simple Japanese Replacement List

Text simplification, defined narrowly, is the process of reducing the linguistic complexity of a text, while retaining the original information contents and meaning (Siddharthan, 2014). Watananabe and Kawamura (2013) introduced a Japanese simplification system with the use of a "Simple Japanese Replacement List". Kaneniwa and Kawamura (2013) used the same list to rewrite difficult vocabulary automatically for Japanese learners who have non-kanji backgrounds. Kajiwara and Yamamoto (2015), constructed an evaluation dataset for Japanese lexical simplification. They extracted 2330 sentences from a newswire corpus and simplified only one difficult word using several Japanese lexical paraphrasing databases. Kodaira et al. (2016) built a controlled and balanced dataset for Japanese lexical simplification. They extracted 2010 sentences with only one difficult word in each sentence from a balanced corpus and collected simplification candidates using crowdsourcing techniques.

Different from the previous research mentioned above, we used a large scale Japanese balanced corpus to extract simplification candidates for difficult words and through manual selection we constructed a "Simple Japanese Replacement List" for Chinese-speaking Japanese language learners. For the levels of word difficulty, we consider levels 3-5 of the new JLPT as easy level, and levels 1-2 as difficult level according to the vocabulary list of the new JLPT, which consists of about 16,000 words. Besides, we consider the words which are not included in the vocabulary list of the new JLPT as difficult words. Since a large number of Kanji characters are used both in Japanese and in Chinese, Chinese-speaking learners can easily understand the Japanese words of Chinese origin (Japanese-Chinese homographs), such as "安全(safety)", "学習(study)", "擁立(support)", or easily guess the meaning of many Japanese original words with the help of Kanji characters, such as "壊す(break)", "打つ(hit)", "取り消す(cancel)". Kanji characters in these Japanese words are also included in Chinese dictionary and have the same or similar meaning with Chinese words. Therefore, we consider these words as easy words for Chinese-speaking learners, although some of these words are difficult words in the vocabulary list of the new JLPT.

We obtain a list of similar words associated with each difficult word which we are going to use for replacement, using Word2vec (https://code.google.com/p/word2vec/). As the training data for the Word2vec model, we use the Balanced Corpus of Contemporary Written Japanese (Maekawa, 2008), which consists of about 5,800,000 sentences in various domains. Based on the list of similar words, we choose easy words which are included in the vocabulary list of new JLPT as simplified words. If there is no appropriate easy word in the vocabulary list of the new JLPT, we use Japanese-Chinese homographs whose meaning is the same, or similar to Chinese words based on Japanese dictionaries (Bunrui goihyo zouhokaiteiban, 2004; Kadokawa ruigo shin jiten, 2002; Kojien 5th Editon, 1998). Japanese-Chinese homographs for simplification are specific for Chinese-natives. Therefore, our "Simple Japanese Replacement List" differs from previous research mentioned above on this aspect.

For simplification of Japanese functional expressions, we rewrite some difficult Japanese functional expressions using easy Japanese functional expressions or easy words in the vocabulary list of the new JLPT based on a Japanese sentence pattern dictionary (Group Jamasi, Xu. 2001).

Original words	Difficulty Level	Part of speech	Simplified words	Difficulty Level
合鍵　(duplicate key)	N1	Noun	鍵　(key)	N5
負け戦　(defeat)	N0	Noun	敗戦　(defeat)	N0
出会う(meet)	N0	Verb	会う　(meet)	N5
胸苦しい　(tough)	N1	Adjective	苦しい　(tough)	N3
が早いか　(when)	N1	Functional Expression	と　(when)	N5
の際には　(when)	N2	Functional Expression	の時　(when)	N5/N5

Table 2: Examples of the Simple Japanese Replacement List

Finally, we created a "Simple Japanese Replacement List," which consists of words and functional expressions. Table 2 shows some examples in the list.

3   Experiment and Evaluation

Our aim is to obtain appropriate example sentences that ease understanding of Japanese functional expressions. We conducted a small-scale experiment for evaluating the method for generating simplified example sentences. For the source data, the Balanced Corpus of Contemporary Written Japanese was used. We removed too short or too long sentences by limiting the sentence length between 3 to 25 words and then used the remaining 4,232,120 sentences for the experimental data.

To identify occurrences of Japanese functional expressions in the extracted sentences, we used a publicly available morphological analyzer MeCab (taku910.github.io/mecab/). We add the two lists we created, "Japanese Functional Expressions List" and "Simple Japanese Replacement List", into the IPA (mecab-ipadic-2.7.0-20070801) dictionary used as the standard dictionary for MeCab, with appropriate part-of-speech information for each expression, hoping that the morphological analyzer MeCab extracts the usages of functional expressions automatically. The accuracy is evaluated in the next section. Table 3 shows some example sentences of Japanese functional expressions and their corresponding simplified sentences.

ID	Original sentences	Simplified sentences
1	そしてそこへ、どこからか小鳥がやって来て、その虫をついばみました。	そしてそこへ、どこからか小鳥が**来**て、その虫を**啄**みました。
2	したがって、いろいろな関係部門、団体等と調整しなければならないことは言うまでもない。	**だから**、**色々**な関係部門、団体等と調整しなければならないことは**言う必要がない**。
3	私はそれ以来、数々の失敗を経てつぎのような結論にたどり着きました。	私はそれ以来、**多く**の失敗を経て**次**のような結論に**到達**しました。
4	つめが伸びていると、皮膚を傷つけるおそれがあるので、気をつけてください。	**爪**が伸びていると、皮膚を傷つける**可能性がある**ので、気をつけてください。
5	その土の中から、冬眠を破られた小さな虫が顔をのぞかせました。	その土の中から、冬眠を破られた小さな虫が顔を**見**せました。

Table 3: Examples of original sentences and simplified sentences. The words with underline are functional expressions and the words in bold are simplified words.

3.1 Evaluation of Japanese functional expressions

In this section, we randomly extract 200 sentences from the experimental data to examine whether the identified Japanese functional expressions are correct or not. Table 4 gives the evaluation results of identification of Japanese functional expressions.

Correct rate	Correctly extracted sentences	171 (85.5%)	
Error rate	Incorrectly extracted sentences	10 (5%)	29 (14.5%)
	Japanese functional expressions are not recognized	19 (9.5%)	
Total		200 (100%)	

Table 4: Evaluation results of Japanese functional expression identification

According to Table 4, we obtained 85.5% accuracy for identifying Japanese functional expressions. Cases of failures of functional expression identification can be viewed from the following three causes. First, the lack of discriminative contextual information causes failure. For example, "をめぐる(with related to)" in "決算 を めぐる 政策評価 の 問題", is incorrectly recognized as a literal usage. Here, both literal usage and functional usage of this expression share almost the same contexts and cannot be distinguished only by the surrounding information used in MeCab. Second is the opposite case where a literal usage is recognized as a functional expression. For example, in "青少年 期 から 身 につけて しまう", "につけて(concerning)" was incorrectly extracted. Third, functional expressions are not included in the current "Japanese Functional Expressions List". For example, a colloquial expression "わけじゃない(it does not mean that)" was not recognized as a functional expression.

3.2 Evaluation of Simplified Sentences

In this section, we evaluate the simplified sentences from the following two aspects, fluency and readability. From the 200 example sentences that include functional expressions, we removed 36 sentences which are easy sentences since they include no difficult words. We do not need to simplify such sentences. We then used the remaining 164 sentences for evaluation.

For the evaluation of fluency, we invited three Japanese natives to check the simplified sentences whether they are natural Japanese sentences. Meanwhile, for readability of the simplified sentences, we invited three Chinese-speaking learners who are all beginners of Japanese language. To compare the readability, we provided them with the Chinese translation of the original sentences and simplified sentences using an online translation software "Google translation" (translate.google.cn). We asked them to read and judge which sentence is easier to understand. Tables 5 and 6 show the evaluation results of fluency and readability respectively.

Natural sentences	142 (86.6%)
Unnatural sentences	22 (13.4%)
Total	164 (100%)

Table 5: Evaluation results of fluency of the simplified sentences

Easy to understand	132 (80.5%)
Difficult to understand	32 (19.5%)
Total	164 (100%)

Table 6: Evaluation results of readability of the simplified sentences

According to the evaluation results in Table 6, 80.5% sentences are simplified appropriately and become easier to understand. Two cases are identified in simplification failure. One is lack of appropriate simplified rules. For example, "請求 しうる" contains a functional expression "うる (possible)" with the difficulty level 2. However, no corresponding simplified word for the functional expression "うる" is found in the current "Simple Japanese Replacement List". This case cannot be coped with by lexical simplification. The other is the usage of inappropriate words, which is the main reason for generation of unnatural simplified sentences. For example, "市内の青果物商を片っ端から尋ねて回った。" was rewritten as "市内の野菜と果物商を一つ一つから尋ねて回った。", which is an unnatural sentence that produces unnatural connections for words.

4 Conclusion

In this paper, we presented our attempt to produce simplified example sentences for learning Japanese functional expressions using "Japanese Functional Expressions List" and "Simple Japanese Replacement List". A small-scale experiment was conducted to verify the effectiveness of the proposed method. The experimental results showed that simplified example sentences are helpful in learning Japanese functional expressions. In the future, we plan to estimate the difficulty level of the extracted example sentences automatically and offer better example sentences for Chinese-speaking learners of Japanese language.

Reference

Dongli Han, and Xin Song. 2011. Japanese Sentence Pattern Learning with the Use of Illustrative Examples Extracted from the Web. *IEEJ Transactions on Electrical and Electronic Engineering*, 6(5):490-496.

Group Jamashi, and Yiping Xu. 2001. *Chubunban Nihongo Kukei Jiten-Nihongo Bunkei Jiten (in Chinese and Japanese)*. Tokyo:Kurosio Publishers.

Tomoyuki Kajiwara, Kazuhide Yamamoto. 2015. Evaluation Dataset and System for Japanese Lexical Simplification. In *Proceedings of the ACL-IJCNLP 2015 Student Research Workshop*, pages 35-40. Beijing, China.

Kumido Kaneniwa, and Yoshiko Kawamura. 2013. Improving the Japanese simplification system for JFL/JSL learners from non-kanji background. *Journal of Japanese language education methods(in Japanese)*, 21(2):10-11.

Tomonori Kodaira, Tomoyuki Kajiwara, Mamoru Komachi. 2016. Controlled and Balanced Dataset for Japanese Lexical Simplification. In *Proceedings of the 54th Annual Meeting of the Association for Computational Linguistics -Student ResearchWorkshop*, pages 1-7, Berlin, Germany.

Kikuo Maekawa. 2008. Balanced Corpus of Contemporary Written Japanese. In *Proceeding of The 6th Workshop on Asian language Resources*, pp.101-102, Stroudsburg, PA, USA.

Suguru Matsuyoshi, Satoshi Sato, and Takehito Utsuro. 2006. Compilation of a dictionary of Japanese functional expressions with hierarchical organization. In *Proc.ICCPOL*, LNAI: Vol.4285, Springer:395-402.

National Institute for Japanese Language and Linguistics. 2004. *Bunrui goihyo zouhokaiteiban (in Japanese)*. Tokyo:Dainihontosho.

Susumu Ohno and Masando Hamanishi. 2002. *Kadokawa ruigo shin jiten (in Japanese)*. Tokyo: Kadokawa shoten.

Takahiro Ohno, Zyunitiro Edani, Ayato Inoue, and Dongli Han. 2013. A Japanese Learning Support System Mathching Individual Abilities. In *Proceeding of the PACLIC 27 Workshop on Computer-Assisted Language Learning*, pages 556- 562.

Lis Pereira and Yuji Matsumoto. 2006. Collocational Aid for Learners of Japanese as a Second Language. In *Proceeding of the 2nd Workshop on Natural Language Processing Techniques for Educational Applications (NLP-TEA-2)*, pages 20-25, Beijing, China.

Takao Shime, Masatoshi Tsuchiya, Suguru Matsuyoshi, Takehito Utsuro and Satoshi Sato. 2007. Automatic Detection of Japanese Compound Functional Expressions and its Application to Statistical Dependency Analysis. *Journal of Natural Language Processing(in Japanese)*, 14(5):167-197.

Izuru Shinmura (Ed. In chief). 1998. *Kojien 5th Editon (in Japanese)*. Tokyo:Iwanani Press.

Advaith Siddharthan. 2014. A survey of research on text simplification. *International Journal of Applied Linguistics*165:2:259-298.

Masatoshi Tsuchiya, Takehito Utsuro, Suguru Matsuyoshi, Satoshi Sato, and Seiichi Nakagawa. 2006. Development and Analysis of An Example Database of Japanese Compound Functional Expressions. *Journal of Information Processing Society of Japan(in Japanese)*, 47(6):1728-1741.

Hyuma Watanabe, and Yoshiko Kawamura. 2013. Basic architecture for a Japanese simplification system. *Journal of Japanese language education methods(in Japanese)*, 20(2):48-49.

Effectiveness of Linguistic and Learner Features to Listenability Measurement Using a Decision Tree Classifier

Katsunori Kotani
Kansai Gaidai University
Hirakata, Osaka, Japan
kkotani@kansaigaidai.ac.jp

Takehiko Yoshimi
Ryukoku University
Otsu, Shiga, Japan
yoshimi@rins.ryukoku.ac.jp

Abstract

In learning Asian languages, learners encounter the problem of character types that are different from those in their first language, for instance, between Chinese characters and the Latin alphabet. This problem also affects listening because learners reconstruct letters from speech sounds. Hence, special attention should be paid to listening practice for learners of Asian languages. However, to our knowledge, few studies have evaluated the ease of listening comprehension (listenability) in Asian languages. Therefore, as a pilot study of listenability in Asian languages, we developed a measurement method for learners of English in order to examine the discriminability of linguistic and learner features. The results showed that the accuracy of our method outperformed a simple majority vote, which suggests that a combination of linguistic and learner features should be used to measure listenability in Asian languages as well as in English.

1   Introduction

An important task of language teachers is to choose reading/listening materials appropriate for the proficiency of their learners so as to prevent decreases in learning motivation. However, this task can be a heavy burden for language teachers when they introduce computer-assisted language learning/teaching (CALL/T) techniques. Although CALL/T allows language teachers to use different reading/listening materials for each learner, it also increases the number of materials that they must evaluate for appropriateness. To address this issue, alternative methods that automatically measure the ease of reading comprehension (readability) have been developed.

However, although the majority of previous studies have addressed the measurement of readability: Japanese by Sato et al. (2008); Chinese by Sung et al. (2015), among others, they have not addressed the ease of listening comprehension (henceforth, listenability). Several studies have examined listenability for English learners (Kiyokawa 1990; Kotani et al. 2014; Kotani & Yoshimi 2016; Yoon et al. 2016); however, to the best of our knowledge, no previous studies on listenability for learners of Asian languages such as Chinese, Korean, and Japanese have been conducted.

The method of Kiyokawa (1990) measured listenability based on the length of sentences and the difficulty of words. It was hypothesized that the listenability of a sentence decreases as it becomes longer and contains more advanced vocabulary words. Kotani et al. (2014) suggested the possibility of using different linguistic elements such as phonological features, and addressed this question by measuring listenability based on various linguistic features, including speech rate and the frequency of phonological modification patterns such as linking. In addition, their method used listening test scores as a learner feature to measure listenability relative to proficiency. This is because sentences with less listenability for learners at the beginner level might be easy for those at the advanced level. However, because that study focused on the accuracy of measurement, the question of discriminability of

Proceedings of the 3rd Workshop on Natural Language Processing Techniques for Educational Applications,
pages 6–10, Osaka, Japan, December 12 2016.

linguistic and learner features for the measurement of listenability remained. The discriminability of linguistic features was examined by Yoon et al. (2016), who used multiple regression analysis to measure listenability; however, they did not examine the discriminability of learner features. Hence, the discriminability of both linguistic and learner features still has yet to be examined.

Given this background, the purpose of this study was to attempt to answer the following two research questions by measuring listenability on the basis of linguistic and learner features:

(1) How accurately can listenability be measured using linguistic and learner features?
(2) Which of linguistic and learner features are discriminative for the measurement of listenability?

To answer these questions, in this study, we developed a listenability measurement method using a decision tree classification algorithm (Quinlan 1992) that classifies sentences into five levels of listenability in order to determine the accuracy of listenability measurement and the discriminability of linguistic and learner features to this classification. Although the linguistic and learner features examined were effective for listenability measurement in English, they were not English-specific, which suggests that they may also be useful for the measurement of listenability in Asian languages.

2   Linguistic and Learner Features

Listenability is measured based on linguistic and learner features. Linguistic features explain the difficulty of a sentence, and learner features explain the proficiency of a learner. The linguistic (Chall 1948; Fang 1966; Kiyokawa 1990; Messerklinger 2006; Kotani et al. 2014; Kotani & Yoshimi 2016; Yoon et al. 2016), and learner features (Kotani et al. 2014; Kotani & Yoshimi 2016) used in this study were originally described elsewhere.

Linguistic features consist of sentence length, mean word length, multiple syllable words, word difficulty, speech rate, and phonological modification patterns. Sentence length is calculated based on the number of words in a sentence. Mean word length is derived from the mean number of syllables per word. Multiple syllable words refer to the number of multiple syllable words in a sentence. Word difficulty is derived from the rate of words absent from Kiyokawa's basic vocabulary list for words in a sentence. Speech rate is calculated in terms of spoken words per minute. Phonological modification patterns are derived from the rate of phonologically modified words in a sentence. The types of phonological modification patterns are: elision (elimination of phonemes), in which vowel sounds immediately follow a stressed syllable, such as the second "o" sound in "chocolate"; reduction (weakening a sound by changing a vowel to a schwa), such as vowel sounds in personal/interrogative pronouns, auxiliaries, modals, prepositions, articles, and conjunctions; contraction (combining word pairs), such as a modal with a subject noun; linkage (connecting final and initial word sounds), such as connected a word ending with an "n" or "r" sound with a word starting with a vowel sound, for example, "in an hour" and "after all"; and deduction (elimination of sounds between words), in which words share the same sound, for example, "good day".

Learner features consist of listening test scores, learning experience, visiting experience, and listening frequency. Listening test score refers to scores on the Test of English for International Communication (TOEIC). Learning experience refers to the number of months for which learners have been studying English. Visiting experience refers to the number of months learners have spent in English-speaking countries. Listening frequency refers to scores on a five-point Likert scale for the frequency of English use (1: infrequently, 2: somewhat infrequently, 3: moderate, 4: somewhat frequently, and 5: frequently).

3   Training/Test Data

Training/test data for a decision tree classification algorithm were constructed using the learner corpus of Kotani et al. (2014), which includes learners' judgment of listenability. Listenability was judged by learners of English as a foreign language using scores on a five-point Likert scale (1: easy, 2: somewhat easy, 3: average, 4: somewhat difficult, or 5: difficult). Scores were judged on a sentence-by-sentence basis where each learner listened to and assigned scores for 80 sentences from four news clips selected from the editorial and special sections for English learners on the Voice of America (VOA) website (http://www.voanews.com). News clips in the special section were intended for learners, while news clips in the editorial section were intended for native speakers of English. The news clips in the special section consisted of short, simple sentences using the VOA's basic vocabulary of 1,500 words; idiomatic expressions were avoided. By contrast, the news clips in the editorial section were made without any restrictions on vocabulary and sentence construction, as long as they were appropriate as news clips for native speakers of English. The speech rate of the news clips in the special section were two-thirds slower than those in the editorial section, which were read aloud at a natural speech rate of approximately 250 syllables per minute (Robb & Gillon 2007).

The learners were 90 university students (48 males, 42 females; mean age ± SD, 21.5 ± 2.6 years) who were compensated for their participation. All learners were asked to submit valid scores from TOEIC tests taken in the current or previous year. The mean TOEIC listening score was 334.78 ± 98.14. The minimum sore was 130 (n = 1), and the maximum score was 495 (n = 8).

Although the training/test data should have consisted of 7,200 instances (90 learners × 80 sentences) for valid listenability measurement, only 6,804 instances were actually observed. Assuming that the missing 396 instances resulted from listening difficulties, these instances were scored as having the lowest listenability. Most instances (25.2%) were scored in the middle range (3) of listenability, and the fewest instances (15.8%) were scored in the high range (2). Listenability scores of 1, 4, and 5 were given by 21.7%, 20.8%, and 16.5% of the learners, respectively.

Table 1 shows the means and SDs of the linguistic and learner features in the training/test data.

Table 1. Descriptive statistics of linguistic (n = 80) and learner features (n = 90)

Type	Feature		Mean	SD
Linguistic	Sentence length		17.6 (words)	7.5
	Mean word length		1.7 (syllables)	0.3
	Multiple syllables		11.2 (words)	7.0
	Difficult words		0.4 (words)	0.1
	Speech rate		199.3 (words per minute)	49.2
	Phonological modification pattern	Elision	0.0 (points)	0.1
		Reduction	0.2 (points)	0.2
		Contraction	0.1 (points)	0.1
		Linking	0.0 (points)	0.0
		Deduction	0.4 (points)	0.2
Learner	Listening test score		334.8 (points)	97.6
	Learning experience		123.2 (months)	36.6
	Visiting experience		11.3 (months)	25.8
	Listening frequency		2.1 (score)	1.1

4   Experiment

Listenability was measured on the basis of linguistic and learner features using a decision tree classification algorithm implemented on C4.5 software (Quinlan 1992). All settings were taken as defaults, and classification was evaluated using five-fold cross validation.

Table 2. Confusion matrix for the test data

Method's / Learner's	Listenability 1	Listenability 2	Listenability 3	Listenability 4	Listenability 5
Listenability 1	1116 (71.4%)	190	169	46	42
Listenability 2	299	293 (25.8%)	348	125	70
Listenability 3	188	307	740 (40.8%)	439	139
Listenability 4	72	161	463	574 (38.3%)	228
Listenability 5	78	59	146	247	661 (55.5%)

The results of the five-fold cross validation tests, as well as the confusion matrix for the test data, where the rows indicate the correct classification and the columns indicate the selected classes, are shown in Table 2. The accuracy of classification rate was 47.0% ((1116+293+740+574+661)/7200) in the test data. Although this might be insufficient for validating our listenability measurement method, we believe that the method can still be judged as valid through a comparison with the accuracy attained by a simple majority vote (25.2%) as a baseline.

We calculated the accuracy for each listenability score from 1 to 5, which is shown as bracketed numbers in Table 2. The accuracy varied from 25.8% (293/(299+293+348+125+70)) to 71.4% (1116/(1116+190+169+46+42)). As this examination was not conclusive, it remains for the future study to examine why the method showed the different accuracies in more detail.

Using the five-fold cross validation test, five decision trees (I–V) were generated. In four of the five decision trees, the same type of linguistic and learner features were allocated at the root nodes, the first-level child nodes (child nodes originating from the root nodes), and the second-level child nodes (child nodes originating from the first-level child nodes). Parts of the decision tree (I–IV) can be seen in Figure 1; the different roots (V) are shown in bold. Part V of the decision tree is shown in Figure 2.

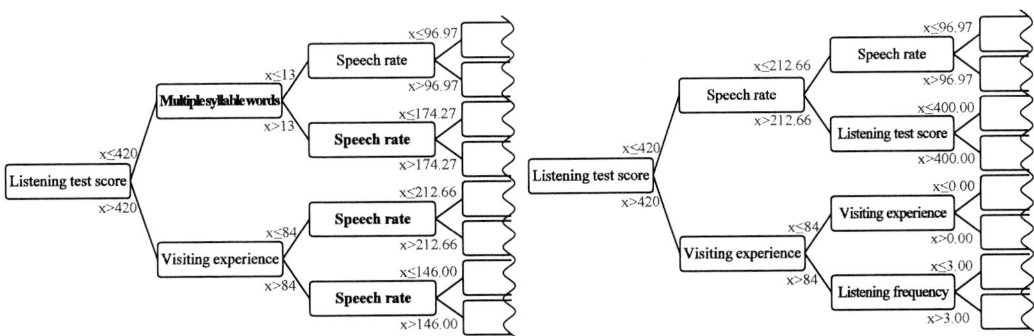

Fig. 1. Decision tree (I–IV)   **Fig. 2.** Decision tree (V)

As the listening test score was allocated at the root node of the five decision trees, this feature was regarded as the most discriminative. Visiting experience was allocated at the first-level child node of the decision trees, and was therefore judged as the second most discriminative feature. The third most discriminative feature was regarded as the speech rate, because it was allocated at either the first- or second-level child node in each tree.

5   Conclusion

In this study, we examined the measurement of listenability for learners of English as a foreign language. We found that learner features were discriminative for the measurement accuracy. This finding suggests that learner features should be taken into account when measuring listenability for learners of Asian languages.

Although the accuracy was not high, our method outperformed a simple majority vote. In the future, using this method as a baseline, we plan on developing a listenability measurement method for Asian languages that would outperform that for English.

Acknowledgements

This work was supported by JSPS KAKENHI Grant Numbers, 22300299, 15H02940.

Reference

Chall, J. S. & Dial, H. E. 1948. Listener Understanding and Interest in Newscasts. *Educational Research Bulletin*, 27(6): 141–153+168.

Fang, I.E. 1966. The Easy Listening Formula. *Journal of Broadcasting & Electronic Media*, 11(1): 63–68.

Kiyokawa, H. 1990. A Formula for Predicting Listenability: the Listenability of English Language Materials 2. *Wayo Women's University Language and Literature*, 24: 57–74.

Kotani, K., Ueda, S., Yoshimi, T., & Nanjo, H. 2014. A Listenability Measuring Method for an Adaptive Computer-assisted Language Learning and Teaching System. *Proceedings of the 28th Pacific Asia Conference on Language, Information, and Computation*: 387–394.

Kotani, K. & Yoshimi, T. 2016 (in press). Learner Feature Variation in Measuring the Listenability for Learners of English as a Foreign Language. *Proceedings of the 1st International Workshop on Emerging Technologies for Language Learning (ETLL 2016)*.

Messerklinger, J. 2006. Listenability. *Center for English Language Education Journal*, 14: 56–70.

Quinlan, J. Ross. *C4.5: Programs for Machine Learning*. Morgan Kaufmann, 1992.

Robb, M. P. & Gillon, G. T. 2007. Speech Rates of New Zealand English- and American English-speaking Children. *Advances in Speech-Language Pathology*, 9(2): 1–8.

Sato, S., Matsuyoshi, S., & Kondoh, Y. 2008. Automatic Assessment of Japanese Text Readability Based on a Textbook Corpus. *Proceedings of the 6th International Conference on Language Resources and Evaluation (LREC 2008)*: 654-660.

Sung, Y. T., Chen, J. L., Cha, J. H., Tseng, H. C., Chang, T. H., & Chang, K. E. 2015. Constructing and Validating Readability Models: the Method of Integrating Multilevel Linguistic Features with Machine Learning. *Behavior Research Methods*, 47(2): 340-354.

Yoon, S-Y., Cho, Y., & Napolitano, D. 2016. Spoken Text Difficulty Estimation Using Linguistic Features. *Proceedings of the 11th Workshop on Innovative Use of NLP for Building Educational Applications*: 267–276.

A Two-Phase Approach Towards Identifying Argument Structure in Natural Language

Arkanath Pathak
Deptt. Computer Sc & Engg.
IIT Kharagpur

Pawan Goyal
Deptt. Computer Sc & Engg.
IIT Kharagpur

Plaban Bhowmick
Centre for Educational Tech.
IIT Kharagpur

`pathak.arkanath@gmail.com` `{pawang@cse, plaban@cet}.iitkgp.ernet.in`

Abstract

We propose a new approach for extracting argument structure from natural language texts that contain an underlying argument. Our approach comprises of two phases: Score Assignment and Structure Prediction. The Score Assignment phase trains models to classify relations between argument units (Support, Attack or Neutral). To that end, different training strategies have been explored. We identify different linguistic and lexical features for training the classifiers. Through ablation study, we observe that our novel use of word-embedding features is most effective for this task. The Structure Prediction phase makes use of the scores from the Score Assignment phase to arrive at the optimal structure. We perform experiments on three argumentation datasets, namely, AraucariaDB, Debatepedia and Wikipedia. We also propose two baselines and observe that the proposed approach outperforms baseline systems for the final task of Structure Prediction.

1 Introduction

The problem of argumentation mining concerns the identification of argument structures in a text. The argument structure is typically represented as a directed graph with textual propositions as nodes and both Support and Attack relations as edges between the propositions. In their influential work, Mochales and Moens (2011) have discussed this problem in detail together with the relevant definitions, frameworks, and terminologies. They define the argumentation structure as consisting of various "arguments", forming a tree structure, where each argument consists of a single conclusion and one or more premise(s). Another widely used framework is the Freeman theory of argumentation structures (Freeman, 1991; Freeman, 2011), which treats an argument as a set of proponent or opponent propositions for a central claim. In the present study, we follow the framework used in (Mochales and Moens, 2011).

The full task of argumentation mining can be divided into four subtasks (Mochales and Moens, 2011):

1. **Segmentation**: Splitting the text into propositions.

2. **Detection**: Identifying the argumentative propositions.

3. **Classification**: Classifying the argumentative propositions into pre-defined classes (e.g. premise or conclusion in the Mochales and Moens' framework and proponent or opponent in the case of Freeman's framework).

4. **Structure Prediction**: Building the structure by identifying the relations (the edges in the argumentative graph structure) between the propositions.

Our work jointly tackles the Classification and Structure Prediction subtasks using a unified approach. Little work has been done as far as Structure Prediction is concerned. We are familiar with only two approaches that can be compared to our work. Lawrence et al. (2014) proposed to form bidirectional edges between propositions in their work on 19th century philosophical texts. They used Euclidean

Proceedings of the 3rd Workshop on Natural Language Processing Techniques for Educational Applications,
pages 11–19, Osaka, Japan, December 12 2016.

distance metric between topic measures derived from a generated topic model for the text to be studied. They achieved a raw accuracy of 33% for linking the edges. However, they do not form directed edges between the argumentation units, which is essential in case of arguments. Peldszus and Stede (2015) jointly predict different aspects of the argument structure. Recent works Persing and Ng (2016; Stab and Gurevych (2016) identified argument relations in the student essays. Discourse features (positional features) have been used in these studies However, absence of these features in argument graph dataset like AraucariaDB (used in our study) makes the relation classification task challenging.

This paper makes the following contributions. i). We propose a data-driven approach for identifying argument structure in natural language text. ii). We present a detailed study over various linguistic, structural and semantic features properties involved in the argument relation classification task. iii). Finally, we propose a metric for evaluating performance of the structure prediction task.

2 Problem Formulation

We have used the AraucariaDB (Reed and Rowe, 2004) dataset[1] to discuss the problem at hand. This corpus consists of 661 argument structures, collected and analysed as a part of a project at the University of Dundee (UK). We found AraucariaDB to be one of the most suitable argumentation datasets, primarily because it is formed from natural language resources like newspapers and magazines. Fig. 1 shows an argument structure from AraucariaDB. The edges in the tree represent a Support relation. For instance, Node 271 and Node 272 are the children of Node 270. Therefore, $271 \rightarrow 270$ as well as $272 \rightarrow 270$ are Support relations. For a given Support relation $n_1 \rightarrow n_2$, we call the node n_1 as the *Text* node and n_2 as the *Hypothesis* node. Our goal can formally be defined as follows:

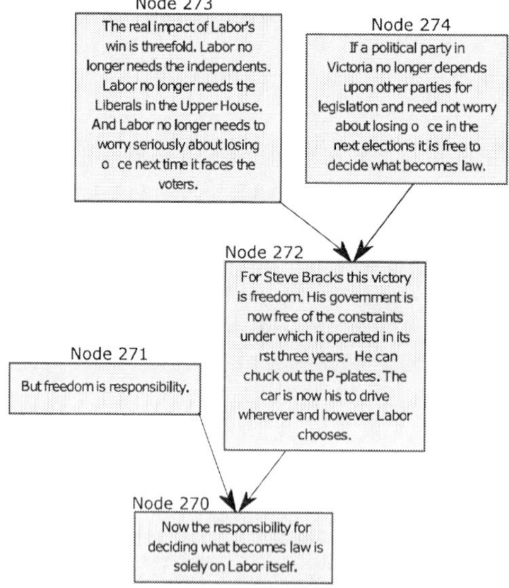

Figure 1: Sample argument (Argument No. 9) from the AraucariaDB.

For a given set of propositions, with an underlying argument structure connecting these propositions, identify the argument structure, that is structurally close to the corresponding gold standard argument.

A measure for structure similarity (which we call $SimScore$) is described in Section 5.2.

3 Proposed Approach

We model an argument structure as a graph, where each node represents a proposition. Given a set of nodes N for an argument, our approach can be divided into two subtasks:[2]

---

[1]The AraucariaDB dataset can be downloaded and visualized with the AIFdb (Lawrence et al., 2012) framework at http://www.arg.dundee.ac.uk/aif-corpora/araucaria.

[2]We assume only Support and Neutral relations between arguments, and the final structure to be a tree. In Section 6, we extend this model to include Attack relations as well as linear structures.

Score Assignment : Assign scores $s_{n_1,n_2} \in [0,1]$ for every pair of nodes $n_1, n_2 \in N$, $n_1 \neq n_2$,. These scores represent the degree of Support relation present in the hypothetical edge connecting n_1 and n_2.

Structure Prediction : Choose the tree T^* with the maximum sum of edge scores, i.e.,

$$T^* = \operatorname*{argmax}_T \sum_{(n_1,n_2) \in E(T)} s_{n_1,n_2}$$

where T can be any tree with the set of nodes N and $E(T)$ denotes the set of edges in T. We use the confidence measures provided by machine learning classifiers as the edge scores in Score Assignment. Specifically, we use binary classification with the classes being *Support* and *Neutral*. The classifier takes as input an ordered pair (n_1,n_2), where n_1 and n_2 are the text nodes.

For Stucture Prediction, our implementation essentially iterates over all possible tree structures (for the given set of nodes) recursively to choose the best tree. A call to the recursive function will already have the tree structure formed upto the last level. The function iterates on all possible sets of nodes (subset of the set of remaining nodes) for the next level. The parent of each node in the next level can be identified (from the last level) as the node which gives rise to the best attachment score. The complexity of our implementation is exponential in the number of nodes in the argument. Therefore, we limit the experiments usually to arguments with 10-15 nodes.

4 Classifier Features

In this section, we describe the set of features chosen for the Score Assignment subtask. The task of Score Assignment is similar to Recognizing Textual Entailment (RTE) or the detection of Natural Language Inference (NLI). However, the problem is still considerably different in the case of arguments since the types of arguments can be much more complex (Walton, 2007). To make this more evident, we have formed a baseline for our experiments (Section 5) where we use a state-of-the-art RTE tool instead for the Score Assignment subtask. We experimented with the features frequently used in NLI, RTE and similar tasks. MacCartney (2009) discusses the features used for the NLI task in detail. However, some of the frequently used features like POS n-grams, the length of propositions, POS of the main verb, etc., are not included in the set of features because they showed insignificant effect on the overall performance in our experiments. We suspect this is due to the fact that many attributes of these features are already captured in the features we have chosen.

Discourse Markers: These are the words that are indicative of argumentative discourse. Discourse markers have persistently been used for both RTE and NLI tasks. Eckle-Kohler et al. (2015) have also discussed the role of discourse markers in the context of argumentation mining. However, we observed that the presence of such words are rare in the AraucariaDB dataset. We have used i). counts of the following words in Text: *as, or, and, roughly, then, since,* and ii). counts of the following words in Hypothesis: *therefore, however, though, but, quite.* This feature set gives rise to 11 (6+5) features.

Modal Features: These are similar to discourse markers but they do not inherently belong to either one of Text or Hypothesis. Therefore, we take the counts of these as features for both Text as well as Hypothesis inputs. We have used the following as the modal words: *can, could, may, might, must, will, would, should.* Modal feature set, therefore, gives rise to 16 (8×2) features.

Longest Common Phrase: The number of words in the longest phrase present in both Text and Hypothesis is considered as a single feature.

Common Wikipedia Entities: In many cases, a specific argument usually revolves around some conceptual entities. For example, Argument 9 (Fig.1) involves the entities *Steve Bracks, Labor,* etc. We have used TAGME (Ferragina and Scaiella, 2010) to annotate a text with Wikipedia entities. After we have the annotations as a vector for both Text and Hypothesis, we take the inner product of the resulting vectors as a single feature.

Word N-grams: Word n-grams are used very frequently as features for NLP tasks. We have used the set of unigrams and bigrams filtered by relative likelihood of presence in Text or Hypothesis nodes in the training data. For instance, the n-grams with higher values of $\frac{p(ngram|Text)}{p(ngram|Hypothesis)}$ will be chosen from Text nodes. The filtering is performed using a constant threshold parameter of the likelihood. We have set the threshold parameter as 3 for all of our experiments. Since we have performed Cross Validation, the number of features for this category will be different for each fold. The mean count for unigrams was

115.4 and that for bigrams was 251.8. Hence, an average of 734.4 ($115.4 \times 2 + 251.8 \times 2$) n-gram features were used over the 5 folds.

Word Vector Embeddings: Word vectors capture a variety of helpful information in the context of natural language. We have directly used the 300-dimensional vectors trained on part of the Google News dataset (Mikolov et al., 2013)[3]. We have used the sum of word vectors over words present in Text node to form a feature vector. To generate another feature vector, a similar process is repeated for Hypothesis node. These vectors are concatenated to give rise to 600 features for an input pair. Using word vectors as features can help with various attributes inherent to Support edges. First, a simple similarity measure can be the difference of the two sum vectors, which can be well captured by using classifiers like linear SVM. Secondly, word vectors trained over an external dataset like Google News can provide the knowledge base for language not present in training set, which is very likely in case of argumentation mining since the arguments are expected to be unrelated. Lastly, since word vectors are based on contextual information, they can infer Support relation from similar contexts in training data.

5 Experiments

All of the experiments in this section are performed on the AraucariaDB arguments. The experiments are performed in a 5-fold cross-validation framework and the mean scores are reported. The folds are over the set of arguments rather than the pairs of text nodes in order to maintain contextual independence between the folds. A subset of AraucariaDB arguments have been used in the following experiments[4].

Measure	type-1 SVM	type-2 SVM	type-2 MLP
$confidence_S$	0.691	0.643	0.678
$confidence_N$	0.425	0.356	0.306
$recall_S$	0.759	0.677	0.677
$recall_N$	0.532	0.681	0.692
$precision_S$	0.193	0.68	0.688
$precision_N$	0.937	0.678	0.681
$accuracy$	0.561	0.679	0.684

Table 1: Classifier Performance: mean values are reported for Support (S) and Neutral (N) relations.

5.1 Classifier Performance (Score Assignment)

Support edges present in the input argument structures are directly taken as Support pair examples for the classifier. However, the generation of Neutral pairs is not so straightforward. To that end, we have experimented with two kinds of frameworks. Please note that the selection of training framework does not affect the ultimate goal of structure prediction. The framework used for training the classifiers is only limited to the Score Assignment phase.

The first framework, which we call the *type-1* framework, considers all the pairs (n_1,n_2) as Neutral such that n_1 and n_2 are text nodes belonging to the same argument and $n_1 \rightarrow n_2$ is not a Support relation. This, however, gives rise to a huge imbalance between the Support and Neutral examples. Many classifiers fail to perform well in such imbalance. Nonetheless, this issue can be resolved in classifiers like linear SVM, by assigning class weights inversely proportional to class frequencies (King and Zeng, 2001) in the input data. We have followed this framework for type-1 SVM. Another way to resolve the problem of imbalance is to down-sample the Neutral relations randomly. However, random sampling did not perform well in our experiments, and thus, we posit that a random subset might not be a good training sample.

To counter this, we devised the *type-2* framework which only considers those pairs (n_1,n_2) as Neutral for which $n_2 \rightarrow n_1$ is a Support relation. This gives a perfectly balanced input dataset with one Neutral example corresponding to each Support example. Thereby, making it suitable for machine learning classifiers. It is difficult to compare the information captured by the two frameworks. While type-1

---

[3]The pre-trained word vectors for Google News dataset are freely available at https://code.google.com/archive/p/word2vec/.

[4]Due to exponential order complexity of Structure Prediction algorithm, we have selected arguments of size 10 nodes or less. Furthermore, arguments involving relations other than Support are ignored.

might seem to capture more information than type-2, type-1 is also prone to more noise since the data is larger as compared to type-2.

A Multi-layer Perceptron (MLP) classifier using the type-2 framework performed better than type-1 and type-2 SVM implementations for arguments with 3 nodes in our experiments. The network is made up of 3 hidden layers with 200 neurons for each layer.

Table 1 summarizes the results for the three classifiers. We have shown 7 performance measures for each classifier. Specifically, we present the mean of the confidence values provided by the classifier for each class label, which is used directly in the Structure Prediction phase. We have scaled the confidence measure[5] linearly between 0 and 1 before using it as scores for Structure Prediction. A mean confidence of 1, therefore, will be the perfect score for Support pairs. Similarly, a mean confidence of 0 will be the perfect score for Neutral pairs. We can observe that each classifier outperforms the others for at least some metric. One can observe that type-2 classifiers perform better in predicting Neutral pairs. The confidence measure is lower than type-1 and the recall is higher as well. However, the precision for Neutral is better for type-1 SVM because of the data imbalance. Type-2 MLP gave the best accuracy in our experiments.

5.2 Structure Prediction Performance

Since the arguments are complex in nature, our approach (Section 3) often fails to predict the entire structure. To counter this, we formulate a measure to evaluate the similarity between the predicted tree and the input tree. The measure, $SimScore$, is defined as:

$$SimScore(T_1, T_2) = \frac{|E(T_1) \cap E(T_2)|}{|E(T_1)|}$$

where T_1 and T_2 have the same set of nodes and $E(T)$ is the set of edges for a tree T. This measure quite intuitively captures the fraction of edges common to both trees. Since the set of nodes are the same, this measure turns out to be directly related to measures like the graph edit distance (Sanfeliu and Fu, 1983).

Since our problem formulation is new, it is difficult to compare the results with existing literature for Structure Prediction in argumentation mining. However, we compare our performance to two baselines. The first baseline, **Random**, is a baseline which randomly chooses any tree structure over the given set of nodes. It can be shown that the expected value of the $SimScore(T_i, T)$ for a given tree T is equal to $1/n$ where n is the number of nodes in T. For the second baseline, **EDITS**, we use the state-of-the-art RTE software package EDITS (Kouylekov and Negri, 2010), instead of the classifiers we proposed, for scoring the edges. However, the metric for scoring structures remains the same as the sum of edge scores. In this case, the entailment relation corresponds to Support relation. EDITS has also been used previously by Cabrio and Villata (2012) in the context of argumentation mining.

Nodes	Arguments	$SimScore$				
		type-1 SVM	**type-2 SVM**	**type-2 MLP**	**EDITS**	**Random**
2	10	**0.9**	0.8	0.8	0.7	0.5
3	187	0.564	0.566	**0.625**	0.363	0.333
4	85	0.529	**0.552**	0.482	0.250	0.250
5	62	**0.446**	0.399	0.435	0.263	0.2
6	72	**0.363**	0.341	0.322	0.263	0.166
7	58	**0.369**	0.323	0.309	0.231	0.142
8	41	**0.230**	0.19	0.199	0.205	0.125
9	19	**0.351**	0.28	0.222	0.265	0.111
10	23	**0.217**	0.188	0.115	0.212	0.1
Any	557	**0.459**	0.442	0.447	0.289	0.234

Table 2: Structure Prediction Performance: Mean of $SimScore$ for the arguments grouped by the number of nodes in the argument. EDITS and Random are baselines whereas type-1 SVM, type-2 SVM and type-2 MLP are proposed approaches.

[5]We have used the SVM and Multi-layer Perceptron classifier implementations provided by the open source library scikit-learn (Pedregosa et al., 2011). For the confidence measure, we have used the decision function in the case of SVM and the predicted probability in the case of MLP. Class imbalance was handled using 'balanced' weighting of classes.

In Table 2, we compare the mean value of $SimScore$ for each classifier. We have further categorized the results based on the number of nodes present in the argument. As evident by the Random baseline, it is expected that the performance will degrade as the number of nodes increase. We can observe that all the three classifiers outperform the EDITS and Random baselines by a considerable factor. For the arguments with 3 nodes, type-2 MLP outperforms type-1 SVM and type-2 SVM. However, for arguments with higher number of nodes, type-1 SVM performs the best. The results reported are statistically significant with a p-value of 0.00198 after performing a two-tailed paired t-test between the type-1 SVM and the EDITS baseline.

5.3 Ablation Study

To test the efficacy of each individual feature/feature group, we have performed a leave-one-out ablation test. In the second column of Table 3, we report the % decrease in the mean SimScore (for any number of nodes) when the type-1 SVM classifier is used. Following observations are made from this study.

- Discourse markers and modal features are observed to be the least effective feature groups.

- Word vectors trained on an external knowledge base are highly effective.

Feature Set	% decrease in $SimScore$	
	With Word Vectors	**Without Word Vectors**
Discourse Markers	0.09%	0.21%
Modal Features	0.27%	0.37%
Wikipedia Similarity	0.59%	0.91%
Word N-grams	1.56%	**21.14%**
Word Vectors	**11.4%**	-
Longest Common Phrase	1.02%	1.22%

Table 3: Ablation Study: The decrease in Structure Prediction performance due to the removal of each kind of feature. The second column corresponds to the experiment with word vectors feature set. The third column corresponds to the experiment in the absence of word vectors feature set.

We conjecture that word vectors encode much more information than n-grams and other linguistic features for Score Assignment. To support this conjecture, we perform another ablation test to judge the effectiveness of other features in absence of word vector feature group. The results are reported in the third column of Table 3. We observe that word n-grams are now influential with a decrease of 21.14%, which was not the case when word vectors were present. Therefore, we can deduce that word vectors were able to capture word n-grams to a great extent. However, discourse markers and modal features are still not very influential. Discourse markers assume 3.21% in the set of terms in AraucariaDB while the modal features are present with 1.89%. We hypothesize the ineffectiveness of discourse markers and modal features to their rarity in AraucariaDB.

6 Arguments with Attack relations

Till now, we have only considered arguments which solely include Support relations. A natural extension of this approach is to support the arguments which include both Support and Attack relations. In an Attack relation, $A \rightarrow B$, statement in node A is used to contradict the statement of node B. We could not find enough argumentation datasets which include attack relations in a significant proportion. We have used two datasets, namely, *Debatepedia* and *Wikipedia* from NoDE (Cabrio and Villata, 2014)[6], a benchmark of natural argument. Although these datasets are pretty small for a machine learning approach, our approach still performs reasonably well for these datasets. The first dataset, *Debatepedia*, consists of data extracted from online debate platforms (debatepedia.org and procon.org). This dataset consists of 260 (140 Support, 120 Attack) relations. Each debate is formed by the responses for a given topic. Fig. 2a shows an example debate from the dataset for the topic of "Violent Games". We will treat such a structure for a given topic as an argument. There are 22 such topics in the dataset. We ignore one topic: "Ground Zero Mosque", because it does not follow a tree structure. The second dataset is built

---

[6]These datasets are described in detail, and are freely available for download, at http://www-sop.inria.fr/NoDE/NoDE-xml.html.

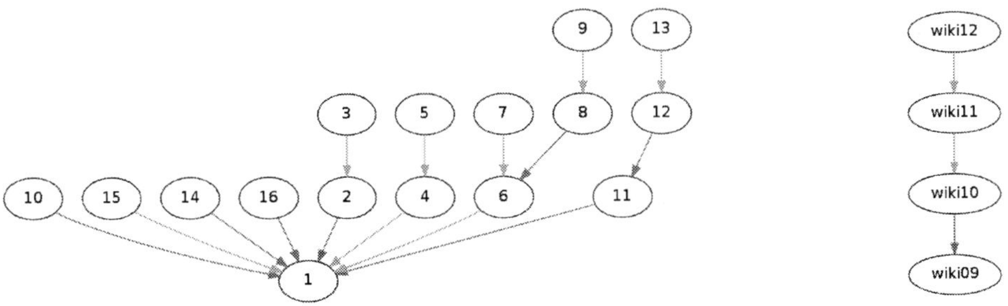

(a) An example debate structure from Debatepedia for the topic of Violent Games.

(b) An example argument from the Wikipedia dataset.

Figure 2: Argument structures with Attack relations. Green edges indicate Support relation whereas red edges indicate Attack relation.

on the Wikipedia revision history over a four-year period, focusing on the top five most revised articles. The Wikipedia dataset consists of 452 pairs (215 Support, 237 Attack). We consider the structure formed by the revision history to be an argument. Therefore, each argument will be a linear graph, as shown in Fig. 2b. To extend our approach for decoding the best possible tree, we need to modify the algorithm to accommodate the fact that the classifiers are no longer binary.

There are now three possible relations for an ordered pair of nodes (a,b): **Support, Attack** and **Neutral**. In the earlier case (AraucariaDB), when we assumed the sole presence of Support relations, distinction between Support and Neutral also included the effect of features that are not related to directional inference, e.g., common Wikipedia entities. However, those features are now common to both Support and Attack relations. To account for these complications, we consider two approaches:

Two-Step Approach: In the first step, a classifier marks the pairs which have either Support or Attack edge. We call it the **Detection** classifier. In a similar fashion, this classifier can also be type-1 or type-2. In the second step, an independent classifier resolves those edges into Support or Attack. We call the second classifier the **Resolver**. In the Structure Prediction phase, the Detection classifier will decide the best tree structure and the Resolver classifier will then resolve the edges into either Support or Attack.

Single-Step Approach: A multi-class classifier resolves all the three relations: Support, Attack or Neutral. Neutral edges are generated using the type-1 framework: any possible edge formed by nodes within the argument which is not an existing Support or Attack edge. In the Structure Prediction phase, the tree structure with the maximum sum of edge scores is chosen. However, the edge score will now be $confidence_S - confidence_N$ instead of $confidence_S$ for each Support edge, where $confidence_S$ and $confidence_N$ are the confidence scores provided by the Single-Step classifier for the Support and Neutral labels, respectively. Similarly, an edge score of $confidence_A - confidence_N$ will be assigned to each Attack edge, where $confidence_A$ is the confidence score assigned by the Single-Step classifier for the Attack label. The $confidence_N$ is deducted due to the missing Neutral edge if a Support edge is chosen. It is evident that assigning $confidence_S - confidence_N$ resolves to assigning $confidence_S$ in Structure Prediction when there are no Attack labels.

For experiments on these approaches, two types of features were included in addition to the features described in Section 3:

1. Negation Discourse Markers: These markers try to capture contrast or negation sentiments in a sentence. Examples of such markers include: *can't, never*, etc. This feature set improved the Single-Step Classifier accuracy by 1.3%.

2. Negation/Contrast Relation Indicators: Features in this category intend to capture negation or contrast relations present in an ordered pair of sentences. We have followed the approaches proposed in (Harabagiu et al., 2006). This feature set improved the Single-Step Classifier accuracy by 6.4%.

In this section, we follow a leave-one-out Cross Validation framework due to the small size of the datasets. Table 4 reports the mean classification accuracies for each classifier for the two datasets. We can see that type-2 framework performs better than type-1 for the Detection classifier. The Two-Step classifier combines the Detection (type-2) and the Resolver classification labels. These results imply that

Classifier	Debatepedia	Wikipedia
Detection (type-1)	0.804	0.535
Detection (type-2)	0.906	0.553
Resolver	0.665	0.719
Two-Step	0.560	0.493
Single-Step	0.761	0.453

Table 4: Classifier Performance for datasets with Attack relations.

Nodes	Arguments	T-S-1	T-S	S-S
7	2	0.83	0.666	0
8	1	0.57 1	0.428	0
9	1	0.875	0.5	0.25
10	2	0.721	0.385	0.055
11	4	0.325	0.225	0.05
12	2	0.545	0.409	0
13	2	0.541	0.333	0
Any	14	0.573	0.387	0.04

Table 5: Mean SimScore for Debatepedia. *T-S-1*: Step 1 of the Two-Step Approach *T-S*: Two-Step Approach *S-S*: Single-Step Approach

a Single-Step classification approach performs better than Two-Step for the Debatepedia dataset[7]. However, we shall see in Table 5 that the Single-Step approach performs poorly in the Structure Prediction phase. Table 5 reports the mean SimScore after the Structure Prediction for the Debatepedia dataset. Similar to Table 2, these results are additionally filtered by the number of nodes in the argument. The third column **T-S-1**, reports performance of the Two-Step approach before the edges are resolved into Support or Attack, i.e. there is no distinction between Support and Attack edges. This is similar to the experiments we performed in Section 5.2. The fourth column **T-S**, reports the overall performance of the Two-Step approach. The fifth column **S-S**, reports the performance of the Single-Step approach. We can see that Single-Step performs poorly as compared to Two-Step approach by a large margin. Table

Nodes	Arg.	T-S-1	T-S	T-S-WL	S-S
2	142	0.507	0.366	0.366	0.274
3	103	0.441	0.305	0.262	0.203
4	34	0.254	0.156	0.176	0.098
Any	279	0.452	0.318	0.304	0.227

Table 6: Mean SimScore for Wikipedia. *T-S-WL*: Two-Step Approach without any restriction for linear structures. Rest of the abbreviations as per Table 5.

6 reports the mean SimScore for the Wikipedia dataset. Here we imposed an additional restriction for the structures to be linear. However, in the fifth column **T-S-WL**, we report the SimScore following the Two-Step approach without any restriction. We observe that the Single-Step approach performs relatively better for the Wikipedia dataset as compared to the Debatepedia dataset. We think this is due to the bigger arguments in Debatepedia.

7 Conclusion

In this paper, we introduced a two-phase approach towards identification of argument structure in natural language text. The first phase involves building models for classifying text-hypothesis pairs into argument relations. The second phase makes use of the classifier confidence scores to construct the argument structure. We have proposed different training models to train the argument relation classifier. With the help of ablation study, we showed that our novel use of word vectors trained on an external corpus can be a crucial feature for such tasks, contributing as much as 11.4% towards the performance. For the final goal of Structure Prediction, our approach predicted almost twice as many correct edges as with the random baseline. We showed that the proposed approach can be extended to arguments containing Attack relations as well, where our experiments predicted an average of 38% edges correctly for Debatepedia dataset.

---

[7]Arguments having size 13 or less are used in this experiment.

References

Elena Cabrio and Serena Villata. 2012. Combining textual entailment and argumentation theory for supporting online debates interactions. In *Proceedings of the 50th Annual Meeting of the Association for Computational Linguistics: Short Papers-Volume 2*, pages 208–212. Association for Computational Linguistics.

Elena Cabrio and Serena Villata. 2014. Node: A benchmark of natural language arguments. *COMMA*, 266:449–450.

Judith Eckle-Kohler, Roland Kluge, and Iryna Gurevych. 2015. On the role of discourse markers for discriminating claims and premises in argumentative discourse. In *Proceedings of the 2015 Conference on Empirical Methods in Natural Language Processing (EMNLP). Association for Computational Linguistics, Lisbon, Portugal, to appear*. Citeseer.

Paolo Ferragina and Ugo Scaiella. 2010. Fast and accurate annotation of short texts with wikipedia pages. *arXiv preprint arXiv:1006.3498*.

James B Freeman. 1991. *Dialectics and the macrostructure of arguments: A theory of argument structure*, volume 10. Walter de Gruyter.

James B Freeman. 2011. *Argument Structure:: Representation and Theory*, volume 18. Springer Science & Business Media.

Sanda Harabagiu, Andrew Hickl, and Finley Lacatusu. 2006. Negation, contrast and contradiction in text processing. In *AAAI*, volume 6, pages 755–762.

Gary King and Langche Zeng. 2001. Logistic regression in rare events data. *Political analysis*, 9(2):137–163.

Milen Kouylekov and Matteo Negri. 2010. An open-source package for recognizing textual entailment. In *Proceedings of the ACL 2010 System Demonstrations*, pages 42–47. Association for Computational Linguistics.

John Lawrence, Floris Bex, Chris Reed, and Mark Snaith. 2012. Aifdb: Infrastructure for the argument web. In *COMMA*, pages 515–516.

John Lawrence, Chris Reed, Colin Allen, Simon McAlister, Andrew Ravenscroft, and David Bourget. 2014. Mining arguments from 19th century philosophical texts using topic based modelling. In *Proceedings of the First Workshop on Argumentation Mining*, pages 79–87. Citeseer.

Bill MacCartney. 2009. *Natural language inference*. Ph.D. thesis, Citeseer.

Tomas Mikolov, Ilya Sutskever, Kai Chen, Greg S Corrado, and Jeff Dean. 2013. Distributed representations of words and phrases and their compositionality. In *Advances in neural information processing systems*, pages 3111–3119.

Raquel Mochales and Marie-Francine Moens. 2011. Argumentation mining. *Artificial Intelligence and Law*, 19(1):1–22.

Fabian Pedregosa, Gaël Varoquaux, Alexandre Gramfort, Vincent Michel, Bertrand Thirion, Olivier Grisel, Mathieu Blondel, Peter Prettenhofer, Ron Weiss, Vincent Dubourg, et al. 2011. Scikit-learn: Machine learning in python. *The Journal of Machine Learning Research*, 12:2825–2830.

Andreas Peldszus and Manfred Stede. 2015. Joint prediction in mst-style discourse parsing for argumentation mining. In *Proc. of the Conference on Empirical Methods in Natural Language Processing*, pages 938–948.

Isaac Persing and Vincent Ng. 2016. End-to-end argumentation mining in student essays. In *Proceedings of NAACL-HLT*, pages 1384–1394.

Chris Reed and Glenn Rowe. 2004. Araucaria: Software for argument analysis, diagramming and representation. *International Journal on Artificial Intelligence Tools*, 13(04):961–979.

Alberto Sanfeliu and King-Sun Fu. 1983. A distance measure between attributed relational graphs for pattern recognition. *Systems, Man and Cybernetics, IEEE Transactions on*, (3):353–362.

Christian Stab and Iryna Gurevych. 2016. Parsing argumentation structures in persuasive essays. *arXiv preprint arXiv:1604.07370*.

Douglas Walton. 2007. Visualization tools, argumentation schemes and expert opinion evidence in law. *Law, Probability and Risk*, 6(1-4):119–140.

Distributed Vector Representations for Unsupervised Automatic Short Answer Grading

Oliver Adams[†‡]   **Shourya Roy**[‡]   **Raghuram Krishnapuram**[§]

[†]The University of Melbourne, Australia
[‡]Xerox Research Center India, Bangalore, India
[§]M. S. Ramaiah Institute of Technology, Bangalore, India
oliver.adams@gmail.com, shourya.roy@xerox.com, raghuk@msrit.edu

Abstract

We address the problem of automatic short answer grading, evaluating a collection of approaches inspired by recent advances in distributional text representations. In addition, we propose an unsupervised approach for determining text similarity using one-to-many alignment of word vectors. We evaluate the proposed technique across two datasets from different domains, namely, computer science and English reading comprehension, that additionally vary between high-school level and undergraduate students. Experiments demonstrate that the proposed technique often outperforms other compositional distributional semantics approaches as well as vector space methods such as latent semantic analysis. When combined with a *scoring scheme*, the proposed technique provides a powerful tool for tackling the complex problem of short answer grading. We also discuss a number of other key points worthy of consideration in preparing viable, easy-to-deploy automatic short-answer grading systems for the real-world.

1 Introduction

Grading is an important task in schools and colleges in order to assess students' understanding and guide teachers in providing instructive feedback. However, answer grading is tedious work and the prevalence of Computer Assisted Assessment has been limited to *recognition* questions with constrained answers such as multiple choice questions. In this paper, we delve into the topic of automatic assessment of students' constructed responses. In particular, we consider *short answers* which are a few words or a few sentences long, including everything in between fill-in-the-gap and essay-type answers (Burrows et al., 2015). Automatic short answer grading (ASAG) involves scoring a student answer given an instructor-provided model (reference) answer. Scoring schemes may optionally be provided to indicate the relative importance of different parts of the model answer. This is a complex natural language understanding task owing to linguistic variations (the same answer could be articulated in different ways), the subjective nature of assessment (multiple possible correct answers or no correct answer) and lack of consistency in human rating. For example, in Table 1, both student answers are correct, but this may not be apparent to a computer system.

In this paper, we employ distributed vector representation of words (Bengio et al., 2003; Mikolov et al., 2013b) for *unsupervised* ASAG, a task where graded student answers are not provided as training data (although a reference answer is still available). This has not yet been systematically explored even though such word embeddings have proven useful in natural language processing. (However, there has been work using embeddings for *supervised* ASAG Sakaguchi et al. (2015), and neural networks for essay grading Alikaniotis et al. (2016).) We conduct an empirical study to compare the proposed method against various other vector aggregation including naive vector addition, Word Mover's Distance (WMD) (Kusner et al., 2015) and paragraph vectors (Le and Mikolov, 2014) using two datasets that come from two different domains. The first is the undergraduate computer science dataset used in Mohler et al. (2011), while the second is a high-school English reading comprehension task which we present and intend to share with the community for future research. An important feature of the latter dataset is the

Proceedings of the 3rd Workshop on Natural Language Processing Techniques for Educational Applications,
pages 20–29, Osaka, Japan, December 12 2016.

Question	What is the unexpected fact stated by the writer? (2)
Model answer	The unexpected fact stated by the writer is that although the modern air-conditioned office is an unlikely place for work related injury, more and more people working in such places complain of disorders involving hands, wrists and other body parts.
Scoring scheme	Working in modern air-conditioned offices leads to more people getting work related injury (1.5)
	People complain of disorders involving hands, wrists and other body parts. (0.5)
Student 1 answer	More no. of white collar workers sitting in high tech offices are complaining of disorders involving hands, wrists, arms, shoulders, neck and back
Student 2 answer	The author states that many white collar workers in hi-tech offices complain of disorders in their hands, wrists etc. But this is very unexpected because an air conditioned office seem an unlike place for an injury to occur.

Table 1: Example of question, model answer, scoring scheme and two student answers from English reading comprehension dataset.

presence of a weighted scoring scheme for each question, which demonstrates promise in improving unsupervised ASAG performance when used.

In ASAG, student answers often contain information beyond the key concepts instructors are looking for, though those extra pieces of text typically do not affect their scores unless they are contradictory or wrong. In order to address the shortcomings of symmetric similarity techniques, we propose an intuitive technique, *Vecalign*, which uses word vector based representations for unsupervised ASAG. Our technique computes an aggregate of word-level distances based on one-to-many word vector alignment using the cosine similarity of the aligned words vectors. Importantly, this allows us to assess similarity of the student answer against the model answer asymmetrically as a textual entailment problem (whether the student answer implies the model answer), which vector space methods such as *paragraph vectors* cannot do. In summary, our contributions include:

1. A comparison of the applicability of popular distributed vector representations of text for unsupervised ASAG across domains.

2. Proposal of an asymmetric word vector alignment method, which exploits weighted scoring schemes. Results indicate that such schemes show promise for improving ASAG reliability by allowing improved expressiveness in specifying answer requirements.

3. An analysis focusing on qualitative assessment of the methods, in light of the shortcomings of correlation metrics such as Pearson's r. To this end, we discuss points of consideration relating to the methods and design of questions for unsupervised ASAG.

2   Background

Our work draws on two foundational bodies of research: that of unsupervised ASAG as well as distributional semantics.

2.1   Unsupervised ASAG

Two recent surveys (Roy et al., 2015; Burrows et al., 2015) provide comprehensive views of research in ASAG, where similarity-based ASAG techniques can be broken into categories including lexical, knowledge-based and vector space. Among the lexical measures, one of the earliest approaches is Evaluating Responses with BLEU (Perez et al., 2004). It adapted the most popular evaluation measure for machine translation, i.e., BLEU, for ASAG with a set of natural language processing techniques such as stemming, closed-class word removal, etc. Mohler and Mihalcea (2009) conducted a comparative study of different semantic similarity measures for ASAG including knowledge-based measures using Wordnet as well as vector space-based measures such as Latent Semantic Analysis (LSA) (Landauer et al., 1998) and Explicit semantic analysis (Gabrilovich and Markovitch, 2006). LSA has remained a popular approach for ASAG and been applied in many variations (Graesser et al., 2000; Wiemer-Hastings and

Zipitria, 2001; Kanejiya et al., 2003; Klein et al., 2011). Lexical and semantic measures have been combined to validate natural complementarity of syntax and semantics for ASAG tasks (Perez et al., 2005). Wael H Gomaa (2012) compared several lexical and corpus-based similarity algorithms (13 string-based and 4 corpus) and their combinations for grading answers on a 0-5 scale. Dzikovska et al. (2013) conducted a 5-way (non-ordinal scale) Student Response Analysis challenge as a part of SemEval-2013. However, the task had more emphasis on giving feedback on student answers, possibly using textual entailment techniques.

2.2 Compositional distributional semantics

In recent years there has been an abundance of distributional text representation techniques based on the distributional hypothesis that words that appear in similar contexts have similar meanings (Harris, 1968). Popular techniques include *word2vec* (Mikolov et al., 2013b) and *Glove* (Pennington et al., 2014) in recent times, but also concepts such as latent semantic analysis (Deerwester et al., 1990) and its variants, as well as measures of distributional similarity (Lee, 1999; Lin, 1998). Compositional techniques building on these word vectors derive vector representations of longer pieces of text, i.e., phrases, sentences, paragraphs and documents. An approach of averaging of bag of word representations of text snippets was employed by early researchers such as (Landauer and Dumais, 1997; Foltz et al., 1998). While they were the first ones to introduce the notion, these approaches do not incorporate word order and have the adaptive capacity to represent the variety of possible syntactic relations in a phrase. Additionally, Erk and Pad (2008) highlighted that a fixed dimensionality vector may suffer from *information scalability* and not able to represent text snippets of arbitrary length. Some related models include holographic reduced representations (Plate, 1995), quantum logic (Widdows, 2008), discrete-continuous models (Clark and Pulman, 2007) and compositional matrix space model (Rudolph and Giesbrecht, 2010). Grefenstette and Sadrzadeh (2011) analyze subject–verb–object triplets and find a matrix-based categorical model to correlate well with human judgments. In recent times there has been a slew of work towards vector composition using neural network models. Notable of those are the paragraph vector of Le and Mikolov (2014) and the recursive deep models of Socher et al. (2013).

Most of the papers mentioned here emphasize obtaining a good generalized vector representation of text snippets. In the case of ASAG, our primary interest is to obtain a measure of similarity between them. We observe that for ASAG not all words in student and model answers are equally important. Rather, pairs of related words which appear in student and model answers are more important than some other words. Hence a measure which identifies and aggregates over such pairs would be meaningful to apply, such as Word Movers Distance (WMD) (Kusner et al., 2015).

3 Techniques

There are a wide range of approaches for generating scores of similarity between documents (Choi et al., 2010). We evaluate a variety of representative distributional semantics based approaches in the task of unsupervised grading and propose an asymmetric method based on aligning word vectors that exploits properties of grading tasks.

3.1 Document vector approaches

We consider two approaches that create document vector representations without composing individual word representations. We use implementations available in the *gensim* Python package (Rehurek, 2010).

Latent semantic analysis: Latent semantic analysis uses matrix factorization to create vector representation of words and documents in the same space. Since it has had a long history of use in ASAG, we consider it as a point of comparison in evaluating the other methods presented here.

Paragraph vectors: A number of more recent approaches have been proposed for creating vector representations of larger units of text (Mitchell and Lapata, 2010; Mikolov et al., 2013a; Grefenstette et al., 2013). The Paragraph vector method of (Le and Mikolov, 2014) provides a way to train vector representations of such larger units by using an approach similar to that of (Mikolov et al., 2013a). Importantly, paragraph vector representations are not compositions of word vectors and they also implicitly consider word order to some extent, which word vector compositions generally do not. We evaluated a variety of configurations, with the *distributed bag of words* model performing the best.

3.2 Word vector based approaches

We also evaluate a number of methods based directly on word vectors of the continuous bag-of-words (CBOW) model (Mikolov et al., 2013b). This method of word vector learning has allowed for word vectors to be trained on larger quantities of data than before, permitting state-of-the-art results in various tasks. Two key practical advantages of this is that the 100 billion word Google News Corpus can be harnessed and that hyperparameters do not need to be tweaked.[1]

Averaging word vectors: A naive approach to creating a document representation is by collapsing word vectors into a single vector through addition or multiplication. In ASAG, this approach has been used in the context of LSA word vectors (Perez et al., 2005). Though composition of few word vectors has demonstrated interesting results, one problem with this method of addition is that the best dimensionality for vectors of a set of paragraphs may not be the same as those for words.

Word mover's distance: This is a measure of similarity between groups of words that is equal to the minimum total distance the word vectors of one document must move in the vector space in order to become the word vectors of another document (Kusner et al., 2015). This method allows words to move to multiple other words, when a mismatch in document sizes occurs.

Targeting scoring schemes with *Vecalign*: We present a vector alignment method, *Vecalign-asym*, designed to capitalize on a feature of assessments: the asymmetry of scoring scheme items and student answer sizes, comparable to the word2vec alignment feature used in the supervised system of Sakaguchi et al. (2015).

Given two texts A and B (model and student answers, respectively), non-open-class words (words that are not nouns, verbs, adjectives or adverbs) are first removed from both. Each word is then replaced by its word vector representation such that we now have A consisting of vectors $(\mathbf{a_1}, \mathbf{a_2}, \ldots, \mathbf{a_m})$ and B consisting of vectors $(\mathbf{b_1}, \mathbf{b_2}, \ldots, \mathbf{b_n})$. We define the one-to-many similarity using the cosine similarity of the component word vectors:

$$asym(A, B) = \frac{\sum_{\mathbf{a}_i \in A} \max_{\mathbf{b}_j \in B}(cos(\mathbf{a}_i, \mathbf{b}_j))}{m} \tag{1}$$

This similarity measure is asymmetric, and is motivated by the observation that model answers are often more concise than student answers, since model answers typically contain only the salient points, while student answers are frequently less to the point, without necessarily being less correct.

If a scoring scheme is available, the awarded score can be defined as the weighted average of the asymmetric Vecalign similarity of each element in the scoring scheme with the student answer. While other methods can similarly be used with scoring scheme, the asymmetry between the size of the student answer and the scoring scheme suits Vecalign-asym well.

We believe that scoring schemes represent a very promising approach for both human grading and ASAG for a variety of reasons: (a) they elicit clearer wording of specifically what the creator of the question is looking for; (b) they allow for explicit weighting of the importance of these components; (c) By introducing smaller scoring scheme items, each of which should be covered in a student answer, they decompose the problem into sub-problems that have a textual entailment flavor, and more readily permit the use of effective asymmetric metrics; (d) We additionally conjecture that scoring schemes improve agreement between graders by making the creator think about the question more carefully by providing clearer guidance to graders.

In addition to the asymmetric Vecalign-asym, a symmetric version can be defined by the average of the asymmetric similarity in both directions. This is similar to the approach of the lexical similarity methods of (Mohler and Mihalcea, 2009). We refer to this measure simply as *Vecalign*.

---

[1] While these vectors were trained in a supervised manner, our proposed method still remains unsupervised analogous to how LSA has been treated as an unsupervised textual similarity measure. An interesting future study would be to train domain specific vectors based on student answer corpora but our datasets were very small for doing the same.

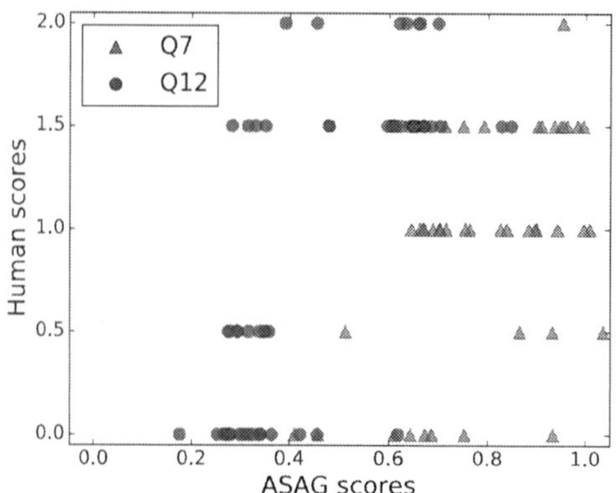

Figure 1: Questions 7 and 12 from the reading comprehension dataset. The ASAG scores come from the *vecalign* approach using the scoring scheme as the gold standard. Overall correlation is less than the average of its parts. Darker circles and triangles represent duplicate datapoints.

4   Data

We evaluate these methods on two datsets. The first is a set of questions (*CSDataset*), model answers and student answers taken from an undergraduate computer science course (Mohler et al., 2011). The dataset comprises of 87 questions from a number of assignments and examinations, with responses from 31 students. The second dataset comes from a high-school reading comprehension task for Class (Standard) XII (12) students as a part of a course on English in the Central Board of Secondary Education (CBSE) in India (*RCDataset*). The dataset comprises 14 questions, each with the recorded responses from 58 students. Along with model answers, questions in this dataset also have fine grained scoring schemes. We will share the dataset with people who are interested in pursuing research in this field and will be benefited by the dataset. Both datasets were tokenized with the *Punkt* tokenizer implementation of NLTK (Bird, 2006) before case normalization and lower-casing.

5   Quantitative evaluation

5.1   Metrics

Pearson's r has been used quite extensively in prior ASAG research. However, the suitability of Pearson's r has been questioned in the context of ASAG (Mohler and Mihalcea, 2009) as well as in general (Willmott, 1982). We too find issue with the use of Pearson's r. Firstly, very different scatter plots can yield similar correlations. Different questions result in different lines of best fit, which sullies the overall correlation. Consider Figure 1, which presents scatter plots of one ASAG system against the human scores. The individual correlations of the questions are both 0.72, but the overall correlation drops to 0.55. For this reason we favour question-wise correlation. Although this means that each number is determined by fewer datapoints and the calculations are statistically less meaningful, we still find that this evaluation is more informative. Furthermore, Pearson's r also penalizes non-linearities. For unsupervised ASAG this is not ideal, as in this case a nonlinear function cannot be learned to optimize for linear correlation. Spearman's ρ, while still subject to the first two problems, avoids this problem and thus we primarily report Spearman's ρ.

Finally, we note that using measures of correlation sidesteps the real-world issue of allocating an actual score to the students. If the ASAG system is used for merely ranking the students, this is not a problem. However, if we need to scale ASAG scores to appropriately grade students, it is a nontrivial problem that is task dependent and likely requires some degree of supervision. The limitations of these metrics motivated us to perform the qualitative evaluation of Section 6, which was influenced largely by manual inspection of the ASAG system outputs and the relationship between scores and the gold-standard average of human scores.

Method	Spearman's ρ of question number													
	All	1	3	12	27	41	45	50	60	69	73	82	84	87
IAA	*.68*	*.76*	*.62*	*.96*	*.99*	*.54*	*.06*	*.47*	*1*	*.52*	*.58*	*und*	*und*	*.85*
VAA	**.50**	.83	**.60**	**.64**	.01	.17	.24	.59	**.72**	**.88**	**.54**	-.04	-.04	.43
VA	.49	**.85**	.55	.58	.25	.19	.08	.62	.34	.55	.51	-.01	.01	.46
W2V-Add	.32	.74	.03	.29	.12	**.21**	**.41**	**.64**	.26	.55	.21	-.04	.01	.18
WMD	.42	**.85**	.02	.57	.35	.02	.17	**.64**	.34	.55	.44	.06	.01	**.65**
Para-Vec	.49	.75	-.14	-.33	.17	.07	.19	.44	.30	.53	.47	**.32**	**.04**	.62
LSA	.39	.65	.07	-.45	**.47**	-.21	.22	.52	.13	.53	-.06	-.08	**.04**	.54

Table 2: Spearman's ρ of the ASAG systems on the CSDataset of Mohler et. al. (2011). There were 87 questions in total, and so only a representative sampling is presented, along with the overall correlation across all 87 questions. Undefined numbers are indicated by *und.* (the correlation is undefined when the variance along any dimension is zero).

Method	Gold	Spearman's ρ of question number													
		All	1	2	3	4	5	6	7	8	9	10	11	12	13	14
IAA	scheme	*.75*	*.73*	*.77*	*.80*	*.27*	*.86*	*und.*	*.71*	*.70*	*.60*	*.61*	*.93*	*.65*	*.55*	*.75*
VAA	scheme	.16	.66	**.75**	**.73**	**.59**	*und.*	*und.*	**.73**	**.69**	.56	**.48**	**.74**	**.69**	**.71**	**.76**
VA	scheme	.09	.62	.51	.70	.55	*und.*	*und.*	.68	.65	.53	.39	.58	.63	.66	**.76**
W2V-Add	scheme	-.16	.66	.37	.72	.46	.21	*und.*	.64	.55	**.57**	.43	.48	.43	.63	.68
WMD	scheme	.08	.56	.16	.58	.52	-.01	*und.*	.51	.37	.45	.36	.60	.59	.58	.68
Para-Vec	scheme	-.04	.54	.09	.61	.04	.10	*und.*	.49	.35	.38	.47	.29	.52	.55	.61
LSA	scheme	.09	.14	.17	.60	.48	**.31**	*und.*	.35	.19	.27	.33	*und.*	.57	.43	.50
VAA	ref.	.29	**.68**	**.75**	.69	.36	.05	*und.*	.71	.49	.48	**.48**	**.74**	.44	**.71**	.66
VA	ref.	.32	.61	.47	.65	.26	-.11	*und.*	.67	.54	.46	.46	.58	.56	.66	.72
W2V-Add	ref.	.13	.65	.74	.62	.38	.03	*und.*	.61	.36	.39	.46	.48	.36	.60	.52
WMD	ref.	.27	.62	.69	.67	.35	-.07	*und.*	.70	.45	.46	.46	.60	.54	.61	.68
Para-Vec	ref.	**.42**	**.68**	.42	.61	.35	-.02	*und.*	.60	.43	.38	**.48**	.32	.45	.46	.45
LSA	ref.	.20	.10	.47	.65	.22	.26	*und.*	.48	.19	.16	.25	.22	.45	.35	.14

Table 3: Overall and question-wise performance of methods on the reading comprehension dataset. *Gold* indicates whether the gold standard is the marking scheme or model answer.

5.2 Observations

Tables 2 and 3 present the overall and question-wise correlations of the ASAG systems against the average of the human scores. Only the reading comprehension dataset had scoring scheme associated, hence Table 3 shows results with respect to both model answer and scoring scheme. We additionally present the annotators' correlation with one another as a point of reference (**IAA**), though these aren't ASAG scores. Due to space constraints, we opted to present a representative sample of the questions from the CSdataset.[2] In each table, we compare vecalign-asym (**VAA**), vecalign (**VA**), WMD (**WMD**), LSA (**LSA**), Paragraph Vectors (**Para-Vec**), and word vector addition (**W2V-Add**). We observe that the relative performance of models stays approximately the same across both datasets. In most cases, Paragraph Vectors and LSA underperform the word2vec based approaches, which is an indication that the large dataset afforded by these methods is a key advantage. Furthermore, note that results of paragraph vector and LSA were from among the best performing hyperparameter configurations, as a number of them were trained.

5.2.1 Comparison with human correlation

Note that the correlation of the ASAG grades cannot be fairly compared with the correlation of the human-assigned grades, since the ASAG grades are evaluated against the *average* of the human scores. However, it is nevertheless meaningful to consider when ASAG correlation is comparable to or exceeds that of humans, as it highlights questions where automated marking might be as effective as manual marking. It is worth noting that in the the RCDataset, the asymmetric approach harnessing the scheme

---

[2]Note, however, that the reported figure for *all* is across all 87 questions.

has a higher correlation than the inter-annotator agreement on 5 out of the 14 questions. In other questions the ASAG system is not so far behind the human agreement. The overall correlation is very low compared to that of humans, since human marks are scored on a consistent scale between questions, whereas ASAG grades are not. As mentioned in Section 5.1, this makes establishing correlation over a number of questions not very informative.

5.2.2 Performance using scoring schemes

As can be seen in Table 3, in 10 out of 14 questions of RCDataset, the asymmetric approach using the scoring scheme is the best performing approach: it has 6 out of 14 questions with a correlation over 0.7 and another 3 are over 0.6. The asymmetric vecalign method has an advantage over the other methods that measured student answers against scheme items, since scoring scheme items are typically far smaller than student answers. The asymmetric vecalign method is also frequently the best performer even when evaluating against the model answer. This is also a reflection on the asymmetry of the model answer. Student answers tend to be longer, while the provided model answer is shorter, capturing only the salient points.

5.2.3 Ensemble performance

We experimented with a few ensemble methods where the score for answers assigned by different methods were averaged to produce a final score. These combinations involved averaging the results of *vecalign* against the model answer along with asymmetric *vecalign* against the scoring scheme (thus intending to harness information both from the scoring scheme and model answer), as well as combinations considering LSA and Paragraph Vectors. However, in all cases, the ensemble approach underperformed the best constituent approach, since different methods implicitly score on different scales.

6 Discussion

We present a discussion involving qualitative assessment of the ASAG systems with respect to selected questions from the CSDataset ("CSQ").

6.1 Questions yielding low or undefined correlations

A number of questions have a low or undefined correlation because of a clear deficiency in the system. For example, the model answer for CSQ27 is "run-time error". Since "run-time" doesn't exist in the vocabulary of the CBOW model trained on the Google News Corpus, only "error" is considered as relevant, and as such responses such as "compilation error" receive high scores, while "run-time" receives none. Note that LSA did not completely fall down on this question.

In other cases, low correlation is not representative of poor system performance. Consider CSQ84. The model answer is "push and pop". This response was present in every student answer, and every student answer was awarded 5/5, except for one who was awarded 4.5. Vecalign-asym awarded almost every student's answer a perfect score, except for one that included "pop-" as a token. Infrequent deviation from perfect scores yields unreliable correlations.

6.1.1 Answer open-endedness and pattern matching

We observe that the more open-ended the expresssion of a legitimate answer can be, the less useful the model answer is. However, open-endedness is an important motivation for short answers as opposed to multiple choice questions. Therefore, a balance must be struck. For CSQ41, the model answer describes the main advantage of linked lists as "the linked lists can be of variable length". The notion of "variable length" can be described in many ways that are not so easily capturable even by semantic vectors. An answer "its resizable" was given a low score by the ASAG system. Other answers described linked lists as being able to be "grown dynamically" and that "elements can be added to a linked list w/o defining any size.".

At the other end of the spectrum, there were questions where the model answer indicated that simple pattern matching approaches for grading would suffice, and perhaps be more effective than distributional semantics based approaches. This is particularly true for jargon such as the previously mentioned "enqueue and dequeue" and "push and pop". Some questions were not suitable for a short answer framework at all, such as yes/no questions. In designing assessments for automatic grading, identifying where simple pattern matching or multiple choice would suffice would improve system performance.

6.1.2 Fundamental limitations of ASAG and question quality

The example of CSQ12 also highlights some fundamental limitations. Student answers that received full marks by graders included answers such as "any number you want" and "as many as needed". However, the model answer was "unlimited number", making it difficult for ASAG.

CSQ45 asks "what is the main advantage of a doubly-linked list over a basic linked list?" and uses the model answer "all the deletion and insertion operations can be performed in constant time, including those operations performed before a given location in the list or at the end of the list". The correlation between human answers for this question was only 0.06, indicating problems with the question and model answer. Since there are multiple advantages and disadvantages of doubly-linked lists, such a question may be more suited to a scoring scheme reference comprised of shorter items that can be matched against the student answer. Another notable reason is that the mention of "speed" and "fast" cannot easily be related to "constant time".

6.1.3 Length of model answer

The model answers in the computer science course were often short and sweet, which is likely why Vecalign-asym outperformed Vecalign. In many cases, student answers elaborated beyond what was in the model and were thus punished by the symmetric method. The asymmetric method avoided this, which explains its significantly better performance on some questions (e.g. CSQ60), where the model answer is a single word.

6.1.4 Text normalization

One key step of normalization that we performed was case normalization, which demonstrated its importance for word vectors. CSQ12 has a model answer "Unlimited number". "Unlimited" has a cosine similarity with "infinite" of only 0.22. But when lowercased, the similarity jumps to 0.48.

6.1.5 Interpretability

Since Vecalign aligns word vectors, it is usually simple to interpret how a score was arrived at for a student answer. However aragraph vectors and LSA are notably more opaque.

6.1.6 Appropriateness of scoring schemes

Use of scoring schemes work well in conjunction with the Vecalign-asym method. However, performance is notably worse when the scoring schemes are used with the other symmetric approaches. Since the elements of the scoring scheme are small, it is a textual entailment problem, which is inherently asymmetric.

7 Conclusion

Although ASAG has been investigated for many years, adoption is not widespread. This is partly because ASAG systems often do not perform adequately and those that do perform well enough for real-world use typically require significant manual supervision (Liu et al., 2014). In order to make ASAG more practicable in the real-world, effort should be placed in situating available models so that it is feasible to create reliable ASAG systems without an overly large amount human of supervision. In this paper, we have made a contribution towards minimizing the impact of this compromise by presenting a simple, effective, and interpretable method of word vector alignment in conjunction with the use of weighted marking schemes, as well as evaluating a variety of alternative approaches. Another important part of making ASAG feasible is examination of which types of questions are amiable to automation. This is an important consideration since questions on which ASAG systems perform poorly are often also the ones on which humans disagree.

References

Dimitrios Alikaniotis, Helen Yannakoudakis, and Marek Rei. 2016. Automatic text scoring using neural networks. In *Proceedings of the 54th Annual Meeting of the Association for Computational Linguistics (Volume 1: Long Papers)*, pages 715–725, Berlin, Germany, August. Association for Computational Linguistics.

Y. Bengio, R. Ducharme, P. Vincent, and C. Janvin. 2003. A neural probabilistic language model. *The Journal of Machine Learning Research*, 3:1137–1155.

S. Bird. 2006. Nltk: the natural language toolkit. In *Proceedings of the COLING/ACL on Interactive presentation sessions*, pages 69–72. Association for Computational Linguistics.

Steven Burrows, Iryna Gurevych, and Benno Stein. 2015. The eras and trends of automatic short answer grading. *International Journal of Artificial Intelligence in Education*, 25(1):60–117.

S. Choi, S. Cha, and C. Tappert. 2010. A survey of binary similarity and distance measures. *Journal of Systemics, Cybernetics and Informatics*, 8(1):43–48.

Stephen Clark and Stephen Pulman. 2007. Combining symbolic and distributional models of meaning. In *AAAI Spring Symposium: Quantum Interaction*, pages 52–55. AAAI.

Scott Deerwester, Susan T. Dumais, George W. Furnas, Thomas K. Landauer, and Richard Harshman. 1990. Indexing by latent semantic analysis. *Journal of the American Society for Information Science*, 41(6):391–407.

Myroslava O Dzikovska, Rodney D Nielsen, Chris Brew, Claudia Leacock, Danilo Giampiccolo, Luisa Bentivogli, Peter Clark, Ido Dagan, and Hoa T Dang. 2013. Semeval-2013 task 7: The joint student response analysis and 8th recognizing textual entailment challenge. Technical report, DTIC Document.

Katrin Erk and Sebastian Pad. 2008. A structured vector space model for word meaning in context. In *EMNLP*, pages 897–906. ACL.

P. W. Foltz, W. Kintsch, and T. K. Landauer. 1998. The measurement of textual coherence with latent semantic analysis. *Discourse Processes*, 25:285–307.

Evgeniy Gabrilovich and Shaul Markovitch. 2006. Overcoming the brittleness bottleneck using wikipedia: Enhancing text categorization with encyclopedic knowledge. In *AAAI*, pages 1301–1306. AAAI Press.

Arthur C. Graesser, Peter M. Wiemer-Hastings, Katja Wiemer-Hastings, Derek Harter, and Natalie K. Person. 2000. Using latent semantic analysis to evaluate the contributions of students in autotutor. *Interactive Learning Environments*, 8(2):129–147.

Edward Grefenstette and Mehrnoosh Sadrzadeh. 2011. Experimental support for a categorical compositional distributional model of meaning. In *Proceedings of the Conference on Empirical Methods in Natural Language Processing*, pages 1394–1404. Association for Computational Linguistics.

E. Grefenstette, G. Dinu, Y. Zhang, M. Sadrzadeh, and M. Baroni. 2013. Multi-step regression learning for compositional distributional semantics. *arXiv preprint arXiv:1301.6939*.

Zellig Harris. 1968. *Mathematical Structures of Language*. John Wiley and Son, New York.

Dharmendra Kanejiya, Arun Kumar, and Surendra Prasad. 2003. Automatic evaluation of students' answers using syntactically enhanced lsa. In *Proceedings of the HLT-NAACL 03 workshop on Building educational applications using natural language processing - Volume 2*, pages 53–60.

Richard Klein, Angelo Kyrilov, and Mayya Tokman. 2011. Automated assessment of short free-text responses in computer science using latent semantic analysis. In *ITiCSE*, pages 158–162. ACM.

Matt J. Kusner, Yu Sun, Nicholas I. Kolkin, and Kilian Q. Weinberger. 2015. From word embeddings to document distances. In Francis R. Bach and David M. Blei, editors, *ICML*, volume 37 of *JMLR Proceedings*, pages 957–966. JMLR.org.

Thomas K. Landauer and Susan T. Dumais. 1997. A solution to Plato's problem: The Latent Semantic Analysis theory of acquisition, induction, and representation of knowledge. *Psychological Review*, 104:211–240.

T. K. Landauer, P. W. Foltz, and D. Laham. 1998. An Introduction to Latent Semantic Analysis. *Discourse Processes*, 25:259–284.

Quoc V Le and Tomas Mikolov. 2014. Distributed representations of sentences and documents. *arXiv preprint arXiv:1405.4053*.

Lillian Lee. 1999. Measures of distributional similarity. In *37th Annual Meeting of the Association for Computational Linguistics*, pages 25–32.

Dekang Lin. 1998. Automatic retrieval and clustering of similar words. In *COLING-ACL98*, Montreal, Canada.

O. Liu, C. Brew, J. Blackmore, L. Gerard, J. Madhok, and M. Linn. 2014. Automated scoring of constructed-response science items: Prospects and obstacles. *Educational Measurement: Issues and Practice*, 33(2):19–28.

T. Mikolov, I. Sutskever, K. Chen, G. Corrado, and J. Dean. 2013a. Distributed representations of words and phrases and their compositionality. In *Advances in neural information processing systems*.

Tomas Mikolov, Kai Chen, Greg Corrado, and Jeffrey Dean. 2013b. Efficient estimation of word representations in vector space. *arXiv preprint arXiv:1301.3781*.

Jeff Mitchell and Mirella Lapata. 2010. Composition in distributional models of semantics. *Cognitive science*, 34(8):1388–1429.

Michael Mohler and Rada Mihalcea. 2009. Text-to-text semantic similarity for automatic short answer grading. In *Proceedings of the 12th Conference of the European Chapter of the Association for Computational Linguistics*, EACL '09, pages 567–575.

Michael Mohler, Razvan C. Bunescu, and Rada Mihalcea. 2011. Learning to grade short answer questions using semantic similarity measures and dependency graph alignments. In *ACL*, pages 752–762.

J. Pennington, R. Socher, and C. Manning. 2014. Glove: Global vectors for word representation. *Proceedings of the Empirical Methods in Natural Language Processing (EMNLP)*, 12:1532–1543.

Diana Perez, Enrique Alfonseca, and Pilar Rodrguez. 2004. Application of the bleu method for evaluating free-text answers in an e-learning environment. In *LREC*. European Language Resources Association.

Diana Perez, Alfio Gliozzo, Carlo Strapparava, Enrique Alfonseca, Pilar Rodriguez, and Bernardo Magnini. 2005. Automatic assessment of students' free-text answers underpinned by the combination of a BLEU-inspired algorithm and latent semantic analysis. In *Proceedings of the Eighteenth International Florida Artificial Intelligence Research Society Conference, FLAIRS*, Clearwater Beach, FL, United states.

T. A. Plate. 1995. Holographic reduced representations. *IEEE Transactions on Neural Networks*, 6:623–641.

R. Rehurek. 2010. Fast and faster: A comparison of two streamed matrix decomposition algorithms.

Shourya Roy, Y Narahari, and Om D Deshmukh. 2015. A perspective on computer assisted assessment techniques for short free-text answers. In *Computer Assisted Assessment. Research into E-Assessment*, pages 96–109. Springer.

Sebastian Rudolph and Eugenie Giesbrecht. 2010. Compositional matrix-space models of language. In *Proceedings of the 48th Annual Meeting of the Association for Computational Linguistics*, pages 907–916. Association for Computational Linguistics.

Keisuke Sakaguchi, Michael Heilman, and Nitin Madnani. 2015. Effective feature integration for automated short answer scoring. *Proceedings of NAACL, Denver, Colorado, USA*.

Richard Socher, Alex Perelygin, Jean Y Wu, Jason Chuang, Christopher D Manning, Andrew Y Ng, and Christopher Potts. 2013. Recursive deep models for semantic compositionality over a sentiment treebank. In *Proceedings of the conference on empirical methods in natural language processing (EMNLP)*, volume 1631, page 1642. Citeseer.

Aly A Fahmy Wael H Gomaa. 2012. Short Answer Grading Using String Similarity And Corpus-Based Similarity. *International Journal of Advanced Computer Science and Applications(IJACSA)*, 3(11).

Dominic Widdows. 2008. Semantic vector products: Some initial investigations. In *Second AAAI Symposium on Quantum Interaction*, volume 26, page 28th. Citeseer.

P. Wiemer-Hastings and I. Zipitria. 2001. Rules for syntax, vectors for semantics. In *Proceedings of the 23rd Annual Conference of the Cognitive Science Society*, Mahwah, NJ. Erlbaum.

C. J. Willmott. 1982. Some comments on the evaluation of model performance. *Bulletin of the American Meteorological Society*, 63:1309–1369, #nov#.

A Comparison of Word Embeddings for English and Cross-Lingual Chinese Word Sense Disambiguation

Hong Jin Kang[1], Tao Chen[2], Muthu Kumar Chandrasekaran[1], Min-Yen Kan[1,2]
[1]School of Computing, National University of Singapore
[2]NUS Interactive and Digital Media Institute

{kanghongjin}@gmail.com
{taochen,muthu.chandra,kanmy}@comp.nus.edu.sg

Abstract

Word embeddings are now ubiquitous forms of word representation in natural language processing. There have been applications of word embeddings for monolingual word sense disambiguation (WSD) in English, but few comparisons have been done. This paper attempts to bridge that gap by examining popular embeddings for the task of monolingual English WSD. Our simplified method leads to comparable state-of-the-art performance without expensive retraining.

Cross-Lingual WSD – where the word senses of a word in a source language e come from a separate target translation language f – can also assist in language learning; for example, when providing translations of target vocabulary for learners. Thus we have also applied word embeddings to the novel task of cross-lingual WSD for Chinese and provide a public dataset for further benchmarking. We have also experimented with using word embeddings for LSTM networks and found surprisingly that a basic LSTM network does not work well. We discuss the ramifications of this outcome.

1 Introduction

A word takes on different meanings, largely dependent on the context in which it is used. For example, the word "bank" could mean "slope beside a body of water", or a "depository financial institution" [1]. Word Sense Disambiguation (WSD) is the task of identifying the contextually appropriate meaning of the word. WSD is often considered a classification task, in which the classifier predicts the sense from a possible set of senses, known as a sense inventory, given the target word and the contextual information of the target word. Existing WSD systems can be categorised into either data-driven supervised or knowledge-rich approaches. Both approaches are considered to be complementary to each other.

Word embeddings have become a popular word representation formalism, and many tasks can be done using word embeddings. The effectiveness of using word embeddings has been shown in several NLP tasks (Turian et al., 2010). The goal of our work is to apply and comprehensively compare different uses of word embeddings, solely with respect to WSD. We perform evaluation of the effectiveness of word embeddings on monolingual WSD tasks from Senseval-2 (held in 2001), Senseval-3 (held in 2004), and SemEval-2007. After which, we evaluate our approach on English–Chinese Cross-Lingual WSD using a dataset that we constructed for evaluating our approach on the translation task used in educational applications for language learning.

2 Related Work

Word Sense Disambiguation is a well-studied problem, in which many methods have been applied. Existing methods can be broadly categorised into supervised approaches, where machine learning techniques are used to learn from labeled training data; and unsupervised techniques, which do not rely on labeled data. Unsupervised techniques are knowledge-rich, and rely heavily on knowledge bases and thesaurus,

---

[1]http://wordnetweb.princeton.edu/perl/webwn?s=bank

Proceedings of the 3rd Workshop on Natural Language Processing Techniques for Educational Applications,
pages 30–39, Osaka, Japan, December 12 2016.

such as WordNet (Miller, 1995). It is noted by Navigli (2009) that supervised approaches using memory-based learning and SVM approaches have worked best.

Supervised approaches involve the extraction of features and then classification using machine learning. Zhong and Ng (2010) developed an open-source WSD system, *ItMakesSense* (hereafter, IMS), which was considered the state-of-the-art at the time it was developed. It is a supervised WSD system, which had to be trained prior to use. IMS uses three feature types: 1) individual words in the context surrounding the target word, 2) specific ordered sequences of words appearing at specified offsets from the target word, and 3) Part-Of-Speech tags of the surrounding three words.

Each of the features are binary features, and IMS trains a model for each word. IMS then uses an support vector machine (SVM) for classification. IMS is open-source, provides state-of-the-art performance, and is easy to extend. As such, our work features IMS and extends off of this backbone.

Training data is required to train IMS. We make use of the One-Million Sense-Tagged Instances (Taghipour and Ng, 2015a) dataset, which is the largest dataset we know of for training WSD systems, in training our systems for the All Words tasks.

WSD systems can be evaluated using either fine-grained scoring or coarse-grained scoring. Under fine-grained scoring, every sense is equally distinct from each other, and answers must exactly match. WordNet is often used as the sense inventory for monolingual WSD tasks. However, WordNet is a fine-grained resource, and even human annotators have trouble distinguishing between different senses of a word (Edmonds and Kilgarriff, 2002). In contrast, under coarse-grained scoring, similar senses are grouped and treated as a single sense. In some WSD tasks in SemEval, coarse-grained scoring was done in order to deal with the problem of reliably distinguishing fine-grained senses.

2.1 Cross-Lingual Word Sense Disambiguation

Cross-Lingual WSD was, in part, conceived as a further attempt to solve this issue. In Cross-Lingual WSD, the specificity of a sense is determined by its correct translation in another language. The sense inventory is the possible translations of each word in another language. Two instances are said to have the same sense if they map to the same translation in that language. SemEval-2010 (Lefever and Hoste, 2010)[2] and SemEval-2013 (Lefever and Hoste, 2013)[3] featured iterations of this task. These tasks featured English nouns as the source words, and word senses as translations in Dutch, French, Italian, Spanish and German.

Traditional WSD approaches are used in Cross-Lingual WSD, although some approaches leverage statistical machine translation (SMT) methods and features from translation. Cross-Lingual WSD involves training by making use of parallel or multilingual corpora. In the Cross-Lingual WSD task in SemEval-2013, the top performing approaches used either classification or SMT approaches.

2.2 WSD with Word Embeddings

In NLP, words can be represented with a distributed representation, such as word embeddings, which encodes words into a low dimensional space. In word embeddings, information about a word is distributed across multiple dimensions, and similar words are expected to be close to each other in the vector space. Examples of word embeddings are Continuous Bag of Words (Mikolov et al., 2013), Collobert & Weston's Embeddings (Collobert and Weston, 2008), and GLoVe (Pennington et al., 2014). We implemented and evaluated the use of word embedding features using these three embeddings in IMS.

An unsupervised approach using word embeddings for WSD is described by Chen (2014). This approach finds representation of senses, instead of words, and computes a context vector which is used during disambiguation.

A different approach is to work on extending existing WSD systems. Turian (2010) suggests that for any existing supervised NLP system, a general way of improving accuracy would be to use unsupervised word representations as additional features. Taghipour (2015b) used C&W embeddings as a starting point and implemented word embeddings as a feature type in IMS. For a specified window, vectors for

---

[2]`http://stel.ub.edu/semeval2010-coref/`
[3]`https://www.cs.york.ac.uk/semeval-2013/`

the surrounding words in the windows, excluding the target word, are obtained from the embeddings and are concatenated, producing $d * (w - 1)$ features, where d is the number of dimensions of the vector, and w is the window size. Each feature is a floating point number, which is the value of the vector in a dimension. We note that (Taghipour and Ng, 2015b) only reported results for C&W embeddings, and did not experiment on other types of word embeddings.

Other supervised approaches using word embeddings include AutoExtend (Rothe and Schütze, 2015), which extended word embeddings to create embeddings for synsets and lexemes. In their work, they also extended IMS, but used their own embeddings. The feature types introduced by this work bear similarities to how Taghipour used word embeddings, but without Taghipour's method of scaling each dimension of the word embeddings.

To conclude, word embeddings have been used in several methods to improve on state-of-the-art results in WSD. However, to date, there has been little work investigating how different word embeddings and parameters affect performance of baseline methods of WSD. As far as we know, there has only been one paper comparing the different word embeddings with the use of basic composition methods in WSD. Iacobacci (2016) performed an evaluation study of different parameters when enhancing an existing supervised WSD system with word embeddings. Iacobacci noted that the integration of Word2Vec (skip-gram) with IMS was consistently helpful and provided the best performance. Iacobacci also noted that the composition methods of average and concatenation produced small gains relative to the other composition strategies introduced. However, Iacobacci did not investigate the use of (Taghipour and Ng, 2015b)'s scaling strategy, which was crucial to improve the performance of IMS.

We also did not find any recent work attempting to integrate modern WSD systems for real-world education usage, and to evaluate the WSD system based on the requirements and suitability for education use. We aim to fill this gap in applied WSD with this work.

3   Methods

As Navigli (2009) noted that supervised approaches have performed best in WSD, we focus on integrating word embeddings in supervised approaches; in specific, we explore the use of word embeddings within the IMS framework. We focus our work on Continuous Bag of Words (CBOW) from Word2Vec, Global Vectors for Word Representation (GloVe) and Collobert & Weston's Embeddings(C&W). The CBOW embeddings were trained over Wikipedia, while the publicly available vectors from GloVe and C&W were used. Word2Vec provides 2 architectures for learning word embeddings, Skip-gram and CBOW. In contrast to Iacobacci (2016) which focused on Skip-gram, we focused our work on CBOW. In our first set of evaluations, we used tasks from Senseval-2 (hereafter SE-2), Senseval-3 (hereafter SE-3) and SemEval-2007 (hereafter SE-2007) to evaluate the performance of our classifiers on monolingual WSD. We do this to first validate that our approach is a sound approach of performing WSD, showing improved or identical scores to state-of-the-art systems in most tasks.

Similar to the work by Taghipour (2015b), we experimented with the use of word embeddings as feature types in IMS. However, we did not just experiment using C&W embeddings, as different word embeddings are known to vary in quality when evaluated on different tasks (Schnabel et al., 2015). We performed evaluation on several tasks. For the Lexical Sample (LS) tasks of SE-2 (Kilgarriff, 2001) and SE-3 (Mihalcea et al., 2004), we evaluated our system using fine-grained scoring. For the All Words (AW) tasks, fine-grained scoring is done for SE-2 (Palmer et al., 2001) and SE-3 (Snyder and Palmer, 2004); both the fine (Pradhan et al., 2007) and coarse-grained were used in (Navigli et al., 2007) AW tasks in SE-2007. In order to evaluate our features on the AW task, we trained IMS and the different combinations of features on the One Million Sense-Tagged corpus (Taghipour and Ng, 2015a).

To compose word vectors, one method (used as a baseline) is to sum up the word vectors of the words in the surrounding context or sentence. We primarily experimented on this method of composition, due to its good performance and short training time. For this, every word vector for every lemma in the sentence (exclusive of the target word) was summed into a context vector, resulting in d features. Stopwords and punctuation are discarded. In Turian's (2010) work, two hyperparameters — the capacity (number of dimensions) and size of the word embeddings — were tuned in his experiments. We follow his protocol and perform the same in our experiments.

As the remaining features in IMS are binary features, they are not comparable to the word embeddings which can have unbounded values, leading to unbalanced influence. As suggested by Turian (2010), we should scale down the word embeddings values to the same range as other features. The embeddings are scaled to control their standard deviations. We implement a variant of this technique as done by Taghipour (2015b), in which we set the target standard deviation for each dimension. A comparison of different values of the scaling parameter, σ is done. For each $i \in \{1, 2, ..d\}$:

$$E_i \leftarrow \sigma \times \frac{E_i}{stdev(E_i)}, \text{ where } \sigma \text{ is a scaling constant that sets the target standard deviation}$$

Similar to Turian (2010) and Taghipour (2015b), we found that a value of 0.1 for σ works well, as seen in Table 1. We evaluate the effect of varying the scaling factor with the feature of the sum of the surrounding word vectors, and find that the summation feature works optimally with 50 dimensions.

Table 1: Effects on accuracy when varying scaling factor on C&W embeddings

Method	SE-2 LS	SE-3 LS
C&W, unscaled	0.569	0.641
C&W, $\sigma_{=0.15}$	0.665	0.731
C&W, $\sigma_{=0.1}$	**0.672**	**0.739**
C&W, $\sigma_{=0.05}$	0.664	0.735

In Table 2, we evaluate the performance of our system on both the LS and AW tasks of SE-2 (held in 2001) and SE-3's (held in 2004), and the AW tasks of SE-2007, which were evaluated on by Zhong and Ng (2010). We obtain statistically significant improvements over IMS on the LS tasks. Our enhancements to IMS to make use of word embeddings also give better results on the AW task than the original IMS, the respective Rank 1 systems from the original shared tasks, and several recent systems developed and evaluated evaluated on the same tasks. We note that although our system increased accuracy on IMS on several AW tasks, the differences were not statistically significant (as measured using McNemar's test for paired nominal data).

It can be seen that the simple enhancement of integrating word embedding using the baseline composition method, followed by the scaling step, improves IMS, and we get performance comparable to or better than the Rank 1 systems in many tasks.

As word embeddings with higher dimensions increases the feature space of IMS, this may lead to overfitting on some datasets. We believe, this is why a smaller number of dimensions work better in the LS tasks. However, as seen in Table 3, this effect was not observed in the AW task. We also note that relatively poorer performance in the LS tasks may not necessarily result in poor performance in the AW task. We see from the results that the combination of (Taghipour and Ng, 2015b)'s scaling strategy and summation produced results better than the proposal in (Iacobacci et al., 2016) to concatenate and average (0.651 and 0.654), suggesting that the scaling factor is important for the integration of word embeddings for supervised WSD.

3.1 LSTM Network

A Long Short Term Memory (LSTM) network is a type of Recurrent Neural Network which has recently been shown to have good performance on many NLP classification tasks. The potential benefit of using an approach using LSTM over our existing approach in IMS is this is that an LSTM network is able to use more information about the sequence of words. For WSD, Kågebäck & Salomonsson (2016) explored the use of bidirectional LSTMs. In our approach, we explore a simpler naïve approach instead.

For the Lexical Sample tasks, we train the model on the training data provided for the task. For the All Words task, we trained the model on the One Million Sense-Tagged dataset. For each task, similar to IMS, we train a model for each word, using GloVe word embeddings as the input layer.

Table 2: Comparison of systems by their accuracy score on both Lexical Sample and All Words tasks. Rank 1 system refers to the top ranked system in the respective shared tasks.

Method	SE-2 LS	SE-3 LS	SE-2 AW	SE-3 AW	SE-2007 Fine-grained	SE-2007 Coarse-grained
IMS + CBOW $\sigma_{=0.1}$ (proposed)	0.680	0.741	0.677	0.679	0.604	0.826
IMS + CBOW $\sigma_{=0.15}$ (proposed)	0.670	0.734	0.673	0.675	**0.615**	**0.828**
IMS	0.653	0.726	0.682	0.674	0.585	0.816
Rothe and Schütze (2015)	0.666	0.736	-	-	-	-
Taghipour and Ng (2015b)	0.662	0.734	-	**0.682**	-	-
(Iacobacci et al., 2016)	**0.699**	**0.752**	0.683	0.682	0.591	-
(Chen et al., 2014)	-	-	-	-	-	0.826
Rank 1 System	0.642	0.729	**0.69**	0.652	0.591	0.825
Baseline (Most Frequent Sense & Wordnet Sense 1)	0.476	0.552	0.619	0.624	0.514	0.789

The performance of the naïve LSTM is poor in both type of tasks, as seen in Table 4. The models converge to just using the most common sense for the AW task. A possible reason for this is overfitting. WSD is known to suffer from data sparsity. Although there are many training examples in total, as we train a separate model for each word, many individual words only have few training examples. We note other attempts to use neural networks for WSD may have run into the same problem. Taghipour and Ng (2015b) indicated the need to prevent overfitting while using a neural network to adapt C&W embeddings by omitting a hidden layer and adding a Dropout layer, while Kågebäck and Salomonsson (2016) developed a new regularization technique in their work.

4   English-Chinese Cross-Lingual Word Sense Disambiguation

We now evaluate our proposal on the Cross-Lingual Word Sense Disambiguation task. One key application of such task is to facilitate language learning systems. For example, *MindTheWord*[4] and *WordNews* (Chen et al., 2015) are two applications that allow users to learn vocabulary of a second language in context, in the form of providing translations of words in an online article. In this work, we model this problem of finding translations of words as a variant of WSD, Cross-Lingual Word Sense Disambiguation, as formalized in (Chen et al., 2015).

In the previous section, we have validated and compared enhancements to IMS using word embeddings. These have produced results comparable to, and in some cases, better than state-of-the-art performance on the monolingual WSD tasks. We further evaluate our approach for use in the Cross-Lingual Word Sense Disambiguation for performing contextually appropriate translations of single words. To accomplish this, we first construct a English–Chinese Cross-Lingual WSD dataset. For our sense inventory, we work with the existing dictionary in the open-source educational application, WordNews (Chen et al., 2015), which contains a dictionary of English words and their possible Chinese translations. We finally deploy the trained system as a fork of the original WordNews.

4.1   Dataset

As far as we know, there is no existing publicly available English–Chinese Cross-Lingual WSD dataset. To evaluate our proposal, therefore, we hired human annotators to construct such an evaluation dataset using sentences from recent news articles. As the dataset is constructed using recent news data, it is a

---

[4]https://chrome.google.com/webstore/detail/mindtheword/fabjlaokbhaoehejcoblhahcekmogbom

Table 3: Accuracy of adding word embeddings to IMS, with different parameters, on SE-2, SE-3 LS and AW tasks and SE-2007 AW task

Type	Size	Compose	Scaling	SE-2 LS	SE-3 LS	SE-2 AW	SE-3 AW	SE-2007 Fine-grained	SE-2007 Coarse-grained
C&W	50	Sum	0.05	0.666	0.734	0.679	0.673	0.594	0.818
			0.1	0.671	0.738	0.678	0.673	0.6	0.819
			0.15	0.666	0.732	0.675	0.672	0.598	0.817
CBOW	50	Sum	0.05	0.672	**0.744**	**0.68**	0.677	0.604	0.824
			0.1	**0.68**	0.741	0.677	0.679	0.604	0.826
			0.15	0.67	0.734	0.673	0.675	**0.615**	**0.828**
GloVe	50	Sum	0.05	0.675	0.738	0.676	0.678	0.596	0.819
			0.1	0.679	0.741	0.678	0.68	0.594	0.819
			0.15	0.674	0.731	**0.68**	0.678	0.591	0.819
CBOW	200	Sum	0.05	0.679	0.742	0.679	0.68	0.602	0.823
			0.1	0.669	0.731	0.676	0.675	0.602	0.82
			0.15	0.651	0.715	0.667	0.673	0.594	0.822
GloVe	200	Sum	0.05	0.682	0.741	0.68	**0.682**	0.6	0.823
			0.1	0.666	0.73	0.677	0.679	0.591	0.827
			0.15	0.654	0.706	0.674	0.675	0.591	0.826
C&W	50	Concat	0.1	0.659	0.724	0.679	0.674	0.585	0.818
CBOW	50	Concat	0.1	0.66	0.725	0.678	0.672	0.581	0.816
	200		0.1	0.667	0.729	0.675	0.67	0.591	0.819
GloVe	50	Concat	0.1	0.657	0.722	0.679	0.671	0.583	0.818
	200		0.1	0.664	0.728	0.677	0.669	0.587	0.817

Table 4: Accuracy of a basic LSTM approach on the Lexical Sample and All Words tasks.

Method	SE-2 LS	SE-3 LS	SE-2 AW	SE-3 AW
LSTM approach (Proposed)	0.458	0.603	0.619	0.623
IMS	0.653	0.726	0.682	0.674
(Kågebäck and Salomonsson, 2016)	0.669	0.734	-	-
Rank 1 System during the task	0.642	0.729	0.69	0.652
Baseline	0.476	0.552	0.619	0.624

good representation for the use case in WordNews. To facilitate future research, we have released the dataset to the public.[5]

To obtain the gold standard for this data set, we hired 18 annotators to select the right translations for a given word and its context. There are 697 instances in total in our dataset, with a total of 251 target words to disambiguate, that were each multiply-annotated by 3 different annotators. Each annotator disambiguated 110+ instances (15 annotators with 116 instances, 3 with 117) in hard-copy. The annotators are all bilingual undergraduate students, who are native Chinese speakers.

For each instance, which contains a single English target word to disambiguate, we include the sentence it appears in and its adjacent sentences as its context. Each instance contains possible translations of the word. The annotators selected all Chinese words that had an identical meaning to the English target word. If the word cannot be appropriately translated, we instructed annotators to leave the annotation blank. The annotators provided their own translations if they believe that there is a suitable translation, but which was not provided by the crawled dictionary.

---

[5] https://kanghj.github.io/english_chinese_news_clwsd_dataset/

The concept of a sense is a human construct, and therefore, as earlier elaborated on when discussing sense granularity, it is may be difficult for human annotators to agree on the correct answer. Our annotation task differs from the usual since we allow users to select multiple labels and can also add new labels to each case if they do not agree with any label provided. As such, applying the Cohen's Kappa as it is for measuring the inter-annotator agreement as it is does not work for our annotated dataset. We are also unable to compute the probably of chance agreement by word, since there are few test instances per word in our dataset.

The Kappa equation is given as $\kappa = \frac{p_A - p_E}{1 - p_E}$. To compute p_A for κ, we use a simplified, optimistic approach where we select one annotated label out of possibly multiple selected labels for each annotator. We always choose the label that results in an agreement between the pair, if such a label exist. For p_E (the probability of chance agreement), as the labels of each case are different, we consider the labels in terms of how frequent they occur in the training data. We only consider the top 3 most frequent senses for each word due to the skewness of the sense distribution. We first compute the probability of an annotator selecting each of the top three frequent senses, p_E is then equals to the sum of the probability that both annotators selected one of the three top senses by chance.

The pairwise value by this proposed method of κ is obtained is 0.42. We interpreted this as a moderate level of agreement. We note that there is a large number of possible labels for each case, which is known to affect the value of κ negatively. This is exacerbated as we allow the annotators to add new labels.

In this annotation task, as we consider the possible translations as fine-grained, the value of agreement is likely to be underestimated in this case. Hence, we believe that clustering of similar translations during annotation is required in order to deal with the issue of sense granularity in Cross-Lingual WSD. To overcome this problem, we used different configurations of granularity during evaluation of our system. For all configurations, we remove instances from the dataset if it does not have a correct sense.

We also noticed that some target words were part of a proper noun, such as the word 'white' in 'White House'. This led to some confusion among annotators, so we omitted instances where the target word is part of a proper noun. Statistics of the test dataset after filtering out different cases are given in Table 5.

Table 5: Statistics of our new annotated Chinese-English crosslingual WSD dataset. Out-of-vocabulary (OOV) annotations refer to annotations added by the annotators

Configuration	# of instances	# of unique target words
Include all	653	251
Exclude instances with OOV annotations	481	206
Exclude instances without at least partial agreement	412	193
Exclude instances without complete agreement	229	136

4.2 Experiments

As previously described, IMS is a supervised system requiring training data before use. We constructed data by processing a parallel corpus, the news section of the UM-Corpus (Tian et al., 2014), and performing word alignment. We used the dictionary provided by (Chen et al., 2015) as the sense inventory, which we further expanded using translations from Bing Translator and Google Translate. For construction of the training dataset, word alignment is used to assign Chinese words as training labels for each English target word. GIZA++ (Och and Ney, 2003) is used for word alignment. To evaluate our system, we compare the results of the method described in (Chen et al., 2015), which uses Bing Translator and word alignment to obtain translations. We use the configuration where every annotation is considered to be correct for our main evaluation since this is closer to a coarse-grained evaluation.

It can be seen that word embeddings improves the performance on Cross-Lingual WSD. Similar to our observations for monolingual WSD, the use of both CBOW and GLoVe improved performance. However, the improvements from the word embeddings feature type over IMS was not statistically significant at 95% confidence level. This is attributed to the small size of the dataset.

Table 6: Results of our systems on the Cross-Lingual WSD dataset, excluding named entities. Instances with out-of-vocabulary annotations are removed. All annotations are considered correct answers.

Method	Accuracy
Bing Translator + word alignment (baseline)	0.559
IMS	0.752
IMS + CBOW, 50 dimensions, $\sigma_{=0.05}$ (proposed)	0.763
IMS + CBOW, 50 dimensions, $\sigma_{=0.1}$ (proposed)	**0.772**
IMS + CBOW, 50 dimensions, $\sigma_{=0.15}$ (proposed)	0.767

4.3 Bing Translator results

We wish to highlight and explain the poor performance of Bing Translator with our annotated dataset as seen in Table 6. This could be because Bing Translator performs translation at the phrase level. Therefore, many of the target words are not translated individually and are translated only as part of a larger unit, making it less suitable for the use case in WordNews where only the translation of single words matter. For example, when translating the word "little" in "These are serious issues and themes, and sometimes **little** kids aren't ready to process and understand these ideas", Bing Translator provides a translation of "这些都是严重的问题和主题，有时小孩 不准备处理和理解这些想法" but does not give an alignment for the word 'little' but instead provides an alignment for the entire multi-word unit "little kids". As such, the translation would not match any of the annotations provided by our annotators. This is an appropriate treatment since a user of an educational app requesting specifically a translation for the single word "little" should not see the translation of the phrase.

5 Conclusion

After we have evaluated the performance of the systems on the this Cross-Lingual WSD dataset, we integrate the top-performing system using word embeddings and the trained models into a fork of the WordNews system. We experimented and implemented with different methods of using word embeddings for supervised WSD. We tried two approaches, by enhancing an existing WSD system, IMS, and by trying a neural approach using a simple LSTM. We evaluated our apporach as well as various methods in WSD, against initial evaluations on the existing test data sets from Senseval-2, Senseval-3, SemEval-2007. In a nutshell, adding any pretrained word embedding as a feature type to IMS resulted in the system performing competitively or better than the state-of-the-art systems on many of the tasks. This supports (Iacobacci et al., 2016)'s conclusion that concluded that existing supervised approaches can be augmented with word embeddings to give better results.

Our findings also validated Iacobacci et al. (2016)'s findings that Word2Vec gave the best performance. However, we also note that, other than Word2Vec, other publicly available word embeddings, Collobert & Weston's embeddings and GLoVe also consistently enhanced the performance of IMS using the summation feature with little effort. Other than on the Lexical Sample tasks, where smaller word embeddings performed better, we also found that the number of dimensions did not affect results as much as the scaling parameter. Unlike Iacobacci et al. (2016), we also found that a simple composition method using summation already gave good improvements over the standard WSD features, provided that the scaling method described in (Taghipour and Ng, 2015b) was performed.

An additional key contribution of our work was to build a gold-standard English-Chinese Cross-Lingual WSD dataset constructed with sentences from real news articles and to evaluate our proposed word embedding approach under this scenario. Our compiled dataset was used as evaluation of the task of translating English words on online news articles. This dataset is made available publicly. We observed that word embeddings also improves the performance of WSD in our Cross-Lingual WSD setting.

As future work, we will examine how to expand the existing dictionary with more English words of varying difficulty and include more possible Chinese translations, as we note that there were several instances in the Cross-Lingual WSD dataset where the annotators did not choose an existing translation.

References

Xinxiong Chen, Zhiyuan Liu, and Maosong Sun. 2014. A unified model for word sense representation and disambiguation. In *Proceedings of the 2014 Conference on Empirical Methods in Natural Language Processing (EMNLP)*, pages 1025–1035, Doha, Qatar. Association for Computational Linguistics.

Tao Chen, Naijia Zheng, Yue Zhao, Muthu Kumar Chandrasekaran, and Min-Yen Kan. 2015. Interactive second language learning from news websites. In *Proceedings of ACL Workshop on Natural Language Processing Techniques for Educational Applications (NLP-TEA'15)*, pages 34–42.

Ronan Collobert and Jason Weston. 2008. A unified architecture for natural language processing: Deep neural networks with multitask learning. In *Proceedings of the 25th international conference on Machine learning*, pages 160–167. ACM.

Philip Edmonds and Adam Kilgarriff. 2002. Introduction to the special issue on evaluating word sense disambiguation systems. *Natural Language Engineering*, 8(04):279–291.

Ignacio Iacobacci, Taher Mohammad Pilehvar, and Roberto Navigli. 2016. Embeddings for word sense disambiguation: An evaluation study. In *Proceedings of the 54th Annual Meeting of the Association for Computational Linguistics (Volume 1: Long Papers)*, pages 897–907. Association for Computational Linguistics.

Mikael Kågebäck and Hans Salomonsson. 2016. Word sense disambiguation using a bidirectional lstm. *arXiv preprint arXiv:1606.03568.*

Adam Kilgarriff. 2001. English lexical sample task description. In *The Proceedings of the Second International Workshop on Evaluating Word Sense Disambiguation Systems*, pages 17–20. Association for Computational Linguistics.

Els Lefever and Véronique Hoste. 2010. Semeval-2010 task 3: Cross-lingual word sense disambiguation. In *Proceedings of the 5th International Workshop on Semantic Evaluation*, pages 15–20, Uppsala, Sweden, July. Association for Computational Linguistics.

Els Lefever and Véronique Hoste. 2013. Semeval-2013 task 10: Cross-lingual word sense disambiguation. In *Second Joint Conference on Lexical and Computational Semantics (*SEM), Volume 2: Proceedings of the Seventh International Workshop on Semantic Evaluation (SemEval 2013)*, pages 158–166, Atlanta, Georgia, USA, June. Association for Computational Linguistics.

Rada Mihalcea, Timothy Anatolievich Chklovski, and Adam Kilgarriff. 2004. The Senseval-3 English lexical sample task. In *Senseval-3: Third International Workshop on the Evaluation of Systems for the Semantic Analysis of Text*. Association for Computational Linguistics.

Tomas Mikolov, Kai Chen, Greg Corrado, and Jeffrey Dean. 2013. Efficient estimation of word representations in vector space. *CoRR*, abs/1301.3781.

George A. Miller. 1995. Wordnet: A lexical database for english. *Commun. ACM*, 38(11):39–41, November.

Roberto Navigli, Kenneth C Litkowski, and Orin Hargraves. 2007. Semeval-2007 task 07: Coarse-grained english all-words task. In *Proceedings of the 4th International Workshop on Semantic Evaluations*, pages 30–35. Association for Computational Linguistics.

Roberto Navigli. 2009. Word sense disambiguation: a survey. *ACM COMPUTING SURVEYS*, 41(2):1–69.

Franz Josef Och and Hermann Ney. 2003. A systematic comparison of various statistical alignment models. *Computational Linguistics*, 29(1):19–51.

Martha Palmer, Christiane Fellbaum, Scott Cotton, Lauren Delfs, and Hoa Trang Dang. 2001. English tasks: All-words and verb lexical sample. In *The Proceedings of the Second International Workshop on Evaluating Word Sense Disambiguation Systems*, pages 21–24. Association for Computational Linguistics.

Jeffrey Pennington, Richard Socher, and Christopher D Manning. 2014. Glove: Global vectors for word representation. In *Proc. of the Empiricial Methods in Natural Language Processing (EMNLP 2014)*, volume 14, pages 1532–43.

Sameer S Pradhan, Edward Loper, Dmitriy Dligach, and Martha Palmer. 2007. SemEval-2007 task 17: English lexical sample, SRL and all words. In *Proceedings of the 4th International Workshop on Semantic Evaluations*, pages 87–92. Association for Computational Linguistics.

Sascha Rothe and Hinrich Schütze. 2015. Autoextend: Extending word embeddings to embeddings for synsets and lexemes. In *Proceedings of the ACL-IJCNLP*, pages 1793–1803.

Tobias Schnabel, Igor Labutov, David Mimno, and Thorsten Joachims. 2015. Evaluation methods for unsupervised word embeddings. In *Proceedings of the Conference on Empirical Methods in Natural Language Processing (EMNLP)*, pages 298–307.

Benjamin Snyder and Martha Palmer. 2004. The English all-words task. In *Senseval-3: Third International Workshop on the Evaluation of Systems for the Semantic Analysis of Text*, pages 41–43.

Kaveh Taghipour and Hwee Tou Ng. 2015a. One million sense-tagged instances for word sense disambiguation and induction. *CoNLL 2015*, pages 338–344.

Kaveh Taghipour and Hwee Tou Ng. 2015b. Semi-supervised word sense disambiguation using word embeddings in general and specific domains. In Rada Mihalcea, Joyce Yue Chai, and Anoop Sarkar, editors, *Proceedings of HLT-NAACL*, pages 314–323. Association for Computational Linguistics.

Liang Tian, Derek F Wong, Lidia S Chao, Paulo Quaresma, and Francisco Oliveira. 2014. UM-Corpus: A Large English-Chinese Parallel Corpus for Statistical Machine Translation. In *Proceeding of the LREC*, pages 1837–1842. European Language Resources Association.

Joseph Turian, Lev Ratinov, and Yoshua Bengio. 2010. Word representations: a simple and general method for semi-supervised learning. In *Proceedings of the 48th annual meeting of the association for computational linguistics*, pages 384–394. Association for Computational Linguistics.

Zhi Zhong and Hwee Tou Ng. 2010. It makes sense: A wide-coverage word sense disambiguation system for free text. In *Proceedings of the ACL 2010 System Demonstrations*, ACLDemos '10, pages 78–83, Stroudsburg, PA, USA. Association for Computational Linguistics.

Overview of NLP-TEA 2016 Shared Task for Chinese Grammatical Error Diagnosis

Lung-Hao Lee[1], Gaoqi Rao[2], Liang-Chih Yu[3,4],
Endong Xun[5], Baolin Zhang[6], Li-Ping Chang[7]

[1]Graduate Institute of Library and Information Studies, National Taiwan Normal University
[2]Center for Studies of Chinese as a Second Language, Beijing Language and Culture University
[3]Department of Information Management, Yuan Ze University
[4]Innovative Center for Big Data and Digital Convergence, Yuan Ze University
[5]College of Information Science, Beijing Language and Culture University
[6]Faculty of Language Sciences, Beijing Language and Culture University
[7]Mandarin Training Center, National Taiwan Normal University

lhlee@ntnu.edu.tw, raogaoqi@blcu.edu.cn, lcyu@saturn.yzu.edu.tw

edxun@126.com, zhangbl@blcu.edu.cn, lchang@ntnu.edu.tw

Abstract

This paper presents the NLP-TEA 2016 shared task for Chinese grammatical error diagnosis which seeks to identify grammatical error types and their range of occurrence within sentences written by learners of Chinese as foreign language. We describe the task definition, data preparation, performance metrics, and evaluation results. Of the 15 teams registered for this shared task, 9 teams developed the system and submitted a total of 36 runs. We expected this evaluation campaign could lead to the development of more advanced NLP techniques for educational applications, especially for Chinese error detection. All data sets with gold standards and scoring scripts are made publicly available to researchers.

1 Introduction

Recently, automated grammar checking for learners of English as a foreign language has attracted more attention. For example, Helping Our Own (HOO) is a series of shared tasks in correcting textual errors (Dale and Kilgarriff, 2011; Dale et al., 2012). The shared tasks at CoNLL 2013 and CoNLL 2014 focused on grammatical error correction, increasing the visibility of educational application research in the NLP community (Ng et al., 2013; 2014).

Many of these learning technologies focus on learners of English as a Foreign Language (EFL), while relatively few grammar checking applications have been developed to support Chinese as a Foreign Language(CFL) learners. Those applications which do exist rely on a range of techniques, such as statistical learning (Chang et al, 2012; Wu et al, 2010; Yu and Chen, 2012), rule-based analysis (Lee et al., 2013) and hybrid methods (Lee et al., 2014). In response to the limited availability of CFL learner data for machine learning and linguistic analysis, the ICCE-2014 workshop on Natural Language Processing Techniques for Educational Applications (NLP-TEA) organized a shared task on diagnosing grammatical errors for CFL (Yu et al., 2014). A second version of this shared task in NLP-TEA was collocated with the ACL-IJCNLP-2015 (Lee et al., 2015). In conjunction with the COLLING 2016, the third NLP-TEA features a shared task for Chinese grammatical error diagnosis again. The main purpose of these shared tasks is to provide a common setting so that researchers who approach the tasks using different linguistic factors and computational techniques can compare their results. Such technical evaluations allow researchers to exchange their experiences to advance the field and eventually develop optimal solutions to this shared task.

Proceedings of the 3rd Workshop on Natural Language Processing Techniques for Educational Applications,
pages 40–48, Osaka, Japan, December 12 2016.

The rest of this paper is organized as follows. Section 2 describes the task in detail. Section 3 introduces the constructed datasets. Section 4 proposes evaluation metrics. Section 5 reports the results of the participants' approaches. Conclusions are finally drawn in Section 6.

2 Task Description

The goal of this shared task is to develop NLP techniques to automatically diagnose grammatical errors in Chinese sentences written by CFL learners. Such errors are defined as redundant words (denoted as a capital "R"), missing words ("M"), word selection errors ("S"), and word ordering errors ("W"). The input sentence may contain one or more such errors. The developed system should indicate which error types are embedded in the given sentence and the position at which they occur. Each input sentence is given a unique sentence number "sid". If the inputs contain no grammatical errors, the system should return: "sid, correct". If an input sentence contains the grammatical errors, the output format should include four items "sid, start_off, end_off, error_type", where start_off and end_off respectively denote the positions of starting and ending character at which the grammatical error occurs, and error_type should be one of the defined errors: "R", "M", "S", and "W". Each character or punctuation mark occupies 1 space for counting positions. Example sentences and corresponding notes are shown as follows.

TOCFL (Traditional Chinese)	HSK (Simplified Chinese)
• Example 1 Input: (sid=A2-0007-2) 聽說妳打算開一個慶祝會。可惜我不能參加。因為那個時候我有別的事。當然我也要<u>參加</u>給你慶祝慶祝。 Output: A2-0007-2, 38, 39, R (Notes: "參加"is a redundant word)	• Example 1 Input: (sid=00038800481)　我根本不能<u>了解这</u>妇女辞职回家的现象。在这个时代，为什么放弃自己的工作，就回家当家庭主妇？ Output: 00038800481, 6, 7, S 　　　　　00038800481, 8, 8, R (Notes: "了解"should be "理解". In addition, "这" is a redundant word.)
• Example 2 Input: (sid=A2-0007-3)　我要送給你一個慶祝禮物。要是<u>兩、三天晚了</u>，請別生氣。 Output: A2-0007-3, 15, 20, W (Notes: "兩、三天晚了"should be "晚了兩、三天")	• Example 2 Input: (sid=00038800464)我真不明白。她们可能是追求一些前代的浪漫。 Output: 00038800464, correct
• Example 3 Input: (sid=A2-0011-1)　我<u>聽到</u>你找到工作。恭喜恭喜！ Output: A2-0011-1, 2, 3, S 　　　　A2-0011-1, 9, 9, M (Notes: "聽到"should be "聽說". Besides, a word "了"is missing. The correct sentence should be "我<u>聽說</u>你找到工作<u>了</u>".	• Example 3 Input: (sid=00038801261)人战胜了饥饿，才努力为了下一代<u>作</u>更好的、更健康的东西。 Output: 00038801261, 9, 9, M 　　　　　00038801261, 16, 16, S (Notes: "能" is missing. The word "作"should be "做". The correct sentence is "才<u>能</u>努力为了下一代<u>做</u>更好的")
• Example 4 Input: (sid=A2-0011-3)　我覺得對你很抱歉。我也很想去，可是沒有辦法。 Output: A2-0011-3, correct	• Example 4 Input: (sid=00038801320)饥饿的问题也是应该解决的。世界上每天<u>由于饥饿很多人</u>死亡。 Output: 00038801320, 19, 25, W (Notes: "由于饥饿很多人" should be "很多人由于饥饿")

Table 1: Example sentences and corresponding notes.

3   Datasets

The learner corpora used in our shared task were taken from two sources: the writing section of the computer-based Test Of Chinese as a Foreign Language (TOCFL) (Lee et al., 2016) and the writing section of the Hanyu Shuiping Kaoshi(HSK, Test of Chinese Level)(Cui et al, 2011; Zhang et al, 2013).

Native Chinese speakers were trained to manually annotate grammatical errors and provide corrections corresponding to each error. The data were then split into two mutually exclusive sets as follows.

(1) Training Set: All sentences in this set were used to train the grammatical error diagnostic systems. Each sentence with annotated grammatical errors and their corresponding corrections is represented in SGML format, as shown in Fig. 1. For the TOCFL track, we provide 10,693 training sentences with a total of 24,492 grammatical errors, categorized as redundant (4,472 instances), missing (8,739), word selection (9,897) and word ordering (1,384). For the HSK track, we provide 10,071 training sentences with a total of 24,797 grammatical errors, categorized as redundant (5,538 instances), missing (6,623), word selection (10,949) and word ordering (1,687).

In addition to the data sets provided, participating research teams were allowed to use other public data for system development and implementation. Use of other data should be specified in the final system report.

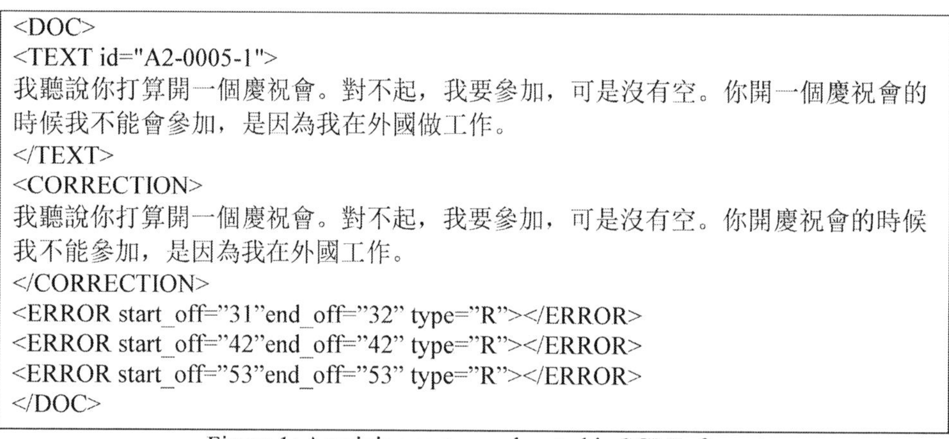

```
<DOC>
<TEXT id="A2-0005-1">
我聽說你打算開一個慶祝會。對不起，我要參加，可是沒有空。你開一個慶祝會的
時候我不能會參加，是因為我在外國做工作。
</TEXT>
<CORRECTION>
我聽說你打算開一個慶祝會。對不起，我要參加，可是沒有空。你開慶祝會的時候
我不能參加，是因為我在外國工作。
</CORRECTION>
<ERROR start_off="31"end_off="32" type="R"></ERROR>
<ERROR start_off="42"end_off="42" type="R"></ERROR>
<ERROR start_off="53"end_off="53" type="R"></ERROR>
</DOC>
```

Figure 1: A training sentence denoted in SGML format.

(2)Test Set: This set consists of testing sentences used for evaluating system performance. Table 2 shows statistics for the testing set for both tracks. About half of these sentences are correct and do not contain grammatical errors, while the other half include at least one error. The distributions of error types (shown in Table 3) are similar with that of the training set.

Track	#Sentences	#Correct	#Erroneous
TOCFL	3,528 (100%)	1,703 (48.27%)	1,825 (51.73%)
HSK	3,011 (100%)	1,539 (51.11%)	1,472 (48.89%)

Table 2: The statistics of testing set for both tracks.

Track	#Error	#R	#M	#S	#W
TOCFL	4,103 (100%)	782 (19.06%)	1,482 (36.12%)	1613 (39.31%)	226 (5.51%)
HSK	3,695 (100%)	802 (21.71%)	991 (26.82%)	1620 (43.84%)	282 (7.63%)

Table 3: The distributions of error types for both tracks.

4   Performance Metrics

Table 4 shows the confusion matrix used for evaluating system performance. In this matrix, TP (True Positive) is the number of sentences with grammatical errors are correctly identified by the developed system; FP (False Positive) is the number of sentences in which non-existent grammatical errors are identified as errors; TN (True Negative) is the number of sentences without grammatical errors that are correctly identified as such; FN (False Negative) is the number of sentences with grammatical errors which the system incorrectly identifies as being correct.

The criteria for judging correctness are determined at three levels as follows.

(1) Detection-level: Binary classification of a given sentence, that is, correct or incorrect, should be completely identical with the gold standard. All error types will be regarded as incorrect.

(2) Identification-level: This level could be considered as a multi-class categorization problem. All error types should be clearly identified. A correct case should be completely identical with the gold standard of the given error type.

(3) Position-level: In addition to identifying the error types, this level also judges the occurrence range of the grammatical error. That is to say, the system results should be perfectly identical with the quadruples of the gold standard.

The following metrics are measured at all levels with the help of the confusion matrix.

- False Positive Rate = FP / (FP+TN)
- Accuracy = (TP+TN) / (TP+FP+TN+FN)
- Precision = TP / (TP+FP)
- Recall = TP / (TP+FN)
- F1 = 2*Precision*Recall / (Precision + Recall)

Confusion Matrix		System Results	
		Positive (Erroneous)	Negative(Correct)
Gold Standard	Positive	TP (True Positive)	FN (False Negative)
	Negative	FP (False Positive)	TN (True Negative)

Table 4: Confusion matrix for evaluation.

For example, for 4 testing inputs with gold standards shown as "00038800481, 6, 7, S", "00038800481, 8, 8, R", "00038800464, correct", "00038801261, 9, 9, M", "00038801261, 16, 16, S" and "00038801320, 19, 25, W", the system may output the result as "00038800481, 2, 3, S", "00038800481, 4, 5, S", "00038800481, 8, 8, R", "00038800464, correct", "00038801261, 9, 9, M", "00038801261, 16, 19, S" and "00038801320, 19, 25, M". The scoring script will yield the following performance.

- False Positive Rate (FPR) = 0 (=0/1)
- Detection-level
  - Accuracy = 1 (=4/4)
  - Precision = 1 (=3/3)
  - Recall = 1 (=3/3)
  - F1 = 1 (=(2*1*1)/(1+1))
- Identification-level
  - Accuracy = 0.8333 (=5/6)
  - Precision = 0.8 (=4/5)
  - Recall = 0.8 (=4/5)
  - F1 = 0.8 (=(2*0.8*0.8)/(0.8+08))
- Position-level
  - Accuracy = 0.4286 (=3/7)
  - Precision = 0.3333 (=2/6)
  - Recall = 0.4 (=2/5)
  - F1 = 0.3636 (=(2*0.3333*0.4)/(0.3333+0.4))

5　Evaluation Results

Table 5 summarizes the submission statistics for the 15 participating teams including 8 from universities and research institutes in P.R.C (ANO, BFSU-TZT, BISTU, CCNU, HIT, PKU, SKY and YUN-HPCC), 4 from Taiwan, R.O.C. (CYUT, NCTU+NTUT, NCYU and NTOU), 2 from European (including Dublin with NTU (TWIRL) and Saarland with Harvard (MAZA) and 1 private firm (Sogou Inc.). In the official testing phase, each team could opt to participate in either one or both of the TOCFL and HSK tracks. Each participating team was allowed to submit at most three runs for each track. Of the 15 registered teams, 9 teams submitted their testing results, for a total of 36 runs including 15 TOCFL runs (denoting as #TRuns) and 21 HSK runs (#HRuns).

Table 6 shows the testing results for the TOCFL track. The NCTU+CYUT team achieved the lowest false positive rate (denoted as "FPR") of 0.1362. Detection-level evaluations are designed to detect whether a sentence contains grammatical errors or not. A neutral baseline can be easily achieved by always reporting all testing sentences as correct without errors. According to the test data distribution, the baseline system can achieve an accuracy of 0.4827. All systems performed above the baseline. The system result submitted by CYUT achieved the best detection accuracy of 0.5955. We use the F1 score to reflect the tradeoffs between precision and recall. The NCYU provided the best error detection results, providing a high F1 score of 0.6779. For identification-level evaluations, the systems need to identify the error types in a given sentences. The system developed by CYUT provided the highest F1 score of 0.3666 for grammatical error identification. For position-level evaluations, CYUT achieved the best F1 score of 0.1248. Perfectly identifying the error types and their corresponding positions is difficult in part because no word delimiters exist among Chinese words in the given sentences.

Table 7 shows the testing results for the HSK track. The CCNU team did not submit the result by the due date. The SKY team achieved the lowest false positive rate of 0.0481. At the detection-level, the accuracy baseline is 0.5111. Eight runs from 5 teams failed to pass the baseline. The system result submitted by SKY achieved the best detection accuracy of 0.6659. For the F1 score, HIT provided the best error detection results, as high as 0.6628. In both the identification-level and position-level evaluations, HIT achieved the best F1 scores of 0.5215 and 0.3855, in different runs. At the position-level, system performance varied considerably among the teams, from 0.0007 to 0.3855. For the HSK track, better F1 scoresat the identification-level and position-level are achieved than in the TOCFL track. Note that, for teams participating in both two tracks, system performances didn't simply increase from TOCFL to HSK, indicating that differences in data sets had a complex impact on system performance.

Participant (Ordered by abbreviations of names)	#TRuns	#HRuns
NLP Lab, Zhengzhou University (**ANO**)	0	2
Beijing Foreign Studies University (**BFSU-TZT**)	0	0
Beijing Information Science and Technology University (**BISTU**)	0	0
Central China Normal University (**CCNU**)	0	1
Chaoyang University of Technology (**CYUT**)	3	3
Harbin Institute of Technology (**HIT**)	0	3
Institute of Computational Linguistics, Peking University (**PKU**)	3	3
Saarland University & Hardvard Medical School (**MAZA**)	0	0
National Chiao Tung University & National Taipei University of Technology (**NCTU+NTUT**)	3	0
National Chiayi University (**NCYU**)	3	3
National Taiwan Ocean University (**NTOU**)	0	0
NLP Lab, Zhengzhou University (**SKY**)	0	3
Beijing Sogou Inc. (**Sogou**)	0	0
Dublin City University & National Taiwan University (**TWIRL**)	0	0
School of Information Science and Engineering, Yunnan University (**YUN-HPCC**)	3	3

Table 5: Submission statistics for all participants.

TOCFL Submission	FPR	Detection-level				Identification-level				Position-level			
		Acc.	Pre.	Rec.	F1	Acc.	Pre.	Rec.	F1	Acc.	Pre.	Rec.	F1
CYUT-Run1	0.3470	**0.5955**	0.6259	0.5419	0.5809	**0.5154**	0.4600	0.3021	0.3647	0.3113	0.1461	0.1089	**0.1248**
CYUT-Run2	0.3558	**0.5955**	0.6236	0.5501	0.5846	0.5133	0.4567	0.3061	**0.3666**	0.3061	0.1432	**0.1092**	0.1239
CYUT-Run3	0.3635	0.5941	0.6205	0.5545	0.5856	0.5078	0.4472	0.3001	0.3592	0.3088	0.1196	0.0768	0.0935
NCTU+NTUT-Run1	**0.1362**	0.5442	**0.6593**	0.2460	0.3583	0.5110	**0.4892**	0.1224	0.1958	**0.4603**	**0.2542**	0.0483	0.0811
NCTU+NTUT-Run2	0.2913	0.5530	0.6000	0.4077	0.4855	0.4793	0.4036	0.1982	0.2659	0.3784	0.1644	0.0639	0.0920
NCTU+NTUT-Run3	0.3200	0.5612	0.6013	0.4504	0.5150	0.4773	0.3993	0.2185	0.2824	0.3613	0.1521	0.0668	0.0928
NCYU-Run1	0.5602	0.5507	0.5559	0.6542	0.6011	0.3577	0.2749	0.2862	0.2805	0.1728	0.0074	0.0056	0.0064
NCYU-Run2	0.9612	0.5218	0.5202	**0.9726**	**0.6779**	0.2328	0.2265	**0.4744**	0.3066	0.0231	0.0129	0.0195	0.0155
NCYU-Run3	0.8491	0.5363	0.5307	0.8959	0.6665	0.2653	0.2384	0.4134	0.3024	0.0580	0.0130	0.0163	0.0145
PKU-Run1	0.2284	0.5210	0.5739	0.2871	0.3828	0.4575	0.3418	0.1173	0.1747	0.3844	0.0996	0.0263	0.0416
PKU-Run2	0.7205	0.5258	0.5292	0.7556	0.6224	0.3242	0.2792	0.3712	0.3187	0.1381	0.0680	0.0824	0.0745
PKU-Run3	0.5250	0.5349	0.5467	0.5907	0.5678	0.3705	0.2729	0.2192	0.2431	0.2331	0.0872	0.0651	0.0745
YUN-HPCC-Run1	0.6289	0.5420	0.5444	0.7014	0.6130	0.2211	0.1588	0.3196	0.2122	0.0886	0.0002	0.0002	0.0002
YUN-HPCC-Run2	0.5931	0.5026	0.5167	0.5918	0.5517	0.2322	0.1675	0.3136	0.2184	0.0991	0	0	null
YUN-HPCC-Run3	0.3382	0.4847	0.5030	0.3195	0.3908	0.4023	0.2810	0.1359	0.1832	0.2797	0.0012	0.0005	0.0007

Table 6: Testing results of TOCFL track.

HSK Submission	FPR	Detection-level				Identification-level				Position-level			
		Acc.	Pre.	Rec.	F1	Acc.	Pre.	Rec.	F1	Acc.	Pre.	Rec.	F1
ANO-Run1	0.5601	0.5473	0.5297	0.6596	0.5876	0.4723	0.4244	0.4292	0.4268	0.3687	0.2910	0.2460	0.2666
ANO-Run2	0.6517	0.4779	0.4738	0.6135	0.5346	0.2977	0.2243	0.2535	0.2380	0.1157	0.0046	0.0046	0.0046
*CCNU-Run1	0.3294	0.4988	0.4811	0.3193	0.3838	0.4012	0.2425	0.1324	0.1713	0.2806	0.0187	0.0089	0.0121
CYUT-Run1	0.4016	0.6141	0.6003	0.6304	0.6150	0.5714	0.5306	0.4376	0.4797	0.3202	0.2037	0.2138	0.2086
CYUT-Run2	0.4191	0.6118	0.5951	0.6440	0.6186	0.5662	0.5238	0.4509	0.4846	0.3143	0.2034	0.2225	0.2125
CYUT-Run3	0.4016	0.6141	0.6003	0.6304	0.6150	0.5715	0.5306	0.4352	0.4782	0.3304	0.1814	0.1440	0.1605
HIT-Run1	0.4334	0.6377	0.6111	0.7120	0.6577	0.5683	0.5146	0.5219	0.5182	0.4781	0.4034	0.3691	**0.3855**
HIT-Run2	0.4327	0.6370	0.6108	0.7099	0.6566	0.5744	0.5224	0.5094	0.5158	0.4756	0.3970	0.3483	0.3711
HIT-Run3	0.4516	0.6370	0.6071	0.7296	**0.6628**	0.5565	0.5002	**0.5447**	**0.5215**	0.4475	0.3695	**0.3697**	0.3696
NCYU-Run1	0.2820	0.5526	0.5629	0.3798	0.4535	0.4554	0.3259	0.1877	0.2382	0.3301	0.0244	0.0095	0.0136
NCYU-Run2	0.9467	0.5042	0.4964	**0.9755**	0.6580	0.2687	0.2588	0.5263	0.3470	0.0312	0.0158	0.0217	0.0183
NCYU-Run3	0.9818	0.4846	0.4864	0.9721	0.6484	0.2227	0.2195	0.3578	0.2721	0.0148	0.0081	0.0089	0.0085
PKU-Run1	0.7706	0.4972	0.4910	0.7772	0.6018	0.3104	0.2717	0.3991	0.3233	0.1106	0.0523	0.0674	0.0589
PKU-Run2	0.8070	0.5022	0.4945	0.8254	0.6185	0.3144	0.2765	0.3594	0.3125	0.1016	0.0595	0.0923	0.0724
PKU-Run3	0.8213	0.5058	0.4968	0.8478	0.6265	0.3062	0.2694	0.3586	0.3076	0.0896	0.0520	0.0863	0.0649
SKY-Run1	0.0695	0.6523	0.8326	0.3614	0.5040	0.6605	0.8235	0.2732	0.4102	0.6073	0.6153	0.1783	0.2765
SKY-Run2	**0.0481**	0.6579	**0.8746**	0.3505	0.5005	0.6765	**0.8821**	0.2972	0.4446	0.6376	0.7054	0.2217	0.3373
SKY-Run3	0.0559	**0.6659**	0.8652	0.3750	0.5232	**0.6849**	0.8744	0.3185	0.4669	**0.6477**	**0.7144**	0.2430	0.3627
YUN-HPCC-Run1	0.5608	0.5191	0.5069	0.6026	0.5506	0.3485	0.2800	0.3879	0.3252	0.0654	0.0024	0.0062	0.0035
YUN-HPCC-Run2	0.7122	0.4949	0.4886	0.7113	0.5793	0.3092	0.2681	0.4565	0.3378	0.0373	0.0022	0.0070	0.0034
YUN-HPCC-Run3	0.2710	0.5058	0.4902	0.2724	0.3502	0.4306	0.2886	0.1448	0.1928	0.2701	0.0010	0.0005	0.0007

Table 7: Testing results of HSK track.

Table 8 summarize the approaches and resources for each of the submitted systems. ANO and CCNU did not submit reports on their develop systems. Though neural networks achieved goodperformances in various NLP tasks, traditional pipe-lines were still widely implemented in the CGED task. CRF, as a sequence labelling model with flexible feature space, was chosen by CYUT, HIT, NCTU+NTUT and SKY in their system pipe-lines. The CRF based systems model with carefully designed feature templates could maintain the performance with neural networks at the same level in the HSK track. The HIT systems using CRF model and LSTM networks achieved the best F1 scores in the three levels. Moreover, CYUT system is simply based onthe CRF model with multiple feature templates in the TOCFL track.

In summary, none of the submitted systems provided superior performance using different metrics, indicating the difficulty of developing systems for effective grammatical error diagnosis, especially in CFL contexts. From organizers' perspectives, a good system should have a high F1 score and a low false positive rate. Overall, the CYUT, NCTU+NTUT, HIT and SKY teams achieved relatively better performances.

Team	Approach	Word/Character Embedding	Additional Resources
CYUT	CRF	---	NLP-TEA-1&NLP-TEA-2
HIT	CRF+LSTM networks	Character Embedding	---
NCTU+NTUT	W2V+CRF	Word Embedding	Sinica Balanced Corpus v4.0 LDC Chinese Gigaword v2 CIRB0303 Taiwan Panorama Magazine TCC300 Wikipedia(ZH_TW) NLP-TEA-1&NLP-TEA-2
NCYU	RNN+LSTM networks	Word Embedding	NLP-TEA-1&NLP-TEA-2
PKU	Bi-LSTM networks	Word Embedding	NLP-TEA-1&NLP-TEA-2
SKY	Ngram+CRF	---	---
YUN-HPCC	CNN/LSTM networks	Word Embedding	Wikipedia(ZH)

Table 8: Summary of approaches and additional resources used by the submitted systems.

6   Conclusions

This study describes the NLP-TEA 2016 shared task for Chinese grammatical error diagnosis, including task design, data preparation, performance metrics, and evaluation results. Regardless of actual performance, all submissions contribute to the common effort to develop Chinese grammatical error diagnosis system, and the individual reports in the proceedings provide useful insights into computer-assisted language learning for CFL learners.

We hope the data sets collected and annotated for this shared task can facilitate and expedite future development in this research area. Therefore, all data sets with gold standards and scoring scripts are publicly available online at http://ir.itc.ntnu.edu.tw/lre/nlptea16cged.htm.

Acknowledgements

We thank all the participants for taking part in our shared task. We would like to thank Kuei-Ching Lee for implementing the evaluation program and the usage feedbacks from Bo Zheng.

This study was partially supported by the Ministry of Science and Technology, under the grant MOST 103-2221-E-003-013-MY3, MOST 103-2410-H-003-043-MY2, MOST 105-2221-E-003-020-MY2, and MOST 105-2221-E-155-059-MY2, and the "Aim for the Top University Project" and "Center of Learning Technology for Chinese" of National Taiwan Normal University, sponsored by the Ministry of Education, Taiwan, R.O.C.

Following grants and projects from P.R.C also supported the study in this paper: Social Science Funding China (11BYY054, 12&ZD173, 16AYY007), Social Science Funding Beijing (15WYA017), National Language Committee Project (YB125-42, ZDI135-3), 863 Key Project (SQ2015AA0100074), MOE Annual Project of Key Research Institutes in Univs "Push Platform in Resources of CSL".

References

Ru-Yng Chang, Chung-Hsien Wu, and Philips Kokoh Prasetyo. 2012. Error diagnosis of Chinese sentences usign inductive learning algorithm and decomposition-based testing mechanism. ACM Transactions on Asian Language Information Processing, 11(1), article 3.

Xiliang Cui, Bao-lin Zhang. 2011. The Principles for Building the "International Corpus of Learner Chinese". Applied Linguistics, 2011(2), pages 100-108.

Robert Dale and Adam Kilgarriff. 2011. Helping our own: The HOO 2011 pilot shared task. In *Proceedings of the 13th European Workshop on Natural Language Generation(ENLG'11)*, pages 1-8, Nancy, France.

Reobert Dale, Ilya Anisimoff, and George Narroway. 2012. HOO 2012: A report on the preposiiton and determiner error correction shared task. In *Proceedings of the 7th Workshop on the Innovative Use of NLP for Building Educational Applications(BEA'12)*, pages 54-62, Montreal, Canada.

Hwee Tou Ng, Siew Mei Wu, Ted Briscoe, Christian Hadiwinoto, Raymond Hendy Susanto, and Christopher Bryant. 2014. The CoNLL-2014 shared task on grammatical error correction. In *Proceedings of the 18th Conference on Computational Natural Language Learning (CoNLL'14): Shared Task*, pages 1-12, Baltimore, Maryland, USA.

Hwee Tou Ng, Siew Mei Wu, Yuanbin Wu, Christian Hadiwinoto, and Joel Tetreault. 2013. The CoNLL-2013 shared task on grammatical error correction. In *Proceedings of the 17th Conference on Computational Natural Language Learning(CoNLL'13): Shared Task*, pages 1-14, Sofia, Bulgaria.

Lung-Hao Lee, Li-Ping Chang, and Yuen-Hsien Tseng. 2016. Developing learner corpus annotation for Chinese grammatical errors. In *Proceedings of the 20th International Conference on Asian Language Processing (IALP'16)*, Tainan, Taiwan.

Lung-Hao Lee, Li-Ping Chang, Kuei-Ching Lee, Yuen-Hsien Tseng, and Hsin-Hsi Chen. 2013. Linguistic rules based Chinese error detection for second language learning. In *Proceedings of the 21st International Conference on Computers in Education*(ICCE'13), pages 27-29, Denpasar Bali, Indonesia.

Lung-Hao Lee, Liang-Chih Yu, and Li-Ping Chang. 2015. Overview of the NLP-TEA 2015 shared task for Chinese grammatical error diagnosis. In *Proceedings of the 2nd Workshop on Natural Language Processing Techniques for Educational Applications (NLP-TEA'15)*, pages 1-6, Beijing, China.

Lung-Hao Lee, Liang-Chih Yu, Kuei-Ching Lee, Yuen-Hsien Tseng, Li-Ping Chang, and Hsin-Hsi Chen. 2014. A sentence judgment system for grammatical error detection. In *Proceedings of the 25th International Conference on Computational Linguistics (COLING'14): Demos*, pages 67-70, Dublin, Ireland.

Chung-Hsien Wu, Chao-Hong Liu, Matthew Harris, and Liang-Chih Yu. 2010. Sentence correction incorporating relative position and parse template language models. IEEE Transactions on Audio, Speech, and Language Processing, 18(6), pages 1170-1181.

Chi-Hsin Yu and Hsin-Hsi Chen. 2012. Detecting word ordering errors in Chinese sentences for learning Chinese as a foreign language. In *Proceedings of the 24th International Conference on Computational Linguistics (COLING'12)*, pages 3003-3017, Bombay, India.

Liang-Chih Yu, Lung-Hao Lee, and Li-Ping Chang. 2014. Overview of grammatical error diagnosis for learning Chinese as foreign language. In *Proceedings of the 1st Workshop on Natural Language Processing Techniques for Educational Applications (NLP-TEA'14)*, pages 42-47, Nara, Japan.

Bao-lin Zhang, Xiliang Cui. 2013. Design Concepts of "the Construction and Research of the Inter-language Corpus of Chinese from Global Learners". Language Teaching and Linguistic Study, 2013(5), pages 27-34.

Chinese Grammatical Error Diagnosis with Long Short-Term Memory Networks

Bo Zheng, Wanxiang Che[*]**, Jiang Guo, Ting Liu**
[†]Research Center for Social Computing and Information Retrieval
Harbin Institute of Technology, China
{bzheng, car, jguo, tliu}@ir.hit.edu.cn

Abstract

Grammatical error diagnosis is an important task in natural language processing. This paper introduces our Chinese Grammatical Error Diagnosis (CGED) system in the NLP-TEA-3 shared task for CGED. The CGED system can diagnose four types of grammatical errors which are redundant words (R), missing words (M), bad word selection (S) and disordered words (W). We treat the CGED task as a sequence labeling task and describe three models, including a CRF-based model, an LSTM-based model and an ensemble model using *stacking*. We also show in details how we build and train the models. Evaluation includes three levels, which are detection level, identification level and position level. On the CGED-HSK dataset of NLP-TEA-3 shared task, our system presents the best F1-scores in all the three levels and also the best recall in the last two levels.

1 Introduction

Chinese has been considered as one of the most difficult languages in the world. Unlike English, Chinese has no verb tenses and pluralities, and there usually exist various ways to express the same meaning in Chinese. Consequently, it is common for non-native speakers of Chinese to make grammatical errors of various types in their writings. The goal of Chinese Grammatical Error Diagnosis (CGED) is to build a system that can automatically diagnose errors in Chinese sentences. Evaluation is carried out in three levels, based on the detection of error occurrences in a sentence, as well as their types and positions.

In this work, we formalize the CGED task as a sequence labeling problem, which assigns each Chinese character in a target sentence with a tag indicating both the error type (R, M, S, W) and position (Beginning, Inside). Therefore, the CGED task can be readily solved with a typical conditional random fields (CRF) model (Lafferty et al., 2001).

However, the main challenge for CGED is that the detection of errors usually requires long-term dependencies. For example, in Table 1, the grammatical error at "表示(represent)" may not be detected until the last word "损害(damage)" shows up. Traditional models with features extracted from a limited context window may not be able to handle these situations.

Neural network-based models have been extensively used in natural language processing (NLP) during recent years, due to their strong capability of automatic feature learning. In particular, the long short-term memory (LSTM) (Hochreiter and Schmidhuber, 1997) based recurrent neural networks (RNN) have been proved to be highly effective in various applications that involves sequence modeling, such as language modeling, named entity recognition (Lample et al., 2016) and parsing (Vinyals et al., 2015), etc. Therefore, in this paper, we propose to use LSTM-based RNNs to solve the CGED problem. In order to leverage both the merits of CRF models and LSTM models, we further present an ensemble model using *Stacking* (Nivre and McDonald, 2008). Evaluations on the NLP-TEA-3 shared task for CGED show that our models achieve the best F1-scores in all levels and the best recall in two levels.

The rest of the paper is organized as follows: Section 2 gives the definition of the CEGD task. Section 3 describes how LSTM network is used to predict errors and what other works we have done. Section 4

---

[*]Email correspondence.

Proceedings of the 3rd Workshop on Natural Language Processing Techniques for Educational Applications,
pages 49–56, Osaka, Japan, December 12 2016.

shows the evaluation results. Section 5 gives some related works. Section 6 gives conclusion and future work of this paper.

2 Task Definition

The shared task of CGED in NLP-TEA-3 is defined as follows: given a Chinese sentence, a CGED system is expected to diagnose four types of grammatical errors, including *redundant words* (R), *missing words* (M), *bad word selection* (S) and *disorder words* (W). Once an error is found, the system should be able to recognize its beginning and ending positions.

Table 1 and Table 2 show two examples in the dataset:

这$_1$种$_2$材$_3$料$_4$表$_5$示$_6$吸$_7$烟$_8$引$_9$起$_{10}$了$_{11}$人$_{12}$们$_{13}$多$_{14}$么$_{15}$大$_{16}$的$_{17}$损$_{18}$害$_{19}$。$_{20}$		
Error Interval	5, 6	12, 13
Error Type	S	R
Correction	这种材料表明吸烟引起了多么大的损害。 This material shows how much harm smoking causes.	

Table 1: Two errors are found in the sentence above, one is bad word selection (S) error from position 5 to 6, the other one is redundant words (R) error from position 12 to 13.

但$_1$是$_2$文$_3$章$_4$中$_5$的$_6$妻$_7$子$_8$是$_9$还$_{10}$有$_{11}$意$_{12}$识$_{13}$的$_{14}$，$_{15}$她$_{16}$还$_{17}$有$_{18}$活$_{19}$的$_{20}$意$_{21}$义$_{22}$。$_{23}$		
Error Interval	9, 10	20, 20
Error Type	W	M
Correction	但是文章中的妻子还是有意识的。她还有活着的意义。 But the wife in the passage is still conscious, she still has a meaning to live.	

Table 2: Two errors are found in the sentence above, one is disordered words (W) error from position 9 to 10, the other one is missing words (M) error in position 20.

3 Methodology

In this work, we treat the CGED task as a sequence labeling problem. Specifically, given a sentence x, our model generates a corresponding label sequence y. Each label in y is a token from a specific tag set. Here we have tag 'O' indicating correct characters, 'B-X' indicating the beginning positions for errors of type 'X' and 'I-X' as middle and ending positions for errors of type 'X'.

We first examine the traditional CRF model and use symbolical represented features. Then we propose our LSTM-based model that use distributed feature representations. At last, we present an ensemble model that combines the two models using *Stacking*.

In this section, we will first introduce how we prepare the data, and then describe the three models we used in this task.

3.1 Data Preparation

Since the CGED task involves identifying the error boundaries, segmenting a sentence into words will bring a lot of misalignments between the words and the endpoints of a corresponding error interval. An example of misalignment is shown in Table 3. Therefore, we decided to solve the problem at character level. Other than the misaligned interval problem, there are many error intervals of different types which may overlap with others. One way to avoid this overlapping problem is to deal with the four types of errors separately. However, we think the four types of errors may have mutual effects on each other, so we pre-processed the training data so that we can keep as many errors as possible by deleting the least numbers of overlapped error intervals. We finally deleted a small part of error intervals which is acceptable. An example of overlapping problem is shown in Table 4.

如$_1$ 果$_2$ 你$_3$ 是$_4$ 青$_5$ 少$_6$ 年$_7$ 你$_8$ 多$_9$ 想$_{10}$ 自$_{11}$ 己$_{12}$ 的$_{13}$ 未$_{14}$ 来$_{15}$ ；$_{16}$ 那$_{17}$ 你$_{18}$ 可$_{19}$ 以$_{20}$ 禁烟$_{21-22}$ 了$_{23}$ 。$_{24}$	
Error Interval	19, 19	21, 21
Error Type	M	S
Correction	如果你是青少年你要多想想自己的未来；那你**就**可以戒烟了。 If you are a teenager you should think about your future so you can quit smoking.	

Table 3: An misalignment example. The two characters "禁(forbid)" and "烟(cigarette)" would be one word after segmenting the sentence into words, which would cause a misalignment problem because only the character "禁(forbid)".

每$_1$ 年$_2$ 暑$_3$ 假$_4$ 是$_5$ 我$_6$ 们$_7$ 运$_8$ 动$_9$ 员$_{10}$ 来$_{11}$ 说$_{12}$ 很$_{13}$ 苦$_{14}$ 的$_{15}$ 时$_{16}$ 候$_{17}$ 。$_{18}$	
Error Interval	5, 12	6, 6
Error Type	W	M
Correction	每年暑假对我们运动员来说是很苦的时候。 Every summer is hard for us athletes.	

Table 4: An overlapping example. The two error intervals are overlapped. In this situation, we will delete the least number of intervals to eliminate the problem.

One kind of features that may be useful in this task is the Part-of-speech (POS) of words. Table 5 shows a snapshot of training data after the pre-processing. Note that our task is being solved at the character level, so we split the POS tag of a word to character level by attaching position indicators ('B-' and 'I-') to the POS of a word.

Character	POS	Label
像	B-p	O
我	B-r	B-W
对	B-p	I-W
不	B-d	B-M
吸	B-n	O
烟	I-n	O
者	I-n	O
来	B-u	O
说	I-u	O

Table 5: A snapshot of our training data after the pre-processing

In the training phase, a sentence is first segmented into terms. Each term is consisted with a character, a corresponding POS tag and an error type tag.

3.2 CRF-Based Model

CRF has been successfully used in various natural language processing applications, especially sequence labeling tasks. Formally, the model can be defined as:

$$P\left(\boldsymbol{y} \mid \boldsymbol{x}\right) = \frac{1}{Z\left(\boldsymbol{x}\right)} exp\left(\Sigma_k \lambda_k f_k\right) \tag{1}$$

where $Z(\boldsymbol{x})$ is the normalization factor, f_k is a set of features, λ_k is the corresponding weight. In this task, $\boldsymbol{x}$ is the input sentence, and $\boldsymbol{y}$ is the corresponding error type label. The feature templates are defined in Table 6. We use stochastic gradient descent (SGD) for training, with L2 regularization to prevent overfitting.

Feature templates
00: $ch_{i+k}, -2 \leq k \leq 2$
01: $ch_{i+k} \circ ch_{i+k+1}, -1 \leq k \leq 0$
02: $pos_{i+k}, -2 \leq k \leq 2$
03: $pos_{i+k} \circ pos_{i+k+1}, -2 \leq k \leq 1$
04: $pos_{i+k} \circ pos_{i+k+1} \circ pos_{i+k+2}, -2 \leq k \leq 0$
Unigram Features
$y_i \circ 00 - 04$
Bigram Features
$y_{i-1} \circ y_i$

Table 6: feature templates of CRF-based model. ch_i refers to the $i_t h$ character, pos_i refers to the POS of $i_t h$ character, y_i refers to the output tag of $i_t h$ character.

3.3 LSTM-Based Model

LSTM network is a variant of recurrent neural network (RNN) and have better ability to capture long-term dependencies. At each time step t, LSTM networks read a current input vector x_t and the hidden state of the previous time step h_{t-1}, and use them to compute a new hidden state h_t.

Vanilla RNNs (Pascanu et al., 2013) typically suffer from the gradient vanishing problem while LSTM networks solve it with an extra memory "cell" (c_t). Specifically, LSTM networks are controlled by three kinds of gates, each gate consists of a sigmoid neural net layer and a point-wise multiplication operation. The three gates are input gate, forget gate and output gate. The input gate controls what proportion of the current input to pass into the memory cell (i_t), and the forget gate controls what proportion of the previous memory cell to "forget" (f_t). When here comes the input x_t, the memory cell is updated as follows:

$$i_t = \sigma \left(W_{ix} x_t + W_{ih} h_{t-1} + W_{ic} c_{t-1} + b_i \right) \tag{2}$$

$$f_t = \sigma \left(W_{fx} x_t + W_{fh} h_{t-1} + W_{fc} c_{t-1} + b_f \right) \tag{3}$$

$$c_t = f_t \odot c_{t-1} + i_t \odot tanh \left(W_{cx} x_t + W_{ch} h_{t-1} + b_c \right) \tag{4}$$

where σ represents point-wise logistic sigmoid function, and $\odot$ is the point-wise Hadamard product.

The output gate (o_t) controls the hidden state h_t at each time step, and they are computed as follows:

$$o_t = \sigma \left(W_{ox} x_t + W_{oh} h_{t-1} + W_{oc} c_t + b_o \right) \tag{5}$$

$$h_t = o_t \odot tanh \left(c_t \right) \tag{6}$$

We use the hidden state h_t to calculate the output label at each time step at last. The architecture of our bidirectional LSTM-based model is illustrated in Figure 1. We used the concatenation of character embeddings and bigram embeddings as lexicalized input features at each position.

The character embeddings are initialized randomly. To obtain the bigram embeddings, we first convert the original character sequence to a bigram sequence. For example, the bigram sequence of sentence "我是中国人" will be ["我是", "是中", "中国", "国人"]. Then we can train bigram embeddings readily using word2vec (Mikolov et al., 2013) on the resulting bigram sequences. In addition, we also used the POS of words as a discrete feature to improve the performance of our model.

We give the comparison between LSTM-based model with unigram feature and LSTM-based model with bigram and also unigram feature in next section. We also adjusted the model by tuning the value of the input dimension of LSTM and the dimension of bigram embeddings.

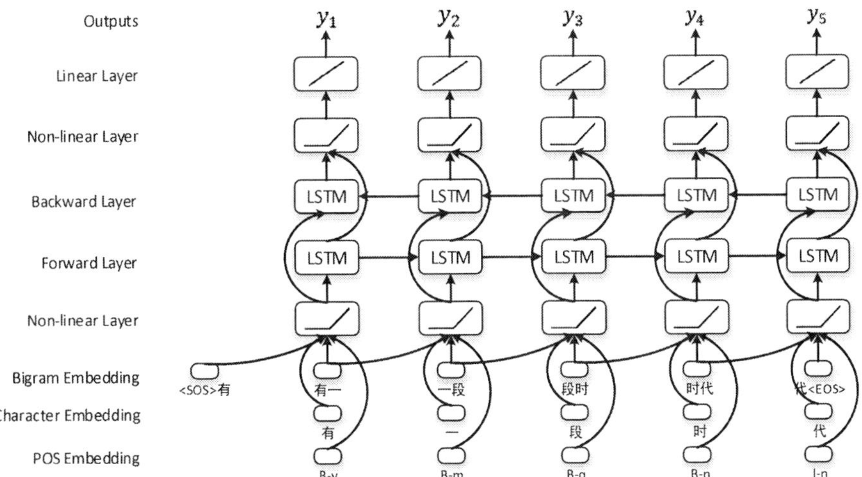

Figure 1: An illustration of the LSTM-based model. The concatenated character embedding, POS embedding and two bigram embeddings are used as the input of the neural network.

3.4 Stacking Model

After preliminary experiments using the two models above, we found that the LSTM-based model has a high recall rate and the CRF-based model has a high precision rate. To take advantage of both models, we further present an ensemble model using *stacking* (Nivre and McDonald, 2008).

We conducted 10-fold cross-validation on the training dataset and obtained the tagging results automatically. Then we put the result of the CRF-based model as a discrete feature to the LSTM layer by adding an additional feature to the input layer of LSTM. We expect that by combining the two models together, the LSTM-based model can achieve higher precision rate.

Results show that after combining the two models, the recall of the LSTM-based model increases, but unfortunately, the precision decreases. The reason could be the results of CRF-based model help LSTM find errors which LSTM-based model wasn't able to find. We will discuss it specifically in the next section.

4 Experiments

4.1 Data and Settings

We obtain the full dataset from the shared task CGED-HSK of NLP-TEA-3 for training and validation, of which 16,142 sentences are used for training and the rest 4000 sentences for validation. The ratio of training dataset size to validation dataset size is about 4:1. Table 7 shows the data distribution in the CGED-HSK training data. In addition, we use the Chinese Gigawords to get the pretrained bigram embeddings. For the CRF-based model, we adopt the CRFsuite toolkit (Okazaki, 2007).

The criterias for evaluation include:

(1) **Detection level**: this is a binary classification of a given sentence, i.e. correct or incorrect should be completely identical with the gold standard. All error types will be regarded as incorrect.

(2) **Identification level**: this could be considered as a multi-class categorization problem. In addition to correct instances, all error types should be clearly identified.

(3) **Position level**: besides identifying the error types, this level also judges the positions of erroneous range. That is, the system results should be perfectly identical with the quadruples of gold standard.

Type	Train	Validation
Redundant	4374	1074
Missing	5250	1203
Selection	8533	2177
Disorder	1196	291
Correct	8086	2002

Table 7: Data statistics.

4.2 Experiment Results

We first conduct experiments with the CRF-based and the LSTM-based model. After that, we examine the effect of *Stacking* by taking the output of the CRF model as features of the LSTM model.

4.2.1 Results on Validation Dataset

We use the validation dataset to select the best hyper-parameters in both the CRF-based model and the LSTM-based model. Table 8 shows the results. As we can see, the LSTM-based model (LSTM (U+B)) has better Recall and F1-score than the CRF-based model, but lower in precision. Besides, the bigram embeddings has a very significant impact on the LSTM-based model.

Model	Detection Level			Identification Level			Position Level		
	P	R	F1	P	R	F1	P	R	F1
CRF	**0.7500**	0.2282	0.3500	**0.7154**	0.1663	0.2699	**0.6507**	0.1296	0.2162
LSTM (U)	0.5188	0.2908	0.3727	0.4458	0.1925	0.2689	0.3329	0.1197	0.1761
LSTM (U+B)	0.6526	0.3629	0.4664	0.5625	0.2484	0.3446	0.4115	**0.1587**	**0.2290**
Stacking	0.6344	**0.3909**	**0.4837**	0.5401	**0.2565**	**0.3478**	0.3797	0.1513	0.2164

Table 8: Results on Validation Dataset. 'U' in the bracket after LSTM refers to using unigram of characters and 'B' refers to using bigram of characters.

4.2.2 Results on Evaluation Dataset

When testing on the final evaluation dataset, we merged our training dataset and validation dataset, and retrain our models. Table 9 shows the results of our three submissions.

Submission	Detection Level			Identification Level			Position Level		
	P	R	F1	P	R	F1	P	R	F1
HIT-Run1	**0.6111**	0.712	0.6577	0.5146	0.5219	0.5182	**0.4034**	0.3691	**0.3855**
HIT-Run2	0.6108	0.7099	0.6566	**0.5224**	0.5094	0.5185	0.397	0.3483	0.3711
HIT-Run3	0.6071	**0.7296**	**0.6628**	0.5002	**0.5447**	**0.5215**	0.3695	**0.3697**	0.3696

Table 9: Results on Evaluation Dataset.

The three models we submitted includes the LSTM-based model (HIT-Run1), Stacking model (HIT-Run2) and LSTM-based model with some post-process (HIT-Run3). The post-process mainly includes changing the 'I-X' errors without a 'B-X' error before it into a single 'B-X' error. This increases the recall rate on three levels but slightly decreases the precision.

The stacking model increases the precision on the identification level while it reduces overall performance. The reason could be that our CRF-based model doesn't have good feature templates or the inherent properties of the task.

Our system presents the best F1 scores in all three levels and also the best recall rates in the last two levels on evaluation dataset. However, the results of this task are not that credible because there are many ways to correct a wrong Chinese sentence. For example, deleting some redundant words may replace errors of missing words.

5 Related Works

In NLP-TEA-1 (Yu et al., 2014) shared task for CGED, there were four types of errors, which were the same as the task of this year. The evaluation was only based on detection of error occurrence, disregarding the recognization of boundaries. In NLP-TEA-2 (Lee et al., 2015) shared task for CGED, the participating systems are required to not only detect the errors but also locate them. Evaluations were focused on traditional Chinese texts rather than simplified Chinese, and one sentence includes one error at most in last two years.

There have been several studies focused on Chinese grammatical error detection. Wu et al. (2010) proposed a method using both Relative Position Language Model and Parse Template Language Model to detect Chinese errors written by US learner. Yu and Chen (2012) proposed a classifier to detect word-ordering errors in Chinese sentences from the HSK dynamic composition corpus. Lee et al. (2013) proposed linguistic rule based Chinese error detection for second language learning. Lee et al. (2014) developed a sentence judgment system using both rule-based and n-gram statistical methods to detect grammatical errors in Chinese sentences. However, all of these previous works used hand-crafted features which may be incomplete and cause the loss of some important information. Comparatively, our neural network approaches have strong capability of automatic feature learning and are completely data-driven.

6 Conclusion

This paper describes our system in the NLP-TEA-3 task for CGED-HSK. We explored the CRF-based model, the LSTM-based model and further used stacking to combine the two models. We achieved highest F1 scores in all three levels and highest Recall rates in identification level and position level.

In our future work, we plan to try more methods such as bagging or adding more features to the CRF-based model. Since Chinese grammar is flexible and irregular, it is difficult to judge the credibility of these results on testing data. In our future work, we will try more models and find better ways to judge the result if possible.

Acknowledgements

This work was supported by the National Key Basic Research Program of China via grant 2014CB340503 and the National Natural Science Foundation of China (NSFC) via grant 61632011 and 61370164.

References

Sepp Hochreiter and Jürgen Schmidhuber. 1997. Long short-term memory. *Neural computation*, 9(8):1735–1780.

John Lafferty, Andrew McCallum, and Fernando Pereira. 2001. Conditional random fields: Probabilistic models for segmenting and labeling sequence data. In *ICML*, volume 1, pages 282–289.

Guillaume Lample, Miguel Ballesteros, Sandeep Subramanian, Kazuya Kawakami, and Chris Dyer. 2016. Neural architectures for named entity recognition. In *NAACL*, pages 260–270, San Diego, California, June.

Lung-Hao Lee, Li-Ping Chang, Kuei-Ching Lee, Yuen-Hsien Tseng, and Hsin-Hsi Chen. 2013. Linguistic rules based chinese error detection for second language learning. In *Work-in-Progress Poster Proceedings of the 21st International Conference on Computers in Education (ICCE-13)*, pages 27–29.

Lung-Hao Lee, Liang-Chih Yu, Kuei-Ching Lee, Yuen-Hsien Tseng, Li-Ping Chang, and Hsin-Hsi Chen. 2014. A sentence judgment system for grammatical error detection. In *COLING (Demos)*, pages 67–70.

Lung-Hao Lee, Liang-Chih Yu, Li-Ping Chang, et al. 2015. Overview of the nlp-tea 2015 shared task for chinese grammatical error diagnosis. *ACL-IJCNLP 2015*, page 1.

Tomas Mikolov, Kai Chen, Greg Corrado, and Jeffrey Dean. 2013. Efficient estimation of word representations in vector space. *International Conference on Learning Representations (ICLR) Workshop*.

Joakim Nivre and Ryan T McDonald. 2008. Integrating graph-based and transition-based dependency parsers. In *ACL*, pages 950–958.

Naoaki Okazaki. 2007. Crfsuite: a fast implementation of conditional random fields (crfs).

Razvan Pascanu, Tomas Mikolov, and Yoshua Bengio. 2013. On the difficulty of training recurrent neural networks. *ICML (3)*, 28:1310–1318.

Oriol Vinyals, Łukasz Kaiser, Terry Koo, Slav Petrov, Ilya Sutskever, and Geoffrey Hinton. 2015. Grammar as a foreign language. In *Advances in Neural Information Processing Systems*, pages 2773–2781.

Chung-Hsien Wu, Chao-Hong Liu, Matthew Harris, and Liang-Chih Yu. 2010. Sentence correction incorporating relative position and parse template language models. *IEEE Transactions on Audio, Speech, and Language Processing*, 18(6):1170–1181.

Chi-Hsin Yu and Hsin-Hsi Chen. 2012. Detecting word ordering errors in chinese sentences for learning chinese as a foreign language. In *COLING*, pages 3003–3018.

Liang-Chih Yu, Lung-Hao Lee, and Li-Ping Chang. 2014. Overview of grammatical error diagnosis for learning chinese as a foreign language. In *Proceedings of the 1st Workshop on Natural Language Processing Techniques for Educational Applications (NLPTEA'14), Nara, Japan*, pages 42–47.

Automatic Grammatical Error Detection for Chinese based on Conditional Random Field

Yajun Liu, Yingjie Han, Liyan Zhuo, Hongying Zan
Natural Language Processing Laboratory
College of Information and Engineering, Zhengzhou University, China
`liuyanjun_gz@163.com, ieyjhan@zzu.edu.cn`
`1967331775@qq.com, iehyzan@zzu.edu.cn`

Abstract

In the process of learning and using Chinese, foreigners may have grammatical errors due to negative migration of their native languages. Currently, the computer-oriented automatic detection method of grammatical errors is not mature enough. Based on the evaluating task ---- CGED2016, we select and analyze the classification model and design feature extraction method to obtain grammatical errors including Mission(M), Disorder(W), Selection (S) and Redundant (R) automatically. The experiment results based on the dynamic corpus of HSK show that the Chinese grammatical error automatic detection method, which uses CRF as classification model and n-gram as feature extraction method. It is simple and efficient which play a positive effect on the research of Chinese grammatical error automatic detection and also a supporting and guiding role in the teaching of Chinese as a foreign language.

1 Introduction

As China's status is improved and its influence in the world is increasing, more and more foreigners begin to learn Chinese. The HSK is an international standardized test for Chinese language proficiency of non-native speakers. From the analysis of the examination papers for many years, we can see that foreigners who study Chinese often make grammatical errors such as Mission(M), Disorder(W), Selection (S) and Redundant (R), owing to their language negative migration, over-generalization, teaching methods, learning strategies and other reasons.

Automatic detection of Chinese grammatical errors is really a challenge for many researchers. There is no space between word and word in Chinese corpus. If words in Chinese corpus are separated from each other, we can use combination of multiple features such as words, part of speech tagging (POS) and word frequency to detect grammatical errors, automatically. But errors of word segmentation and part of speech tagging will be accumulated in, and then have a negative effect on automatic detection of grammatical errors.

Examples are as follows:

The original sentence:

a) 他现在的工作是研究生物   His present job is studying biology

b) 他站起身来   He stands up

c) 他明天起身去北京   He leaves Beijing tomorrow

After word segmentation:

a) 他/现在/的/工作/是/研究/生物   His / present / job / is / studying / biological

b) 他站/起/身/来   He stands / up

c) 他/明天/起身/去/北京   He / leaves for / Beijing / tomorrow

Proceedings of the 3rd Workshop on Natural Language Processing Techniques for Educational Applications,
pages 57–62, Osaka, Japan, December 12 2016.

In example a, the "研究生物 (study biology)" will arise segmentation ambiguity, in example b and c, "起身 (get up)" has two different way of divisions which has a bad effect on automatic detection of grammatical errors. In this respect, current automatic detection methods have poor performance, we need actively explore effective automatic detection methods which can help reduce workload of artificial detection and play a positive guiding role in teaching Chinese as a foreign language. With some grammatical errors and error cause found by these methods, teaching Chinese as a foreign language will be well guided.

For many researchers, CGED evaluating task provides a platform to study automatic detection of Chinese grammatical errors. CGED 2016 evaluating task divides the Chinese grammatical errors into four categories: Mission(M), Disorder(W), Selection (S) and Redundant (R), and includes three tasks such as Detection Level, Identification Level and Position Level.

In order to achieve Chinese grammatical error automatic detection, we first consider the problem of Chinese grammatical errors as a classification problem, and then use rule-based method, statistical learning method or the fusion of multiple classification methods. Through analysis and comparison, we use CRF to complete three tasks including Detection Level, Identification Level and Position Level.

The rest of this paper is organized as follows: Section 2 briefly introduces related work in this field. Section 3 introduces the statistical learning method CRF and its tools. Section 4 discusses the realization of Chinese grammatical error automatic detection which includes data preprocessing, data feature extraction, model selection and result analysis. Finally, conclusion and prospects are arranged.

2   Related work

In the aspect of automatic detection of grammatical errors, the study of English is more deep. Anubhav Gupta (2014) proposed a rule-based approach that relies on the difference in the output of two POS taggers, to detect verb forms, lexical and spelling errors, but fuzzy or erroneous input of the POS tagger could result in an erroneous output. In order to solve context-sensitive spelling correction, an algorithm combining Winnow variable and weighted majority voting was proposed by Andrew R. Golding (1999), but in this way we need to improve the adaptability of the algorithm to unfamiliar test sets. Anoop Kunchukuttan (2014) proposed two enhancements based on statistical machine translation for all types of errors. Although it is possible to use a simple set of methods to increase recall rate, it also leads to a decrease in precision.

Relevant works related to Chinese grammatical error detection are much less compared with that of English. Chi Hsin Yu and Hsin-Hsi (2012) proposed a classifier based on CRF model to detect Chinese text disorder. Shuk-Man Cheng (2014) proposed a support vector machine model to further explore the problem of word order reordering. Yang Xiang and Xiaolong Wang (2015) used an ensemble learning method which learns and trains the corpus to identity the grammatical errors and error types, but the detection of the error location is not ideal. Xiupeng Wu and Peijie Huang (2015) used a hybrid model that integrates rule-based and N-gram statistical method to detect the Chinese grammatical errors, which can identify the error types well and point out error position, but rules are needed summarizing manually. Lung-Hao Lee and Liang-Chih Yu (2014) introduced a sentence-level detection system that integrates multiple rules and N-gram statistical features. Generally speaking, relevant rule are needed in most of the Chinese grammatical error automatic detection summarizing manually, and these existing methods on the error position are not ideal at present.

3   CRF

3.1 CRF model

CRF (Random Field Conditional) is a distinguished indirect graph model. In an indirect graph $G = (V, E)$, where V be the set of end point, E be the set of indirect edges, $Y = \{Y_v | v \in V\}$, that is, each node in V corresponds to a random variable which is in the range of possible tag set $\{y\}$. If we observe the sequence X as a condition and each random variable Y_v satisfies the following Markov characteristic:

$$p(Y_v | X, Y_w, w \neq v) = p(Y_v | X, Y_w, w \sim v) \qquad (1)$$

where denotes that two nodes are adjacent in graph G, then (X, Y) is a conditional random field. Model diagram is shown in Figure 1.

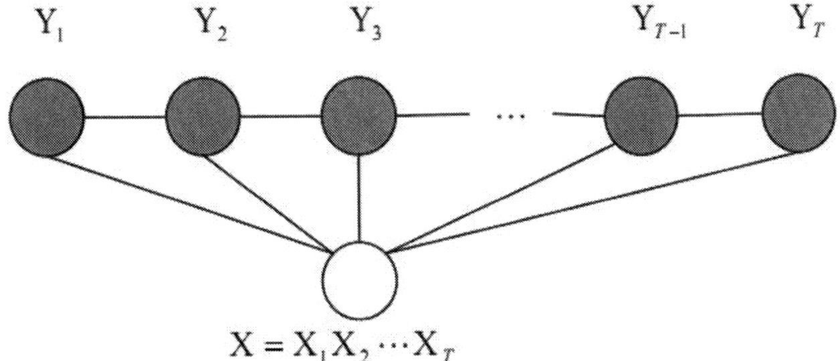

Fig.1 Schematic diagram of conditional random field model

For the first time, Lafferty introduced CRF into natural language processing, and the choice of CRF potential function is greatly influenced by the maximum entropy model, and first-order chain structure is applied to construct the CRF model. In graph $G = (V, E)$, the largest group which is the edge in graph G contains only two adjacent nodes.

We define the form of each potential function as follows:

$$\emptyset_{y_c}(y_c) = \exp(\textstyle\sum_k \lambda_k f_k(c, y|c, x)) \qquad (2)$$

Where $y|c$ denotes the random variable corresponding to the node in the C group, $f_k(c, y|c, x)$ is a Boolean feature function, then p (y | x) is:

$$p(y|x) = \frac{1}{Z_{(x)}} \exp(\textstyle\sum_{c \in C} \sum_k \lambda_k f_k(c, y_c, x)) \qquad (3)$$

where $Z_{(x)}$ is the normalization factor.

$$Z_{(x)} = \textstyle\sum_y \exp(\textstyle\sum_{c \in C} \sum_k \lambda_k f_k(c, y_c, x)) \qquad (4)$$

3.2 CRF ++ tool selection

CRF-based tools are currently available such as crf++, flexcrf, pocket crf.

First of all, crf++ is the first order crf, flexcrf is the second order crf, because n-order crf training time required (p is the number of markers, T is the first order crf training time, N is the order), so compared with crf++, flexcrf needs more training time.

Second, pocket crf does not provide a command line, and there is only one example that shows how to complete the training and testing, and pocket crf does not identify the space, so pocket crf string input file must be strictly separated by 0x09. In contrast, crf++ has a command line, and can ignore all spaces and 0x09 between the columns. So in this experiment, we use the CRF++ tool 0.58 version[1].

4   CRF-based automatic detection of Chinese grammatical errors

According to the above discussion, we choose CRF as the statistical learning method and CRF++ as the tool of automatic detection. Through data preprocessing, feature selection, training and cross validation, the automatic detection result of test data, result analysis are given.

4.1 Data preprocessing

The main work of data preprocessing is to preprocessing the training data set of CGED 2016, and then the training corpus format is adjusted to the input format required by CRF++. The correct sentences and the wrong sentences are extracted from the corpus according to artificial annotation, and then the corpus are automatically marked according to the wrong position and the wrong type.

Example of original training corpus:

<DOC>

<TEXT id="200405109523100360_2_6x2">

---

[1] https://code.google.com/archive/p/crfpp/downloads.

妈妈对爸爸劝戒烟的原因就是我的健康。非吸烟者比吸烟者得病率更高，这个所有的人知道。
</TEXT>

<CORRECTION>

妈妈劝爸爸戒烟的理由就是我的健康。非吸烟者比吸烟者得病率更高，这个所有的人都知道。

</CORRECTION>

<ERROR start_off="3" end_off="3" type="R"></ERROR>

<ERROR start_off="4" end_off="6" type="W"></ERROR>

<ERROR start_off="10" end_off="11" type="S"></ERROR>

<ERROR start_off="39" end_off="39" type="M"></ERROR>

</DOC>

Preprocessed training corpus:

妈/C 妈/C 对/R 爸/W 爸/W 劝/W 戒/C 烟/C 的/C 原/S 因/S 就/C 是/C 我/C 的/C 健/C 康/C 。/C 非/C 吸/C 烟/C 者/C 比/C 吸/C 烟/C 者/C 得/C 病/C 率/C 更/C 高/C ，/C 这/C 个/C 所/C 有/C 的/C 人/C 知/M 道/C 。/C

妈/C 妈/C 劝/C 爸/C 爸/C 戒/C 烟/C 的/C 理/C 由/C 就/C 是/C 我/C 的/C 健/C 康/C 。/C 非/C 吸/C 烟/C 者/C 比/C 吸/C 烟/C 者/C 得/C 病/C 率/C 更/C 高/C ，/C 这/C 个/C 所/C 有/C 的/C 人/C 都/C 知/C 道/C 。/C

Note: 1. /C, /M, /W, /S, /R represent Correct, Mission, Disorder, Selection and Redundant.
　　　 2. punctuation, letters, etc. are also followed by the corresponding label.

4.2 Feature Selection

In practice, the feature selection directly affects the performance of the model. The more features are selected, the more time is required when the feature is analyzed and the model is trained, may be the more complex the model is. Therefore, selecting better features not only can simplify the model, but also can reduce the running time. In the statistical machine learning method CRF, this experiment adopts feature length of 5 and 7, then uses bi-gram and tri-gram model to extract features. We conduct cross validation for two kinds of sequence length features, and results are shown in the table1.

Sequence length		5	7
False Positive Rate		0.0518	0.0811
Detection Level	Precision	0.7192	0.6623
	Recall	0.1284	0.1489
	F1-Score	0.2179	0.2431
Identification Level	Precision	0.6142	0.5588
	Recall	0.0798	0.0962
	F1-Score	0.1413	0.1641
Position Level	Precision	0.3981	0.4286
	Recall	0.0332	0.0569
	F1-Score	0.0612	0.1005

Table 1 cross validation results

Through the comparison of Precision, Recall and F1-Score, False Positive Rate has an increase of 2.93% when the sequence length is 7, but there are different levels of promotion in the recall rate of Detection Level, Identification Level and Position Level, F1 is also better than the sequence length 5.

4.3 Results and analysis

The results of the closed test with the training data of CGED2016 are shown in Table 2. Considering the influence of the size of the training data on the model, we add 2015 TOCFL training data to 2016 HSK training data for closed test, the results are shown in Table 2.

Training corpus		2016 HSK data	2015 TOCFL and 2016 HSK data
False Positive Rate		0.0759	0.0596
Detection Level	Precision	0.7055	0.6515
	Recall	0.1323	0.1361
	F1-Score	0.2227	0.2252
Identification Level	Precision	0.6258	0.5516
	Recall	0.0923	0.0896
	F1-Score	0.1609	0.1541
Position Level	Precision	0.4381	0.3414
	Recall	0.0430	0.0377
	F1-Score	0.0784	0.0680

Table 2 closed test results

We compare and analyze the closed results, and then select the HSK data of 2016 and TOCFL data of 2015 as training data, as shown in Table 3.

Training corpus	Correct	Error				Sum
		R	S	M	W	
2016 HSK	10072	5532	10942	6619	1691	20144
2015 TOCFL	2205	430	849	620	306	4410

Table 3 Training data distribution table

Note: 1. Each of these error statements may contain multiple types of errors or include multiple identical types of errors.
2. 2015 TOCFL corpus is converted to HSK for use

In the three results we submitted, SKY_Run2.txt and SKY_Run3.txt are generated by model which is strained by feature template with the sequence length of 5 and 7. These two submitted results have best performance on all three tasks, especially False Positive Rate, Accuracy and Precision indicators, but work badly in recall rate. Our team achieved the lowest false positive rate of 0.0481 in 2016 CGED evaluating task.

The evaluation results are as follows:

Submission results		SKY_Run1.txt	SKY_Run2.txt	SKY_Run3.txt
False Positive Rate		0.0695	**0.0481**	0.0559
Detection Level	Accuracy	0.6523	0.6579	**0.6659**
	Precision	0.8326	**0.8746**	0.8652
	Recall	0.3614	0.3505	0.3750
	F1-Score	0.5040	0.5005	0.5232
Identification Level	Accuracy	0.6605	0.6765	**0.6849**
	Precision	0.8235	**0.8821**	0.8744
	Recall	0.2732	0.2972	0.3815
	F1-Score	0.4132	0.4446	0.4669
Position Level	Accuracy	0.6073	0.6376	**0.6477**
	Precision	0.6153	0.7054	**0.7144**
	Recall	0.1783	0.2217	0.2430
	F1-Score	0.2765	0.3373	0.3627

Table 4 Evaluation results

From the analysis of the results, we can see that feature templates with two kinds of sequence length use bigram and trigram models to extract features and select more features, thus greatly improve Precision, but have a serious impact on recall rate.

As for Position Level task, SKY_Run3.txt plays better than SKY_Run2.txt, and has good performance on Accuracy, Precision, Recall and F1-Score indicators, so feature template with sequence length

7 plays better. When the length of the sequence becomes longer, the effect of position level task is better. But if the length is too long, the learning process will become difficult and the model will become more complex. Compared with the first two tasks, the results in Position Level are not ideal. Since the open source tool based on the statistical machine learning method CRF only supports chained sequences, when the sequence length is 5 and 7, the long sentences can't be analyzed on the whole, which affects the automatic detection of Chinese grammatical errors.

5   Conclusion and prospect

In this paper, we use statistical learning method CRF and n-gram feature extraction method to achieve Chinese grammatical error automatic detection. It can be seen from the evaluation results that the CRF model has a good performance in the automatic detection of Chinese grammatical errors, especially False Positive Rate and Precision. But in the overall quantity of Chinese grammatical errors, the errors that are detected are too few, which affects the overall performance.

In general, CRF has great potential in automatic detection of Chinese grammatical errors. Compared with HMM (Hidden Markov Model), it has no strict independence assumption, and its feature design is flexible. Compared with the regular method, it can predict more flexible grammatical errors. It is also simpler than multiple classifier fusion methods. The only thing we need to do is to manually mark the corpus for CRF learning. In the following work, we will collect more corpus of Chinese grammatical errors to improve the performance of the model, and we will also consider mutual information and other methods for feature extraction.

Reference

Chang, Ru-Yng, Chung-Hsien Wu, and Philips Kokoh Prasetyo. 2012. Error diagnosis of Chinese sentences using inductive learning algorithm and decomposition-based testing mechanism. ACM Transactions on Asian Language Information Processing (TALIP), 11(1), 3.

Cheng, Shuk-Man, Chi-Hsin Yu, and Hsin-Hsi Chen. 2014. Chinese Word Ordering Errors Detection and Correction for Non-Native Chinese Language Learners. In COLING (pp. 279-289).

Della Pietra, Stephen, Vincent Della Pietra, and John Lafferty. 1997. Inducing features of random fields. IEEE transactions on pattern analysis and machine intelligence, 19(4), 380-393.

Golding, Andrew R., and Dan Roth. 1999. A winnow-based approach to context-sensitive spelling correction. Machine learning, 34(1-3), 107-130.

Gupta, Anubhav. 2014. Grammatical Error Detection and Correction Using Tagger Disagreement. CoNLL-2014, 21860(26282), 49.

Kunchukuttan, Anoop, Sriram Chaudhury, and Pushpak Bhattacharyya. 2014, May. Tuning a Grammar Correction System for Increased Precision. In CoNLL Shared Task (pp. 60-64).

Lafferty, John, Andrew McCallum, and Fernando Pereira. 2001, June. Conditional random fields: Probabilistic models for segmenting and labeling sequence data. In Proceedings of the eighteenth international conference on machine learning, ICML (Vol. 1, pp. 282-289).

Lee, Lung-Hao, Liang-Chih Yu, and Li-Ping Chang. 2015. Overview of the NLP-TEA 2015 Shared Task for Chinese Grammatical Error Diagnosis. ACL-IJCNLP 2015, 1.

Lee, Lung-Hao, et al. 2014, July. A Sentence Judgment System for Grammatical Error Detection. In COLING (Demos) (pp. 67-70).

Ng, Hwee Tou, et al. 2014, May. The CoNLL-2014 Shared Task on Grammatical Error Correction. In CoNLL Shared Task (pp. 1-14).

Sha, Fei, and Fernando Pereira. 2003, May. Shallow parsing with conditional random fields. In Proceedings of the 2003 Conference of the North American Chapter of the Association for Computational Linguistics on Human Language Technology-Volume 1 (pp. 134-141). Association for Computational Linguistics.

Xiang, Yang, et al. 2015. Chinese grammatical error diagnosis using ensemble learning. ACL-IJCNLP 2015, 99.

Yu, Liang-Chih, Lung-Hao Lee, and Li-Ping Chang. 2014, November. Overview of grammatical error diagnosis for learning Chinese as a foreign language. In Proceedings of the 1st Workshop on Natural Language Processing Techniques for Educational Applications (NLPTEA'14), Nara, Japan (pp. 42-47).

CYUT-III System at Chinese Grammatical Error Diagnosis Task

Po-Lin Chen, Shih-Hung Wu*
Chaoyang University of Technology,
Taichung, Taiwan, R.O.C

streetcatsky@gmail.com

Liang-Pu Chen, Ping-Che Yang
IDEAS, Institute for Information Industry,
Taipei, Taiwan, ROC.

{eit, maciaclark}@iii.org.tw

*Contact author: shwu@cyut.edu.tw

Abstract

This paper describe the CYUT-III system on grammar error detection in the 2016 NLP-TEA Chinese Grammar Error Detection shared task CGED. In this task a system has to detect four types of errors, including redundant word error, missing word error, word selection error and word ordering error. Based on the conditional random fields (CRF) model, our system is a linear tagger that can detect the errors in learners' essays. Since the system performance depends on the features heavily, in this paper, we are going to report how to integrate the collocation feature into the CRF model. Our system presents the best detection accuracy and Identification accuracy on the TOCFL dataset, which is in traditional Chinese. The same system also works well on the simplified Chinese HSK dataset.

1   Introduction

Chinese essay writing is hard for foreign learners, not only on the aspect of learning pictograph Chinese characters but also on that of learning Chinese grammar that has no strong syntax rules. An automatic grammar error detection system might help the learners to get instant feedback when they are writing an essay in a computer aided language learning environment (Shiue and Chen, 2016).

In order to develop a grammar error detection system with the statistical natural language processing technology, developers need a large learner corpus (Chang et al., 2012). However, currently there is no publicly available large leaner corpus in Chinese essay writing. That puts off the research in this field. The NLP-TEA workshop has been holding a Chinese Grammar Error Detection (CGED) shared task in the workshop for two years since 2014 (Yu et al., 2014) (Lee et al. 2015). They provides a set of learner corpus and a clear definition on 4 major Grammar error types in the foreign learner corpus. The shared tasks stimulated the research and drew many participants.

The goal of the shared task is to develop a system that can detect the four types of grammar errors in learner corpus. Comparing to the task definition of CGED in 2014 and 2015, the major difference in this year is the sentences might contain multiple errors. And the organizers provide two data sets: one is in traditional Chinese, the TOCFL dataset; the other is in simplified Chinese, the HSK dataset. Figure 1 and 2 are examples of the four error types, where redundant word is abbreviated 'R', missing word 'M', word selection error 'S', and word ordering error 'W'.

Based on the conditional random fields (CRF) model, we build a linear tagger that can detect the errors in learners' essays. The major improvement of our system is integrating the collocation feature into the CRF model. Since there is no publicly available Chinese collocation dataset, we will also report how we collect collocation.

The paper is organized as follows: Section 2 describes our methodology, section 3 shows our system architecture, section 4 is the discussion, and the final part is the conclusions.

Proceedings of the 3rd Workshop on Natural Language Processing Techniques for Educational Applications,
pages 63–72, Osaka, Japan, December 12 2016.

TOCFL (Traditional Chinese)
Example 1:
Input: (sid=A2-0007-2) 聽說妳打算開一個慶祝會。可惜我不能參加。因為那個時候我有別的事。當然我也要參加給你慶祝慶祝。
Output: A2-0007-2, 38, 39, R
(Note: "參加" is a redundant word)

Example 2:
Input: (sid=A2-0007-3) 我要送給你一個慶祝禮物。要是兩、三天晚了，請別生氣。
Output: A2-0007-3, 15, 20, W
(Note: "兩、三天晚了" should be "晚了兩、三天")

Example 3:
Input: (sid=A2-0011-1) 我聽到你找到工作。恭喜恭喜！
Output: A2-0011-1, 2, 3, S
       A2-0011-1, 9, 9, M
(Notes: "聽到" should be "聽說". Besides, a word "了" is missing. The correct sentence should be "我聽說你找到工作了")

Example 4:
Input: (sid=A2-0011-3) 我覺得對你很抱歉。我也很想去，可是沒有辦法。
Output: A2-0011-3, correct

Figure 1. Examples of TOCFL (Traditional Chinese) from 2016 NLP-TEA CGED shared task
[http://nlptea2016.weebly.com/shared-task.html]

HSK (Simplified Chinese)
Example 1:
Input: (sid=00038800481) 我根本不能了解这妇女辞职回家的现象。在这个时代，为什么放弃自己的工作，就回家当家庭主妇？
Output: 00038800481, 6, 7, S
       00038800481, 8, 8, R
(Notes: "了解" should be "理解". In addition, "这" is a redundant word.)

Example 2:
Input: (sid=00038800464) 我真不明白。她们可能是追求一些前代的浪漫。
Output: 00038800464, correct

Example 3:
Input: (sid=00038801261) 人战胜了饥饿，才努力为了下一代作更好的、更健康的东西。
Output: 00038801261, 9, 9, M
       00038801261, 16, 16, S
(Notes: "能" is missing. The word "作" should be "做". The correct sentence is "才能努力为了下一代做更好的")

Example 4:
Input: (sid=00038801320) 饥饿的问题也是应该解决的。世界上每天由于饥饿很多人死亡。
Output: 00038801320, 19, 25, W
(Notes: "由于饥饿很多人" should be "很多人由于饥饿")

Figure 2. Examples of HSK (Simplified Chinese) from 2016 NLP-TEA CGED shared task
[http://nlptea2016.weebly.com/shared-task.html]

2. Methodology

Our system is based on the conditional random field (CRF) (Lafferty et al., 2001). CRF model can cooperate with various kind of linguistic features. We believe that the word itself, its POS, and the appearance of collocation words or not are the major components. In our system, we use the template technology to generate 49 combinatorial features. The technology is briefly described in the following sub-sections.

2.1. Conditional Random Fields

CRF has been used in many natural language processing applications, such as named entity recognition, word segmentation, information extraction, and parsing. To perform different tasks, it requires different feature sets and labelled training data. The CRF can be regarded as a sequential labelling tagger. Given a sequence data X, the CRF can generate the corresponding label sequence Y based on the trained model. Each label Y is taken from a specific tag set, which needs to be defined in different tasks. X is a data sequence to be labelled, and output Y is a corresponding label sequence. While each label Y is taken from a tag set, how to define and interpret the label is a task-depended work for the developers. Mathematically, the model can be defined as:

$$P(Y|X) = \frac{1}{Z(X)} \exp(\sum_k \lambda_k f_k) \tag{1}$$

where Z(X) is the normalization factor, f_k is a set of features, λ_k is the corresponding weight. In this task, X is the input sentence, and Y is the corresponding error type label. As in the previously work, we define the tag set as: {O, R, M, S, D}, corresponding to no error, redundant, missing, selection, and word ordering respectively (Chen et al., 2015). Figure 3 shows a snapshot of our working file. The first column is the input sentence X, and the fourth column is the labelled tag sequence Y. The second column is the Part-of-speech (POS) of the word in the first column. The combination of words and the POSs will be the features in our system. The POS set used in our system is listed in Table 1, which is a simplified POS set provided by CKIP[1].

Our system is built on the base of CRF++ (Kudo, 2007), a linear-chain CRF model software developed by Kudo[2]. In the training phase, a training sentence is first segmented into terms. Each term is labelled with the corresponding POS tag and error type tag. Then our system uses the CRF++ leaning algorithm to train a model. The features used in CRF++ can be expressed by templates. The format of each template is %X[row, col], where row is the number of rows in a sentence and column is the number of column as we shown in Figure 3. The feature templates used in our system are the combination of terms and POS of the input sentences. All the templates are listed in Table 2. An example on how a sentence is represented is given in Table 3. For example, the first feature template is "Term+POS": if an input sentence contains the same term with the same POS, the feature value will be 1; otherwise the feature value will be 0. The second feature template is "Term+Previous Term": if an input sentence contains the same term bi-gram, the feature value will be 1; otherwise the feature value will be 0.

Term	POS	collocation	Tag
一	DET	N	O
個	M	N	O
小時	N	N	O
以前	POST	Y	O
我	N	Y	O
決定	Vt	Y	O
休息	Vi	N	O

Figure 3 A Snapshot of a training sentence example in our system

---

[1] http://ckipsvr.iis.sinica.edu.tw/

[2] http://crfpp.sourceforge.net/index.html

Table 1. Simplified CKIP POS tags[3]

POS	
A	Adjective
C	Conjunction
POST	Postposition
ADV	Adverb
ASP	Tense marker
N	Noun and pronoun
DET	Article and Numeral
M	Chinese classifier
Nv	Nominalization
T	Chinese particles
P	Preposition
Vi	Intransitive verbs
Vt	Transitive verbs

2.2. Collocation

Collocation is useful lexicon knowledge for error correction in language learning (Ferraro et al., 2014). In his computational linguistic research papers, Smadja defined that collocations has four characteristics (Smadja, 1993). Firstly, collocations are arbitrary combinations of any lexicon, not syntactic or grammatical combinations. Secondly, collocations are domain depended, which means collocations are like terminology in one domain and it is hard to understand for outsider. Thirdly, collocations are recurrent, that means collocations are not exceptions, but rather often are repetitions in a given context. Lastly, collocations are cohesive lexical clusters, the presence of one word of a collocation often implies the rest of the collocation will appear in the context.

(Manning and Schütze, 1999) defined that a COLLOCATION is an expression consisting of two or more words that correspond to some conventional way of idea delivering. And there are three characteristics. The first is the non-compositionality, i.e. the meaning of the expression cannot be predicted from the meaning of the parts. The second is the non-substitutability, i.e. substitute near-synonyms for the components of a collocation will not be a collocation. The last is the Non-modifiability that is collocations cannot be freely modified with additional lexical material or through grammatical transformations.

2.3. The collection of Chinese collocation pairs

In the experiments, two methods are used to collect collocation pairs. The first is to select manually some collocation pairs from publicly available printed collocation dictionaries. We collect 80,040 collocation pairs (Chen et al., 2016). The second method is to use T-score to determine if the pair in a corpus is collocation or not.

We extract collocation from 874 correct sentences provided by NLP-TEA2. After word segmentation and POS tagging, our system focuses on content words, i.e. nouns, verbs, adverbs and adjectives only. Using the T-test technic, our system extracts 7,746 collocation pairs from all possible 10,581 pairs. The null hypothesis is: two terms appears independently, not a collocation pair.

The T-test formula is:

$$t = \frac{\bar{x} - \mu}{\sqrt{\frac{s^2}{N}}} \tag{2}$$

where $\bar{x}$ is the sample mean, s^2 is the sample variance, N is the sample size, and μ is the mean of the distribution. If the t statistic is above a threshold, we can reject the null hypothesis. The null hypothesis here is that the two words are independent (Manning and H. Schütze, 1999).

---

[3] National Digital Archives Program, "CKIP POS," http://ckipsvr.iis.sinica.edu.tw/

Table 2. Sample statistics of word frequency in the training set

Sample pairs	Term 1	# of term 1	Term 2	# of term 2	# of term 1 and 2 in one sentence
Pair 1	繼續(continue)	7	工作(work)	14	4
Pair 2	媽媽(Mother)	9	台灣(Taiwan)	26	1

For example, in our corpus with total N=4869 terms, the frequency of the term "continue" is 7, the frequency for term " work" is 14, and the frequency of " continue work" is 4, then we can calculate the t-score as follows:

$$H_0: \text{P(continue work)=P(continue)*P(work)}=\frac{7}{4869}*\frac{14}{4869}=4.1337*10^{-6}=\mu$$

Since $4.1337*10^{-6}$ is near 0, thus $s^2 = P(1-P) \approx$ P. There are 4 times these two terms appear together in one sentence, therefore:

$$\bar{x}=\frac{4}{4869} \approx 8.21523 * 10^{-4}. \text{ Then we can get the T-score:}$$

$$\text{T-Score(continue work)}=\frac{\bar{x}-\mu}{\sqrt{\frac{s^2}{N}}} \approx \frac{8.21523*10^{-4}-4.1337*10^{-6}}{\sqrt{\frac{8.21523*10^{-4}}{4869}}} \approx 1.98994.$$

This t value of 1.98994 is larger than 0.96817, the threshold we chose. So we can reject the null hypothesis that "continue work" occurs independently and it is a collocation.

For the second example, frequency of the term "Mother" is 9, the frequency for term "Taiwan" is 26, and the frequency of "Mother Taiwan" is 1, then we can calculate the t-score as follows:

$$\mu = \text{P(Mather Taiwan)} = \text{P(Mather)} * \text{P(Taiwan)} = \frac{9}{4869}*\frac{26}{4869} \approx 9.870435 * 10^{-6}$$

And $\bar{x}=\frac{1}{4869} \approx 2.05380 * 10^{-4}$

Again, according to Bernoulli trial, since $\bar{x}$ is very small, $s^2 \approx \bar{x}$.

$$\text{T-Score(Mather Taiwan)}=\frac{\bar{x}-\mu}{\sqrt{\frac{s^2}{N}}} \approx \frac{2.05380*10^{-4}-9.870435*10^{-6}}{\sqrt{\frac{2.05380*10^{-4}}{4869}}} \approx 0.95194.$$

This t value of 0.95194 is not larger than 0.96817, the threshold we chose. So we cannot reject the null hypothesis that "Mother Taiwan" occurs independently and it is not a collocation.

Table 3. Templates and the corresponding value

Template	Corresponding Features
U01:%x[0,0]/%x[0,1]	Term+POS
U02:%x[0,0]/%x[-1,0]	Term+previous Term
U03:%x[0,0]/%x[-1,1]	Term+previous POS
U04:%x[0,1]/%x[-1,0]	POS+previous Term
U05:%x[0,1]/%x[-1,1]	POS+previous POS
U06:%x[0,0]/%x[-1,0]/%x[-1,1]	Term+previous Term+previous POS
U07:%x[0,1]/%x[-1,0]/%x[-1,1]	POS+previous Term+previous POS
U08:%x[0,0]/%x[-2,0]	Term+previous previous Term
U09:%x[0,0]/%x[-2,1]	Term+previous previous POS
U010:%x[0,1]/%x[-2,0]	POS+previous previous Term
U011:%x[0,1]/%x[-2,1]	POS+previous previous POS
U012:%x[0,0]/%x[-2,0]/%x[-2,1]	Term+previous previous Term+previous previous POS
U013:%x[0,1]/%x[-2,0]/%x[-2,1]	POS+previous previous Term+previous previous POS
U014:%x[0,0]/%x[1,0]	Term+next Term
U015:%x[0,0]/%x[1,1]	Term+next POS
U016:%x[0,1]/%x[1,0]	POS+next Term
U017:%x[0,1]/%x[1,1]	POS+next POS

U018:%x[0,0]/%x[1,0]/%x[1,1]	Term+next Term+next POS
U019:%x[0,1]/%x[1,0]/%x[1,1]	POS+next Term+next POS
U020:%x[0,0]/%x[2,0]	Term+next next Term
U021:%x[0,0]/%x[2,1]	Term+next next POS
U022:%x[0,1]/%x[2,0]	POS+next next Term
U023:%x[0,1]/%x[2,1]	POS+next next POS
U024:%x[0,0]/%x[2,0]/%x[2,1]	Term+next next Term+next next POS
U025:%x[0,1]/%x[2,0]/%x[2,1]	POS+next next Term+next next POS
U026:%x[0,0]/%x[0,2]	Term+C
U027:%x[0,0]/%x[-1,2]	Term+previous C
U028:%x[0,2]/%x[-1,2]	C+previous C
U029:%x[0,0]/%x[-1,0]/%x[-1,1]/%x[-1,2]	Term+previous Term+previous POS+previous C
U030:%x[0,1]/%x[-1,0]/%x[-1,1]/%x[-1,2]	POS+previous Term+previous POS+previous C
U031:%x[0,0]/%x[-2,2]	Term+previous previous C
U032:%x[0,1]/%x[-2,2]	POS+previous previous C
U033:%x[0,0]/%x[1,2]	Term+next C
U034:%x[0,1]/%x[1,2]	POS+next C
U036:%x[0,1]/%x[2,2]	POS+next next C
U037:%x[0,0]/%x[-2,0]/%x[-2,1]/%x[-2,2]	Term+previous previous Term+previous previous POS+previous previous C
U038:%x[0,1]/%x[-2,0]/%x[-2,1]/%x[-2,2]	POS+previous previous Term+previous previous POS+previous previous C
U039:%x[0,0]/%x[1,0]/%x[1,1]/%x[1,2]	Term+next Term+next POS+next C
U040:%x[0,1]/%x[1,0]/%x[1,1]/%x[1,2]	POS+next Term+next POS+next C
U041:%x[0,0]/%x[2,0]/%x[2,1]/%x[2,2]	Term+next next Term+next next POS+next next C
U042:%x[0,1]/%x[2,0]/%x[2,1]/%x[2,2]	POS+next next Term+next next POS+next next C
U043:%x[-1,1]/%x[0,1]/%x[1,1]	previous POS+POS+next POS
U044:%x[-1,0]/%x[0,0]/%x[1,0]	previous Term+Term+next Term
U045:%x[-1,0]/%x[0,0]/%x[1,1]	previous Term+Term+next POS
U046:%x[-1,0]/%x[0,1]/%x[1,2]	previous Term+POS+next POS
U047:%x[-1,1]/%x[0,0]/%x[1,0]	previous POS+Term+next Term
U048:%x[-1,1]/%x[0,0]/%x[1,1]	previous POS+Term+next POS
U049:%x[-1,1]/%x[0,1]/%x[1,0]	previous POS+POS+next Term
U050:%x[-1,0]/%x[0,1]/%x[1,1]	previous Term+POS+next Term

3. System architecture

Our system flowchart is shown in Figure 4. The training phrase consists of two steps: 1. Collecting collocation. 2. Training the CRF with the help of collocation detection, word segmentation and POS tagging results. In the first training phrase, a large Chinese corpus is used as the training set. After the word segmentation and POS tagging, the corpus is used to collect collocations as we described in section 2.2. In the second training phrase, the collocations appeare in the same sentence or not is used as one separate feature for CRF tagger training.

The test phrase is straightforward. The test sentence is first segmented into words with POS tag, after detecting the appearance of collocation terms or not, the sentence is prepared as the input of CRF model. The CRF model will give one output tag to each term. The tag indicate error detection, error type, and also error position at the same time.

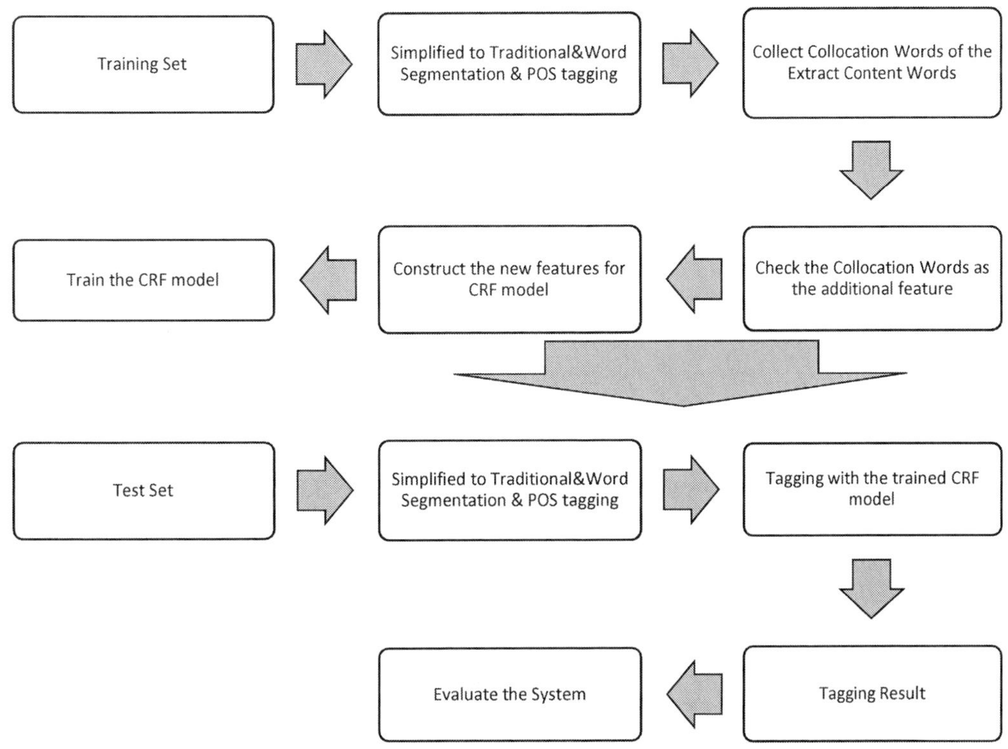

Figure 4.System Flowchart

4. Experiments

The system evaluation metrics of CGED shared task includes three levels. We focus on the identification level: this level is a multi-class categorization problem. All error types should be identified, i.e., Redundant, Missing, Word ordering, and Selection. The metrics used are accuracy, precision, recall, and F1-score.

4.1. Experiment Settings

We send respectively three runs for both data set this year, and the major difference for each experiment settings is the size of training set. Our system is based on traditional Chinese processing, the simplified Chinese is translated into traditional Chinse by Microsoft Word in advance. Our training data consists of data from NLP-TEA1(Chang et al.,2012) Training Data, Test Data, and the Training Data from NLP-TEA2 and NLP-TEA3. Table 4 shows the number of sentences in our training set.

Run1 settings: Use all the available data as the training set. For TOCFL, the training set is the union of the training sets in the NLP-TEA1, NLP-TEA2, and TOCFL in NLP-TEA3. For HSK, the training set is the union of the one used for TOCFL and HSK in NLP-TEA3.

Run2 settings: Almost the same as those in Run1, the only difference is the correct sentences are excluded from the training set. We believe that they provide no help for finding errors.

Run3 settings: Almost the same as those in Run1. The difference is how our system treats the continuous errors. If two errors of the same type occurred continuously, our system will combine them as one longer error. For example, two errors of the same type:

A2-0019-1, 10, 12, S

A2-0019-1, 13, 13, S

will be reported as:

A2-0019-1, 10, 13, S.

Table 4. Training set size

size	NLP-TEA1	NLP-TEA2	NLP-TEA3
Redundant	1830	434	10010
Correct	874	0	0
Selection	827	849	20846
Disorder (word ordering)	724	306	3071
Missing	225	622	15701

4.2. Experimental results

In the formal run of NLP-TEA-3 CGED shared task, there are 5 participants, and each team submits 3 runs in TOCFL, totally 15 runs. There are 8 participants in HSK, totally 21 runs. Table 5 shows the false positive rate. Our system has 0.082 false positive rate. The average of all runs is calculated from 15 runs for TOCFL and 21 runs for HSK.

Table 6, Table 7, and Table 8 show the formal run result of our system compared with the average in Detection level, Identification level, and Position level respectively. Our system achieves the highest Accuracy in Detection Level(TOCFL) and Identification-Level (TOCFL). The numbers in boldface are the best performance among all formal runs.

Table 5: The false positive rate in Detection Level (the lower the better)

Submission	False Positive Rate (TOCFL)	False Positive Rate (HSK)
CYUT&III-Run1	0.3470	0.4016
CYUT&III-Run2	0.3558	0.4191
CYUT&III-Run3	0.3635	0.4016
Average of all runs	0.4812	0.4956

Table 6: Performance evaluation in Detection Level

	Detection Level(TOCFL)				Detection Level(HSK)			
	Accuracy	Precision	Recall	F1	Accuracy	Precision	Recall	F1
Run1	**0.5955**	0.6259	0.5419	0.5809	0.6141	0.6003	0.6304	0.615
Run2	**0.5955**	0.6236	0.5501	0.5846	0.6118	0.5951	0.644	0.6186
Run3	0.5941	0.6205	0.5545	0.5856	0.6141	0.6003	0.6304	0.615
Average of all formal runs	0.5442	0.5700	0.5679	0.5455	0.5627	0.5807	0.6237	0.5688

Table 7: Performance evaluation in Identification Level

	Identification-Level (TOCFL)				Identification-Level (HSK)			
	Accuracy	Precision	Recall	F1	Accuracy	Precision	Recall	F1
CYUT-Run1	**0.5154**	0.46	0.3021	0.3647	0.5714	0.5306	0.4376	0.4797
CYUT-Run2	0.5133	0.4567	0.3061	**0.3666**	0.5662	0.5238	0.4509	0.4846
CYUT-Run3	0.5078	0.4472	0.3001	0.3592	0.5715	0.5306	0.4352	0.4782
Average of all formal runs	0.39118	0.32647	0.27321	0.2716	0.4555	0.4310	0.3705	0.3720

Table 8: Performance evaluation in Position Level.

	Position-Level (TOCFL)				Position-Level (HSK)			
	Accuracy	Precision	Recall	F1	Accuracy	Precision	Recall	F1
CYUT-Run1	0.3113	0.1461	0.1089	**0.1248**	0.3202	0.2037	0.2138	0.2086
CYUT-Run2	0.3061	0.1432	**0.1092**	0.1239	0.3143	0.2034	0.2225	0.2125
CYUT-Run3	0.3088	0.1196	0.0768	0.0935	0.3304	0.1814	0.144	0.1605
Average of all formal runs	0.2402	0.0846	0.0459	0.0597	0.2892	0.2059	0.1366	0.1529

5. Discussion and Conclusions

This paper reports our approach to the NLP-TEA-3 CGED Shared Task evaluation. By integrating the collocation as an additional feature into CRF model, we build a system that can achieve the task. The approach uniformly deals with the four error types: Redundant, Missing, Selection, and Word ordering.

Our system presents the best accuracy in detection level, best accuracy and F1 in identification level, and best recall and F1 in position-level at the TOCFL official run.

Due to the limitation of time and resource, our system is not tested under different experimental settings. In the future, we will use a larger corpus to extract more collocations to improve the performance on error diagnosis.

Acknowledgments

This study is conducted under the "Online and Offline integrated Smart Commerce Platform (3/4)" of the Institute for Information Industry which is subsidized by the Ministry of Economic Affairs of the Republic of China.

References

Ru-Yng Chang, Chung-Hsien Wu, and Philips Kokoh Prasetyo. 2012. Error Diagnosis of Chinese Sentences Using Inductive Learning Algorithm and Decomposition-Based Testing Mechanism. ACM Transactions on Asian Language Information Processing, 11(1), article 3, March.

Tao-Hsing Chang, Yao-Ting Sung, Jia-Fei Hong, Jen-I chang. 2014. KNGED: a Tool for Grammatical Error Diagnosis of Chinese Sentences.

Po-Lin Chen, Wu Shih-Hung, Liang-Pu Chen, Ping-Che Yang, Ren-Dar Yang. 2015. Chinese Grammatical Error Diagnosis by Conditional Random Fields, in Proceedings of The 2nd Workshop on Natural Language Processing Techniques for Educational Applications, pages 7–14, Beijing, China, July.

Po-Lin Chen, Wu Shih-Hung, Liang-Pu Chen, Ping-Che Yang. 2016. Improving the Selection Error Recognition in a Chinese Grammar Error Detection System, IEEE IRI 2016, Pittsburgh, Pennsylvania, USA, July.

Gabriela Ferraro, Rogelio Nazar, Margarita Alonso Ramos, and Leo Wanner. 2014. Towards advanced collocation error correction in Spanish learner corpora. Lang. Resour. Eval. 48, 1, pp. 45-64.

Michael Gamon. 2011. High-Order Sequence Modeling for Language Learner Error Detection, in Proceedings of the Sixth Workshop on Innovative Use of NLP for Building Educational Applications, pages 180–189, Portland, Oregon, June.

Lafferty, A. McCallum, and F. Pereira. 2001. Conditional random fields: Probabilistic models for segmenting and labeling sequence data. In Intl. Conf. on Machine Learning.

Lee, Lung-Hao, Liang-Chih Yu, and Li-Ping Chang. 2015. Overview of the NLP-TEA 2015 shared task for Chinese grammatical error diagnosis. In Proceedings of the 2nd Workshop on Natural Language Processing Techniques for Educational Applications (NLP-TEA 2015). 1-6.

Manning, C. D. and H. Schütze. 1999. Foundations of Statistical Natural Language Processing, The MIT Press.

National Digital Archives Program, "CKIP POS," http://ckipsvr.iis.sinica.edu.tw/, 2015.

F. Smadja. 1993. "Retrieving Collocation from Text: Xtract," Computational Linguistics, Vol. 19, No. 1, pp. 143-177.

Yow-Ting Shiue and Hsin-Hsi Chen. 2016. "Detecting Word Usage Errors in Chinese Sentences for Learning Chinese as a Foreign Language." Proceedings of 10th Language Resources and Evaluation Conference, 23-28 May 2016, Portorož, Slovenia.

Taku Kudo. 2007. "CRF++: Yet Another CRF toolkit", https://taku910.github.io/crfpp/.

Jui-Feng Yeh, Yun-Yun Lu, Chen-Hsien Lee, Yu-Hsiang Yu, Yong-Ting Chen. 2014. Detecting Grammatical Error in Chinese Sentence for Foreign.

Yu, Liang-Chih, Lung-Hao Lee, and Li-Ping Chang. 2014. Overview of grammatical error diagnosis for learning Chinese as a foreign language. In Proceedings of the 1st Workshop on Natural Language Processing Techniques for Educational Applications (NLP-TEA 2014). 42-47.

Chung-Hsien Wu, Chao-Hong Liu, Matthew Harris, and Liang-Chih Yu. 2010. *Sentence Correction Incorporating Relative Position and Parse Template Language Models*. IEEE Transactions on Audio, Speech, and Language Processing, 18(6), 1170-1181.

Shih-Hung Wu, Hsien-You Hsieh. 2012. Sentence Parsing with Double Sequential Labeling in Traditional Chinese Parsing Task. Second CIPS-SIGHAN Joint Conference on Chinese Language Processing, pages 222–230.

Word Order Sensitive Embedding Features/Conditional Random Field-based Chinese Grammatical Error Detection

Wei-Chieh Chou, Chin-Kui Lin,
Yih-Ru Wang
Department of Electrical Engineering,
National Chiao Tung University, Hsinchu,
Taiwan, ROC

m0450743.eed04g@g2.nctu.edu.tw,lck199
382.eed04g@g2.nctu.edu.tw,yrwang@mail
.nctu.edu.tw

Yuan-Fu Liao
Department of Electronic Engineering
National Taipei University of Technology
Taipei, Taiwan, ROC

yfliao@ntut.edu.tw

Abstract

This paper discusses how to adapt two new word embedding features to build a more efficient Chinese Grammatical Error Diagnosis (CGED) systems to assist Chinese foreign learners (CFLs) in improving their written essays. The major idea is to apply word order sensitive Word2Vec approaches including (1) structured skip-gram and (2) continuous window (CWindow) models, because they are more suitable for solving syntax-based problems. The proposed new features were evaluated on the Test of Chinese as a Foreign Language (TOCFL) learner database provided by NLP-TEA-3&CGED shared task. Experimental results showed that the new features did work better than the traditional word order insensitive Word2Vec approaches. Moreover, according to the official evaluation results, our system achieved the lowest (0.1362) false positive (FA) and the highest precision rates in all three measurements among all participants.

1 Introduction

In recent years, the rise of Asian economies and nearly 20 years of rapid development of China has led to a corresponding interest in the study of Standard Chinese ("Mandarin") as a foreign language, the official language of mainland China and Taiwan.

However, it might be a great challenge for those CFLs to learn how to write an essay or report in Chinese. Because approximately 3,000 Chinese characters and 5,000 words are required for receiving Test of Chinese as a Foreign Language (TOCFL) certificate in advanced level[1]. Beside, Chinese is an analytic language, in that they depend on syntax (word order and sentence structure) rather than morphology, i.e., changes in form of a word, to indicate the word's function in a sentence. And Chinese also makes heavy use of grammatical particles to indicate aspect and mood, such as like 了 (le , perfective), 還 (hái, still), 已經 (yǐjīng, already), and so on.

CFLs often make four types of grammatical errors, including (1) disorder, (2) missing, (3) redundant and (4) selection, for example:

- Disorder: 我要送給你一個慶祝禮物。要是兩、三天晚了，請別生氣 ("兩、三天晚了" should be "晚了兩、三天")
- Missing: 我聽說你找到工作。恭喜恭喜！("工作" should be "工作了")
- Redundant: 今天是我大學畢業了 ("今天是" should be "今天")
- Selection: 我等在教室沒那麼久老師就來了 ("那麼" should be "多")

To detect those grammatical errors is not an easy task. Recently, researchers have proposed many approaches for CGED task. They could be roughly divided into two categories including (1) hybrid linguistic rules+language modelling and (2) pure classification-based methods.

---

[1] http://www.sc-top.org.tw/english/eng_index.php

73

Proceedings of the 3rd Workshop on Natural Language Processing Techniques for Educational Applications,
pages 73–81, Osaka, Japan, December 12 2016.

For example, Lee et al. (2013) applied a set of handcrafted linguistic rules with syntactic information to detect errors occurred in Chinese sentences written by CFLs. Lee et al. (2014) then further implemented a sentence judgement system that integrated both rule-based an and n-gram statistical methods to detect grammatical errors in Chinese sentences. Lin and Chen (2015) proposed a system which measured the likelihood of sentences generated by deleting, inserting, or exchanging characters or words in which two sentence likelihood functions were proposed based on frequencies of space removed version of Google n-grams.

On the other hand, Xiang (2015) utilized an ensemble classifier random feature subspace method for CGED task. Cheng et al. (2014) proposed a CRF-based method to detect word ordering errors and a ranking SVM-based model to suggest the proper corrections. Finally, Chen et al. (2015) and Yeh et al. (2015) also adopt CRFs and collected a set of common grammatical error rules for building CGED systems.

Among these two methods, the classification-based approach, especially the CRF-based one is quite promising. Because, CRFs treat the CGED problem as a sequence-to-sequence mapping task, it could then model well the word ordering and sentence structure. However, traditional CRF-based approaches often only take current and few neighbouring words and their POS tags as the input features. This may limit CRFs' horizon vision. Besides, word-based features will result in the sparse training data problem, since the total number of Chinese words is more than $160,000^2$.

To alleviate these two difficulties, this paper would like to discuss how to adapt word embedding features to alleviate the sparseness issue and especially how to extract two new word order sensitive embedding features proposed by Wang (2015) to capture ordering information. The major idea is to apply word order sensitive Word2Vec approaches including (1) Structured Skip-gram and (2) CWindow models. Because they seriously take word ordering information into account and are therefore more suitable for solving syntax-based problems. By this way, we hope we could build a more efficient CGED system.

2   System Implementation for NLP-TEA-3&CGED shared task

The block diagram of our proposed system is shown in Fig. 1. It has a CRF-based traditional Chinese parser for word segmentation and POS tagging frontend and a CRF-based CGED backend. But the major enhancement comparing with other CRF-based approaches is that it applies the word order sensitive Word2Vec module to extract word embedding vectors and then does word clustering to generate input features for CRF-based CGED module.

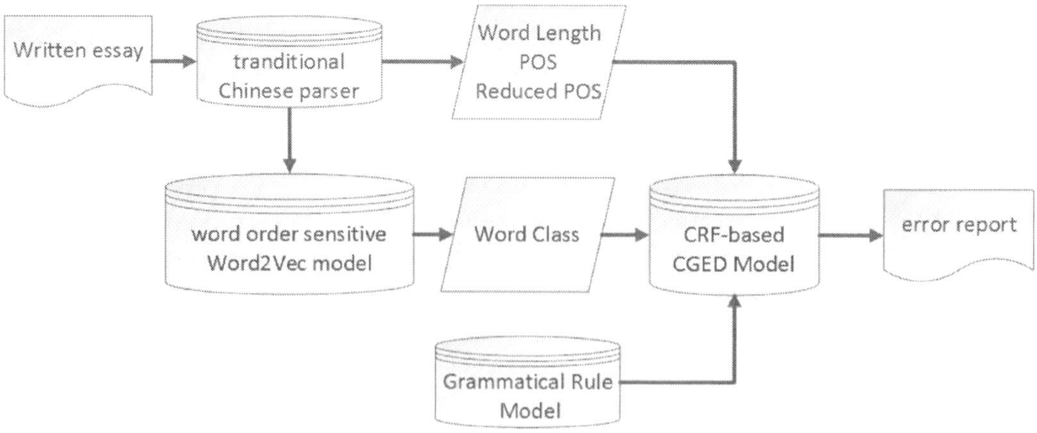

Figure 1: The block diagram of the proposed word ordering sensitive embedding feature/CRF-based Chinese Grammatical Error Detection system.

In the following subsections, several system components will be discussed in more detail, including (1) traditional Chinese parser, (2) word order sensitive Word2Vec, (3) grammatical rule and (4) CRF-based CGED models.

2.1 Traditional Chinese Parser

The parser used in this system (as shown in Fig. 2) is a CRF-based system for traditional Chinese. It has three main modules including (1) text normalization, (2) word segmentation and (3) POS tagging.

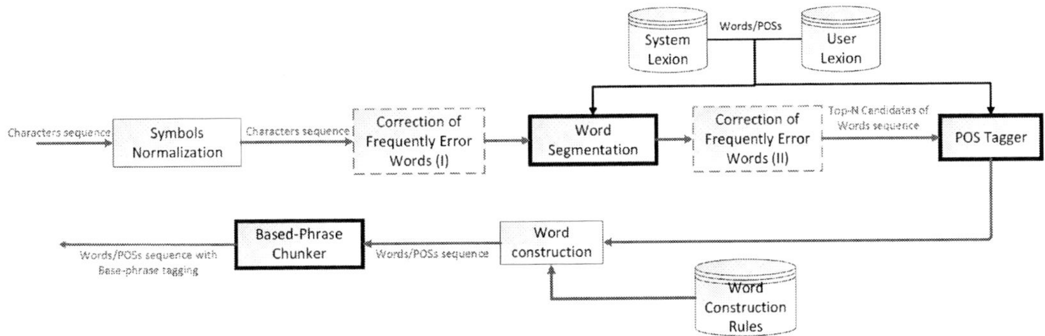

Figure 2: The schematic diagram of the proposed Chinese parser.

This parser was trained using Sinica Balanced Corpus ver. 4.0^{3}. Its performance is as follows: The F-measure of the word segmentation is 96.72% for the original database and 97.50% for the manually corrected corpus. The difference between precision and recall rate is less than 0.06%. The accuracy of the POS (47-type) tagging is 94.97%.

It is worth noting that this CRF-based Chinese word segmentation and parser is originally built for automatic speech recognition (ASR). So another purpose of this study is to examine how generalization and sophistication our parser is. Since Chinese words are not well defined (without word boundaries), a high quality Chinese word segmentation and parser is essential for building an effective word embedding representation and a good CGED system.

2.2 Word Order Sensitive Embedding Feature Extraction

One way to alleviate the sparse training data problem is to use word classes instead of words themselves as the input features for CRF-based CGED system. The most widely used tools for building word clustering are the models described in (Mikolov 2013a, b, c), including the "Skip-gram" and the "Continuous Bag-of-Words" (CBOW) models. However, since these models only give a word a single embedding feature vector, they are insensitive to word order and may not be suitable for CGED tasks.

Therefore, in this paper, we will adopt two new word order sensitive embedding approaches including (1) CWindow and (2) Structured Skip-gram (see Fig. 3) models proposed by Wang (2015) to take word ordering information into account.

Basically, CWindow defines a output predictor $O \in \mathbb{R} (|V| \times (2c \times d))$ that takes a $(2c \times d)$-dimensional vector $[e(w_{-c}), \ldots, e(w_{-1}), e(w_1), \ldots, e(w_c)]$ (the embeddings of the context words) as input. Words in different position hence have different weights. Structured Skip-gram, on the other hand, defines a set of $c \times 2$ output predictors $(O_{-c}, \ldots, O_{-1}, O_1, O_c)$, with size $O \in \mathbb{R} <(|V|) \times d$, to predict the outputs according to their positions. These two models then will generate word order sensitive embeddings features. By this way, it should be easier for CGED system to detect abnormal word ordering or sentence structures.

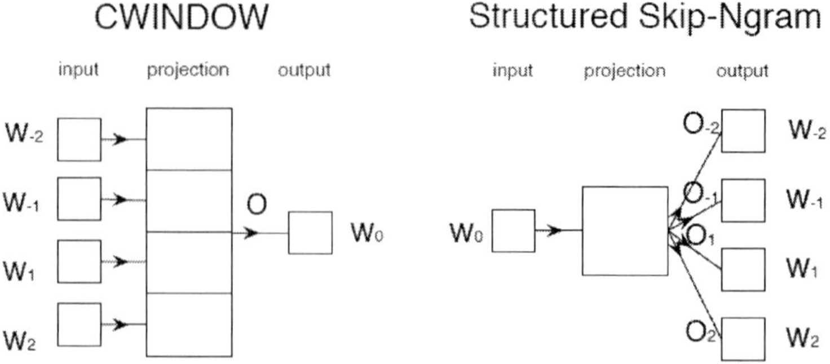

Figure 3: Illustration of the CWindow and Structured Skip-gram models.

2.3   Error-Prone Words

To detect some common grammatical errors often made by CFLs, a set of error patterns could be used to assist CGED system. For example, Yeh (2015) checked the following words in his CRF-based CGED system:

- Quantifiers
    - ✓   #. of human: "位" or "個"
    - ✓   #. of animals: "隻", "匹", "頭", or "條"
    - ✓   #. of things: "件"
    - ✓   #. of buildings: "座" or "棟"
    - ✓   #. of vehicle: "臺", "輛", "架" or "艘"
- Error-prone words (word + POS)
    - ✓   "把 (let)" + "Nh" or "Na" or "Nep"
    - ✓   "跟(with)" + "VA" or "Nh" or "Na"
    - ✓   "應該(maybe)" or "好像(like)" or "到底(at last)" + "Nh" or "Na"
    - ✓   "已經(already)" + "Neqa" or "Neu"
    - ✓   "Neqa" or "Neu" + "P" or "Na" or "VA"

After some literature survey, it is found that CFLs also often use "是(is)", "的(of)" and "了(finish)" incorrectly. Therefore, this work will specially considers a set of 9 error-prone words including "把(let)", "跟(with)", "應該(maybe)", "好像(like)", "到底(in the end)", "已經(already)", "是(is)", "的(of)" and "了(finish)". Here are some real error examples produced by CFLs (from TOCFL learner corpus):

- Redundant: "把(let)", "是(is)" or "的(of)" or "了"
    - ✓   看著我把搖搖頭。("看著我把搖搖頭" should be "看著我搖搖頭")
    - ✓   她是很漂亮。("她是很漂亮" should be "她很漂亮")
    - ✓   張愛文住在台北，他是十六歲。("他是十六歲" should be "他十六歲")
    - ✓   我想請你在日本料理的餐廳吃飯，好不好？("我想請你在日本料理的餐廳吃飯" should be "我想請你在日本料理餐廳吃飯")
    - ✓   幸虧沒有別的人先買走了。 ("幸虧沒有別的人先買走了" should be "幸虧沒有別的人先買走")
- Disorder: "跟(with)", "應該(should)", "好像(seem)", "到底(in the end)"
    - ✓   要不要下了課去西門跟我看電影？("要不要下了課去西門跟我看電影" should be "要不要下了課跟我去西門看電影")
    - ✓   家長也應該不讓小孩子亂玩網路遊戲。("家長也應該不讓小孩子亂玩網路遊戲" should be "家長也不應該讓小孩子亂玩網路遊戲")
    - ✓   到底我哪裡有錯？("到底我哪裡有錯" should be "我到底哪裡有錯")

    ✓   現在我跟這瑞典人的關係是已經很好的朋友。("現在我跟這瑞典人的關係是已經很好的朋友" should be "現在我跟這瑞典人的關係已經是很好的朋友")

- Selection: "好像"
    - ✓ 我覺得為了知道他們的想法，學生應該學他們的文化。好像他們的生活方式，歷史甚麼的。("好像他們的生活方式" should be "例如他們的生活方式")
- Missing: "了(finish)"
    - ✓ 你找到工作，恭喜恭喜！("你找到工作" should be "你找到工作了")

2.4 CRF-based Chinese Grammatical Error Detection

The performance of CRF-based model is mainly decided by the quality of feature engineering. In this work, five different features and four sets of feature templates are designed for building our CRF-based CGED system.

First, the five features are (1) word length, (2) POS, (3) reduced POS[4], (4) word class index, (5) error-prone word indicator. Fig. 4 shows an example of how these features are putting together with the grammatical error-type ground-truth to form a training data file.

```
你      1       Nh      N       84      0       0
開      1       VC      Vt      546     0       0
一      1       Neu     DET     374     0       B-R
個      1       Nf      M       624     0       I-R
慶祝會   3       Na      N       834     0       0
的      1       DE2     T       752     的      0
時候     2       Na      N       126     0       0
我      1       Nh      N       84      0       0
不能     2       D       ADV     715     0       0
會      1       D       ADV     834     0       B-R
參加     2       VC      Vt      952     0       0
，      1       PM      PM      -2      0       0
是      1       SHI     Vt      622     是      0
因為     2       Cbb     C       622     0       0
我      1       Nh      N       84      0       0
在      1       P       P       116     0       0
外國     2       Nc      N       6       0       0
做      1       VC      Vt      546     0       B-R
工作     2       Na      N       81      0       0
```

Figure 4: An example list of features and error-type ground-truth for training our CRF-based CGED model. The columns from left to right are word, word length, POS, reduced POS, word class index, error-prone word indicator and grammatical error-type ground-truth, respectively.

Second, the four sets of feature templates are specified in Table 1. They consider some combinations of the five features (and their n-grams). It is worth noting that the fourth template "(POS_{n-1} $EPWI_n$ POS_{n+1})" could be treated as a generalization of the "Error-prone words (word + POS)" pattern proposed in Yeh (2015) (mentioned in previous subsection).

Features	Features Templates
Word Class	C_{n-2}, C_{n-1}, C_n, C_{n+1}, C_{n+2}, (C_{n-2} C_{n-1} C_n), (C_n C_{n+1} C_{n+2}), (C_{n-1} C_n C_{n+1}), (C_{n-2} C_{n-1} C_n C_{n+1} C_{n+2})
POS+RPOS	($RPOS_{n-2}$ $RPOS_{n-1}$ POS_n), ($RPOS_{n-1}$ POS_n $RPOS_{n+1}$), (POS_n $RPOS_{n+1}$ $RPOS_{n+2}$)
RPOS+Word Class	($RPOS_{n-2}$ $RPOS_{n-1}$ C_n), ($RPOS_{n-1}$ C_n $RPOS_{n+1}$), (C_n $RPOS_{n+1}$ $RPOS_{n+2}$)
Error-Prone Word Indicator	(POS_{n-1} $EPWI_n$ POS_{n+1})

Table 1: List of feature templates designed for building our CRF-based CGED system. Here "C" , "POS", RPOS and EPWI are the word class index, POS, reduced POS and error-prone word indicator, respectively.

---

[4] http://ckipsvr.iis.sinica.edu.tw/cat.htm

3 NLP-TEA 3 & CGED Shared Task

The goal of the NLP-TEA3&CGED shared task is to develop systems to automatically diagnose Chinese sentences written by CFLs. The systems should indicate where and what type of errors are embedded in CFLs' sentence.

In the following experiments, the effectiveness of the error-prone word templates was first checked. Then the performance of the new "CWindow" and "Structured Skip-gram" were compared with the original "Skip-gram" and the "CBOW" models. Finally, the official evaluation results of our three CWindow-based submissions were discussed.

3.1 TOCFL learner database

The TOCFL learner database (NLP-TEA3) provided by the organizers was used to develop our CGED system. In order to enlarge the pool of training samples, the data sets of the two previous editions of this shared task, i.e., NLP-TEA1 (Yu et al. (2014)) and NLP-TEA2 (Lee et al. (2015)) are also added together. In the end, there are in total 63,462 sentences for system development. Table 2 shows the statistics of different grammatical error types on the development dataset.

Error-type	#. of errors
Disorder	1,980
Redundant	4,971
Missing	90
Selection	10,686
Correct	35,141

Table 2: Statistics of the numbers of error-types made by CFLs on our training corpus.

The development data was further divided into a training and a testing subsets by a ratio of 9:1. Therefore, there are 57,116 and 6,346 sentences in the training and testing subsets, respectively.

3.2 Model Settings

Four types of embedding representations including CBOW, Skip-gram, Structured Skip-gram and CWindow models were built using the modified Word2Vec toolkit[5,6]. They were all trained using the same set of text corpora including (1) LDC Chinese Gigaword Second Edition[7], (2) Sinica Balanced Corpus ver. 4.0, (3) CIRB0303[8] (Chinese Information Retrieval Benchmark, version 3.03), (4) Taiwan Panorama Magazine[9], (5) TCC300[10] and (6) Wikipedia (ZH_TW version).

In all methods, the vector size was set to 300 and using a context window of 13 (6+1+6) words. To speed up the computation, the probability of a target word was estimated with the hierarchy Softmax method. After the vector space is established, k-mean algorithm was utilized to cluster all words into 1,024 classes.

Finally, the CRF++ toolkit developed by Kudo[11] was utilized to build our CRF-based CGED system. It is worth noting although there are four different Word2Vec frontends but the CRF backend is the same (except the input word class features) for all following experiments.

3.3 Preliminary Results on Development Dataset

First of all, Table 3 shows the impact of (with and without) error-prone words evaluated using a CWindow/CRF-based system. According the results, it indicates that those special words did help to

---

[5] https://code.google.com/p/word2vec/

[6] https://github.com/dav/word2vec

[7] https://catalog.ldc.upenn.edu/LDC2005T14

[8] http://www.aclclp.org.tw/use_cir.php

[9] http://www.aclclp.org.tw/use_gh_c.php

[10] http://www.aclclp.org.tw/use_mat.php - tcc300edu

[11] https://taku910.github.io/crfpp/

improve the performance of our CRF-based CGED system. Therefore, those error-prone words will be considered in all systems reported below.

Approach	Accuracy	Precision	Recall	F1
Without	89.91%	52.17%	10.69%	17.75%
With	89.89%	52.32%	10.89%	18.03%

Table 3: Performance comparison on the effectiveness of adding the error-prone words feature templates on a CWindow/CRF-based CGED system.

Second, Table 4 showed the performance of the Structured Skip-gram-, CWindow-, Skip-gram- and CBOW-based CGED systems (all take error-prone words into account). It is found that CWindow achieved the best F1-score. Because F1-score is the most balanced performance measurement, all our submissions will use the CWindow-based approach.

Approach	Accuracy	Precision	Recall	F1
Skip-gram	89.59%	44.57%	10.49%	16.98
CBOW	89.91%	52.00%	10.32%	17.22
Structured Skip-gram	90.02%	56.97%	10.19%	17.29
CWindow	89.89%	52.32%	10.89%	18.03

Table 4:Performance of the Structured Skip-gram-, CWindow-, Skip-gram- and CBOW-based CGED systems (all take error-prone words into account).

3.4   Official Evaluation Results

Three runs (NCTU+NTUT-Run1, Run2 and Run3) were submitted to NLP-TEA 2016 CGED shared task for official evaluation. All submissions are CWindow-based systems, since CWindow achieved the best performance in preliminary experiments. The only difference between these three runs is that they have different FA performance (i.e., different operating points). Table 5 shows the official evaluation results of our three submissions.

Among three submissions, Run1 has the lowest FA and highest precision rate in all three measurements comparing with other participants. Especially, Run1 achieved 0.1362 FA, 0.4603 accuracy, 0.2542 precision and 0.0483 recall rate in position-level. Since FA is the most important factor that influences users' experiences on CGED applications, the proposed approach is quite promising.

Team-Run	False Positive Rate	Detection-Level				Identification-Level				Position-Level			
		Accuracy	Precision	Recall	F1	Accuracy	Precision	Recall	F1	Accuracy	Precision	Recall	F1
NCYU-Run1	0.5602	0.5507	0.5559	0.6542	0.6011	0.3577	0.2749	0.2862	0.2805	0.1728	0.0074	0.0056	0.0064
NCYU-Run2	0.9612	0.5218	0.5202	0.9726	0.6779	0.2328	0.2265	0.4744	0.3066	0.0231	0.0129	0.0195	0.0155
NCYU-Run3	0.8491	0.5363	0.5307	0.8959	0.6665	0.2653	0.2384	0.4134	0.3024	0.058	0.013	0.0163	0.0145
CYUT-Run1	0.347	0.5955	0.6259	0.5419	0.5809	0.5154	0.46	0.3021	0.3647	0.3113	0.1461	0.1089	0.1248
CYUT-Run2	0.3558	0.5955	0.6236	0.5501	0.5846	0.5133	0.4567	0.3061	0.3666	0.3061	0.1432	0.1092	0.1239
CYUT-Run3	0.3635	0.5941	0.6205	0.5545	0.5856	0.5078	0.4472	0.3001	0.3592	0.3088	0.1196	0.0768	0.0935
PKU-Run1	0.2284	0.521	0.5739	0.2871	0.3828	0.4575	0.3418	0.1173	0.1747	0.3844	0.0996	0.0263	0.0416
PKU-Run2	0.7205	0.5258	0.5292	0.7556	0.6224	0.3242	0.2792	0.3712	0.3187	0.1381	0.068	0.0824	0.0745
PKU-Run3	0.525	0.5349	0.5467	0.5907	0.5678	0.3705	0.2729	0.2192	0.2431	0.2331	0.0872	0.0651	0.0745
NCTU+NTUT-Run1	0.1362	0.5442	0.6593	0.246	0.3583	0.511	0.4892	0.1224	0.1958	0.4603	0.2542	0.0483	0.0811
NCTU+NTUT-Run2	0.2913	0.553	0.6	0.4077	0.4855	0.4793	0.4036	0.1982	0.2659	0.3784	0.1644	0.0639	0.092
NCTU+NTUT-Run3	0.32	0.5612	0.6013	0.4504	0.515	0.4773	0.3993	0.2185	0.2824	0.3613	0.1521	0.0668	0.0928
YNU-HPCC-Run1	0.6289	0.542	0.5444	0.7014	0.613	0.2211	0.1588	0.3196	0.2122	0.0886	0.0002	0.0002	0.0002
YNU-HPCC-Run2	0.5931	0.5026	0.5167	0.5918	0.5517	0.2322	0.1675	0.3136	0.2184	0.0991	0	0	null
YNU-HPCC-Run3	0.3382	0.4847	0.503	0.3195	0.3908	0.4023	0.281	0.1359	0.1832	0.2797	0.0012	0.0005	0.0007

Table 5: Official TOCFL evaluation results of NLP-TEA3&CGED shared task.

4   Conclusion

In this paper, a word order sensitive embedding features/CRF-based CGED system was proposed and implemented for participating the NLP-TEA-3&CGED shared task. The experimental results showed that the proposed new features did work better than the traditional word order insensitive Word2Vec approaches. Moreover, according to the official evaluation results, our system achieved the lowest FA (0.1342) and the highest precision rates in all three measurements among all participants. Therefore, the proposed approach is a promising one and will be further explored in the near future. Finally, the latest version of our traditional Chinese parser is available on-line at http://parser.speech.cm.nctu.edu.tw.

Acknowledgment

This work was supported by the Ministry of Science and Technology, Taiwan with contract 105-2221-E-009-142-MY2, 104-2221-E-027-079 and 105-2221-E-027-119

Reference

Chen, Po-Lin, Wu, Shih-Hung. (2015). Chinese Grammatical Error Diagnosis by Conditional Random Fields. Proceedings of The 2nd Workshop on Natural Language Processing Techniques for Educational Applications, pages 7–14.

Cheng, Shuk-Man, Yu, Chi-Hsin, Chen, Hsin-Hsi. (2014) Chinese Word Ordering Errors Detection and Correction for Non-Native Chinese Language Learners. Proceedings of COLING 2014, the 25th International Conference on Computational Linguistics: Technical Papers.

Lafferty, J., McCallum, A., and Pereira, F. (2001). Conditional random fields: Probabilistic models for segmenting and labeling sequence data. In Proc. of ICML, pp.282-289, 2001

Lee, Lung-Hao, Chang, Li-Ping, Lee, Kuei-Ching, Tseng, Yuen-Hsien, and Chen, Hsin-Hsi (2013). Linguistic Rules Based Chinese Error Detection for Second Language Learning. In Work-in-Progress Poster Proceedings of the 21st International Conference on Computers in Education (ICCE'13), Denpasar Bali, Indonesia, 18-22 November, 2013, pp. 27-29.

Lee, Lung-Hao, Yu, Liang-Chih, Lee, Kuei-Ching, Tseng, Yuen-Hsien, Chang, Li-Ping, and Chen, Hsin-Hsi. (2014). A Sentence Judgment System for Grammatical Error Detection. In Proceedings of the 25th International Conference on Computational Linguistics (COLING'14), Dublin, Ireland, 23-29 August, 2014, pp. 67-70.

Lee, Lung-Hao, Liang-Chih Yu, and Li-Ping Chang. 2015. Overview of the NLP-TEA 2015 shared task for Chinese grammatical error diagnosis. In Proceedings of the 2nd Workshop on Natural Language Processing Techniques for Educational Applications (NLP-TEA 2015). 1-6.

Lin, Chuan-Jie, and Chen, Shao-Heng. (2015). NTOU Chinese Grammar Checker for CGED Shared Task. Proceedings of The 2nd Workshop on Natural Language Processing Techniques for Educational Applications, pages 15–19,

Mikolov, Tomas, Chen, Kai, Corrado, Greg, and Dean, Jeffrey. (2013a). Efficient Estimation of Word Representations in Vector Space. In Proceedings of Workshop at ICLR.

Mikolov, Tomas, Sutskever, Ilya, Chen, Kai, Corrado, Greg, and Dean, Jeffrey. (2013b). Distributed Representations of Words and Phrases and their Compositionality. In Proceedings of NIPS.

Mikolov, Tomas, Yih, Wen-tau, and Zweig, Geoffrey. (2013c). Linguistic Regularities in Continuous Space Word Representations. In Proceedings of NAACL HLT.

Wang, Ling, Dyer, Chris, Black, Alan, and Trancoso, Isabel, (2015). Two/Too Simple Adaptations of Word2Vec for Syntax Problems. Proceedings of the 2015 Conference of the North American Chapter of the Association for Computational Linguistics: Human Language Technologies.

Wang, Yih-Ru, and Liao, Yuan-Fu (2015). Word Vector/Conditional Random Field-based Chinese Spelling Error Detection for SIGHAN-2015 Evaluation. Proceedings of the Eighth SIGHAN Workshop on Chinese Language Processing (SIGHAN-8), pages 46–49, Beijing, China, July 30-31.

Xiang, Yang, Wang, Xiaolong, Han, Wenying, and Hong, Qinghua. (2015). Chinese Grammatical Error Diagnosis Using Ensemble Learning. Proceedings of The 2nd Workshop on Natural Language Processing Techniques for Educational Applications, pages 99–104.

Yeh, Jui-Feng, Yeh, Chan-Kun, Yu, Kai-Hsiang, Li Ya-Ting, and Tsai, Wan-Ling. (2015). Condition Random Fields-based Grammatical Error Detection for Chinese as Second Language. Proceedings of The 2nd Workshop on Natural Language Processing Techniques for Educational Applications, pages 105–110.

Yu, Liang-Chih, Lung-Hao Lee, and Li-Ping Chang. 2014. Overview of grammatical error diagnosis for learning Chinese as a foreign language. In Proceedings of the 1st Workshop on Natural Language Processing Techniques for Educational Applications (NLP-TEA 2014). 42-47.

81

A Fluctuation Smoothing Approach for Unsupervised Automatic Short Answer Grading

Shourya Roy[†]   **Sandipan Dandapat**[‡]   **Y. Narahari**[§]

[†]Xerox Research Centre India, Bangalore
[‡]Microsoft India, Hyderbad,
[§]Indian Institute of Science, Bangalore

shourya.roy@xerox.com, sadandap@microsoft.com, hari@csa.iisc.ernet.in

Abstract

We offer a fluctuation smoothing computational approach for unsupervised automatic short answer grading (ASAG) techniques in the educational ecosystem. A major drawback of the existing techniques is the significant effect that variations in model answers could have on their performances. The proposed fluctuation smoothing approach, based on classical sequential pattern mining, exploits lexical overlap in students' answers to any typical question. We empirically demonstrate using multiple datasets that the proposed approach improves the overall performance and significantly reduces (up to 63%) variation in performance (standard deviation) of unsupervised ASAG techniques. We bring in additional benchmarks such as (a) paraphrasing of model answers and (b) using answers by k top performing students as model answers, to amplify the benefits of the proposed approach.

1 Introduction

In this paper, we deal with the problem of automatic assessment of students' constructed answers in natural language in an educational environment. In particular, we are interested in *short answers*: a few words to a few sentences long (everything in between fill-in-the-gap and essay type answers (Burrows et al., 2015)) and refer to the task as *Automatic Short Answer Grading* (ASAG). An example ASAG task is shown in Table 1. This is a non-trivial task owing to: linguistic variations (a given answer could be articulated in many different ways); subjective nature of assessment (multiple possible correct answers or no correct answer); lack of consistency in human rating (non-binary scoring on an ordinal scale within a range); etc.

Question	How are overloaded functions differentiated by the compiler?
Model Ans	Based on the function signature. When an overloaded function is called, the compiler will find the function whose signature is closest to the given function call.
Stud#1	It looks at the number, types, and order of arguments in the function call
Stud#2	By the number, and the types and order of the parameters.

Table 1: A question, model answer, and student answers from a computer science course (Mohler and Mihalcea, 2009). These will be used as a running example in the paper.

The number and type of its parameters.
The compiler selects the proper functions to execute based on number, types and order of arguments in the function call.
It selects the proper function to execute based on number, types and order of arguments in the function call.
The compiler selects proper function to execute based on number, types and order of arguments in the function call.
Is based on number, types, and order of arguments in the function call.
Compiler selects proper function to execute based on number, types and order of arguments in the function call.

Table 2: A few other possible model answers to the same question shown in Table 1.

Two recent survey papers by Roy et al. (2015) and Burrows et al. (2015) provide comprehensive views of research in ASAG. Both papers have grouped prior research based on the types of approaches used as well as the extent of human supervision needed. They report that a large fraction of prior work in ASAG uses various textual similarity measures (lexical, semantic etc.) to obtain a similarity value between student and model answers and convert those values to grades appropriately. Such *unsupervised ASAG techniques* largely reduce the need of instructor involvement either for training the ASAG system (as done in supervised ASAG (Sukkarieh et al., 2011; Madnani et al., 2013; Ramachandran et

Proceedings of the 3rd Workshop on Natural Language Processing Techniques for Educational Applications,
pages 82–91, Osaka, Japan, December 12 2016.

al., 2015)) or for providing all possible variations of model answers (e.g. concept mapping based approaches (Burstein et al., 1999; Leacock and Chodorow, 2003)). However, the unsupervised ASAG techniques suffer from two shortcomings which motivate the main contribution of this work. First, variations in model answers can significantly affect their performance. Consider a few *equivalent* model answers in Table 2 of our running example question (shown in Table 1). Replacing the instructor provided model answer with any of these is not expected to change human evaluation of student answers. However doing so make unsupervised ASAG techniques exhibit alarming fluctuations. An intrigued reader may make a forward reference to Figure 3 to see the fluctuation in performance of four unsupervised ASAG techniques against equivalent model answers to the question. This is a pragmatic concern as it shows that unsupervised ASAG techniques' performance significantly fluctuate depending on how model answers are specified. We will address this shortcoming in this paper. The second shortcoming is that there is no standardization in respect of how model answers are written across datasets or even within a dataset. The model answer in Table 1 is more detailed and self-contained than the model answer `"Abstraction and reusability"` for another question `"What are the main advantages associated with object-oriented programming?"` from the same dataset. Owing to such variation and key additional factors such as types of questions (*definition, interpretation, comparison* etc.), it is unlikely that any one of these ASAG techniques that rely solely on model answers would work well across all types of questions. While this is an important problem to be addressed, we do not deal with it in this paper.

There are two reasons behind the first shortcoming of the unsupervised ASAG techniques. The first is, all words (generally, n-grams) in the model answer are given equal importance to compute the score of a student answer, whereas instructors typically give emphasis on certain key words (or concepts). Second, there can be diverse ways to express a correct answer but the model answer may not capture all possible ways. These lead to the primary contribution of this work, which is to propose a *fluctuation smoothing* approach to make unsupervised ASAG techniques more consistent and effective. The proposed approach is generic; it works across lexical, knowledge based, and vector space based ASAG techniques. It is based on an intriguing finding that short answers to a question typically contain significant lexical overlap among them and such overlapping text portions are usually coupled to the correct answer to the question.[1] Based on similar motivation, Ramachandran et al. demonstrated effectiveness of using students' answers to a question to extract patterns for short answer scoring (2015). They used a graph based approach to extract patterns from groups of questions and their answers towards constructing regular expression alike patterns for short answer scoring. While they used a supervised approach using the extracted patterns as features, our approach is completely unsupervised - hence easier to test on new datasets and in real life. Secondly, we opine that regular expression based features can be constraining towards generalization and real life usage for free text answers.

Our approach is implemented in two steps. In the first step, we propose a variant of the sequential pattern mining problem (Agrawal and Srikant, 1995) to identify n-grams with high *support* that are more common (than the rest of the n-grams) among student answers. In the second step, we deduce our fluctuation smoothing approach by re-weighing different parts of the model answers in a manner proportional to their support values which in turn are used by the unsupervised ASAG techniques. Intuitively, the proposed technique brings in diversity by upweighing certain *scoring* words (n-grams) in the model answer (for our running example, the upweighed words include *call* and *overload*) and introducing new words (n-grams) which are not present in the model answer (e.g. *parameter, argument, type*) but have possibly affected instructors' scores. In the sequel, we use the words *approach, method,* and *technique* synonymously. We also use the phrases *fluctuation smoothing* and *stabilization* synonymously.

Our contributions: The contributions and novelty of this work are summarized below.

- We present vulnerabilities of unsupervised ASAG techniques arising from their sole dependence

---

[1]We hasten to add that this finding may not always be true. For example, occasionally, instructors design difficult and tricky questions to mislead students towards incorrect answers. However, we have empirically found lexical overlap to pervade the answers in our datasets. Additionally, we propose a *conservative* variant of our fluctuation smoothing approach that does not get affected by common mistakes made by a large number of students.

on the way model answers are written by instructors. These are potential roadblocks for practical adoption of these techniques and motivate our work in this paper.

- We propose a fluctuation smoothing approach, based on sequential pattern mining (Agrawal and Srikant, 1995), for unsupervised ASAG techniques by leveraging textual overlap between students' short answers. (§ 2.2)
- We empirically demonstrate on multiple datasets that the proposed approach improves the overall performance and significantly reduces the variation in performance. We bring in additional benchmarks such as (a) paraphrasing of model answers and (b) using top-k best answers by students as model answers, to convincingly demonstrate the efficacy of the proposed approach (§ 3.3)
- We create and offer a new dataset on high-school English reading comprehension task in a Central Board of Secondary Education (CBSE) school in India. (§ 3.1)

2 Proposed Approach for ASAG

In this section, we first describe unsupervised ASAG techniques building upon popular lexical, knowledge based, and vector space based methods. In the following section, we describe the proposed fluctuation smoothing approach.

2.1 Unsupervised ASAG Techniques

The basic premise of unsupervised ASAG techniques is: higher the similarity between the model and a student answer, higher the score the latter receives. Typically these measures output a score between 0 and 1 which are subsequently scaled by the maximum attainable score for a question. Building on these measures, we present an unsupervised technique leveraging the asymmetric nature of ASAG tasks i.e. student answers to be evaluated against the model answer and not the other way. Given two texts, model answer M and a student answer S, we conduct standard pre-processing operations such as stopword removal and stemming. The score of S with respect to M is then defined as:

$$asym(M, S) = \frac{1}{k} \sum_{i=1}^{k} \max_{\mathbf{s}_j \in S}(sim(\mathbf{m}_i, \mathbf{s}_j)) \tag{1}$$

where $\mathbf{m}_i$ and $\mathbf{s}_j$ are pre-processed n-grams of M and S respectively and k is the number of n-grams in M. For $n = 1$, $\mathbf{m}_i$ and $\mathbf{s}_j$ are words of M and S; and k is the length of M with respect to number of words. $sim(.,.)$ is a textual similarity measure of one of the following types:

- **Lexical**: In this category, we consider lexical overlap (**LO**) between model and student answers. It is a simple baseline measure which looks for exact match for every content words (post pre-processing e.g. stopword removal and stemming).
- **Knowledge based**: These measures employ a background ontology to arrive at word level semantic similarity values based on various factors such as distance between two words, lowest common ancestor, etc. Mohler and Mihalcea (2009) compared eight different knowledge-based measures to compute similarities between words in the model and student answers using Wordnet. We select the best performing one in this category, the measure proposed by Jiang and Conrath (**JCN**) (Jiang and Conrath, 1997) as shown below:

$$sim(m_i, s_j) = [IC(m_i) + IC(s_j) - 2 \times IC(LCS(m_i, s_j))]^{-1}$$

where, $LCS(m_i, s_j)$ is the least common subsumer of m_i and s_j in Wordnet (Miller, 1995), $IC(w) = -log\ P(w)$ and $P(w)$ is the probability of encountering an instance of word w in a large corpus.
- **Vector space based**: In this category, we have chosen one of the most popular measures of semantic similarity, namely, Latent Semantic Analysis (**LSA**) (Landauer et al., 1998) trained on a Wikipedia dump. We also consider the recently popular word2vec tool (**W2V**) (Mikolov et al., 2013) to obtain vector representation of words which are trained on 300 million words of Google news dataset and are of length 300. Both LSA and W2V build on several related ideas towards capturing importance of context to obtain vector representation of words e.g. the distributional hypothesis "Words will

occur in similar contexts if and only if they have similar meanings" (Harris, 1968). Similarity between words is the measured as the cosine distance between corresponding word vectors in the resultant vector space using the well known dot product formula.

2.2 Fluctuation Smoothing

2.2.1 Intuition

In unsupervised ASAG techniques, each student answer is compared against the model answer **independently** to arrive at a score indicating goodness of the student answer. These techniques give equal importance to each word of the model answer, whereas an instructor would often look for certain key words (equivalently, concepts, phrases etc.) such as the word *signature* in the model answer shown in Table 1. Second, there could be alternate ways of expressing equivalent correct answers different from the instructor provided model answer, such as the notion of *(function) signature* being rightly expressed by *number, types and order of arguments* for our running example. Both of these phenomena contribute towards fluctuations in performance of unsupervised ASAG techniques.

Towards addressing this issue, we exploit a fact that student answers to a question, as a collection, are expected to share more **commonalities** than any random collection of text snippets. Furthermore, we observe that such commonalities are likely to influence instructor given scores irrespective of whether or not they are a part of the model answer. Hence, extracting and incorporating these commonalities in an ASAG technique should help smoothing the fluctuation exhibited by unsupervised ASAG techniques relying solely on instructor given model answers. In the first step of the proposed two-step fluctuation smoothing approach, we apply a variant of the *sequential pattern mining* algorithm (Agrawal and Srikant, 1995) to identify frequent common n-grams in student answers. In the second step, we either upweigh n-grams present in the model answer or add new n-grams, with weights proportional to their support.

2.2.2 Technique

Sequential patterns in the context of text has been used to capture non-contiguous sequence of words for classification and clustering (Jaillet et al., 2006). Prior work has reported that for such tasks, sequential patterns have more reliable statistical properties than commonly used lexical features e.g. n-grams in NLP domain (Sebastiani, 2002). For short answers too, our observation was that sequential patterns are more statistically significant and less noisy than n-grams and hence developed our approach based on sequential patterns. The following two steps, namely, *mining high support n-grams* and *updating unsupervised ASAG scoring* are repeated for all questions.

Step 1: Mining High Support n-grams

The objective of this step is to extract commonly occurring patterns and quantify the notion of commonalities using *support*:

1. A student answer (s_i) is converted to a sequence of words ($w_1^i, w_2^i, \ldots, w_k^i$) by performing standard pre-processing operations such as stopword removal and stemming as well as task specific pre-processing viz. question word demoting.

2. An n-gram p, is a sequence of n consecutive tokens from s_i i.e. $p = w_j^i, w_{j+1}^i, \ldots, w_{j+n-1}^i$. It is imperative to note that these n-grams are not n consecutive words from the original model answer. Hence they may not make semantic sense when considered in isolation. For example, a few frequent n-grams for various n of our running example are `(number, type, order, argument, call)`, `(base, number, type, order)`, `(proper, execute, base)`.

3. The support of p is defined as $sup(p) = \frac{|\{s_i : p \in s_i\}|}{|\{s_i\}|}; \forall i$ i.e. the fraction of student answers containing p. Connecting to our intuition, n-grams with high support are commonalities among answers we are looking for.

Step 2: Updating Unsupervised ASAG Scoring

1. Sort n-grams in decreasing order of their support.

2. For every n-gram p assign a weight w, where $w = sup(p) \times f + count(p, M)$ and the function $count(.,.)$ returns the number of times the n-gram p appears in M (0, if it does not). The multiplicative factor f ensures differential weighing of the same n-gram appearing in multiple questions. The intuition being in the longer model answer, an n-gram obtained the same support amidst larger number of n-grams hence should have higher weights. Experimentally we find that average length of answers gives the best performance across various datasets.

3. Update the asymmetric similarity measure as below by incorporating the weights and with appropriate normalization.

$$asym(M, S) = \frac{1}{\sum_{i=1}^{k'} w_i} \sum_{i=1}^{k'} w_i \max_{\mathbf{s}_j \in S} (sim(\mathbf{m}_i, \mathbf{s}_j)) \tag{2}$$

where w_i is the weight of $\mathbf{m}_i$ and k' is the new length of M with respect to the number of n-grams.

To illustrate, for our running example's model answer, some of the words which get higher weights are (in decreasing order of weights) are `function`, `overloaded`, `call`, `compiler` etc. whereas new words such as `type`, `argument`, `number`, `order`, `parameter`, `proper` etc. get added to the model answer. In a *conservative* smoothing variant, we increase the support of n-grams which has $count(.,.) > 0$ i.e. only the word which appear in the instructor provided model answer. We call this conservative as it prevents introducing n-grams which might arise from a common misconception among large number of students.

3 Performance Evaluation

In this section, we present empirical answers to the following questions. Given n *valid* model answers to a question, what is the extent of fluctuation exhibited by the unsupervised ASAG techniques and smoothing achieved by the proposed approach (**Fluctuation Smoothing Performance**)? Secondly, are there alternate ways of bringing in diversity instead of relying on single instructor provided model answer? How do they compare against the proposed approach of leveraging student answers as a source of diversity (**Aggregate Performance**)?

3.1 Datasets

We evaluate the proposed fluctuation smoothing technique on three datasets. (i) **CSD:** This is one of the earliest ASAG datasets consisting of 21 questions with 30 student answers evaluated each on a scale of 0-5 from an undergraduate computer science course (Mohler and Mihalcea, 2009). Student answers were independently evaluated by two annotators and automatic techniques are measured against their average. (ii) **X-CSD:** This is an extended version of CSD with 81 questions by the same authors (Mohler et al., 2011). (iii) **RCD:** We created a new dataset on a reading comprehension assignment for Standard-12 students in Central Board of Secondary Education (CBSE) in India. The dataset contains 14 questions answered by 58 students. The answers were graded by two expert human raters based on model answers, again on a scale of 0-5 and optional scoring scheme.

All datasets have less than (total number of questions $\times$ total number of students) answers as presumably some students did not answer some questions. We mark such missing entries as "No Answer" and corresponding groundtruth scores as zero.

3.2 Performance Metric

A wide variety of metrics have been used in the ASAG literature with no standard one. Pearson's r and quadratic weighted Cohen's κ are the two most popular one which we use, though the suitability of the former for ASAG has been questioned (Mohler and Mihalcea, 2009). For every question we compute r and κ and reported values are average over all questions for each dataset.

3.3 Quantitative Results

Fluctuation Smoothing Performance: Towards generating valid model answers for each question, we select those student answers which were graded as perfect 5/5 by the instructor with respect to the model answer. We consider each of them (and the instructor provided model answer) as a model answer in turn and score all student answers using the unsupervised ASAG techniques - with and without fluctuation smoothing (i.e. Equation (1) and Equation (2) respectively). For our running example, there are 20 perfect scoring student answers (some of those are shown as examples in Table 2). Resultant Pearson's r of scores and associated fluctuations can be seen in Figure 3. Firstly, it is clear that all techniques suffer from fluctuation in performance as they rely solely on the model answers to score student answers (red dashed lines). Secondly, it is visually evident that the fluctuation smoothed technique (blue solid lines) shows significantly less variability than respective non-smoothed ones. Corresponding standard deviation (SD) values clearly support the observation. Table 3 shows aggregate SD in performance of all methods for three datasets under no smoothing and the proposed smoothing technique along with its conservative variant. Each big cell, bordered with double lines, shows the SD numbers for a (technique, metric) combination. It is evident that the proposed smoothing technique reduces fluctuations across all settings, often significantly, going up to 63% for (LSA,CSD) combination. This is a clear demonstration of the efficacy of the proposed fluctuation smoothing approach. Expectedly, the conservative approach gives less smoothing effect supporting our intuition that student answers bring in diverse views not captured in instructor provided model answers.

Aggregate Performance: At the core of it, the proposed fluctuation smoothing technique is essentially synthesizing a *super* model answer for every question. It does so by bringing in additional and diverse snippets of possible correct answers from the corresponding student answers. Next we ask the question if there are other possible ways of bringing in diverse views of correct answers. Towards that we consider the following two possible variants:

Paraphrasing: Using freely available paraphrase generators [2] we created four different paraphrases for each model answer and applied the proposed smoothing technique. For example, for the model answer of our running example (Table 1), one paraphrased model answer is "`Predicated on the function signature. When an overloaded function is called, the compiler will find the function whose signature is most proximate to the given function call.`"

Answers of top-k Students: We selected five best performing students for each dataset and their answers are chosen as model answers. Note that their answers to all questions may not be necessarily correct, but their overall performances were better than the rest of the students.

Each of these options is used as a source of diversity to reweigh different parts of the model answer (as shown in Equation 2). Figures 1 and 2 show Pearson's r and Cohen's κ for CSD with unsupervised ASAG techniques. Default refers to the scenario when no diversity source is used (Equation 1) and the remaining are with various diversity options described. Across all settings, we note that average performance of unsupervised techniques are comparable. The "stabilized-proposed" option emerges as the best, albeit jointly in some cases, though the differences are significant. However, by bringing in diversity we can reduce fluctuation in performance as we already demonstrated in Table 3 and Figure 3. We make similar observations on XCSD and RCD.

Finally, we obtain better r value for CSD compared to the values reported by Mohler and Mihalcea in their paper (2009) for these two techniques. We believe that this is owing to bigger size of Wikipedia corpus on which LSA was trained (compared to what it was in 2009) as well as our asymmetric similarity measure (compared to their symmetric measure) and possibly difference in preprocessing (we used WordnetLemmatizer instead of more commonly used Porter stemmer etc.).

4 Prior Art

Recent survey papers by Roy et al.(2015) and Burrows et al. (2015) provide comprehensive views of research in ASAG. Both of them have grouped prior research based on types of approaches used as

---

[2] http://paraphrasing-tool.com/; http://www.goparaphrase.com/; https://spinbot.com/; http://paraphrase.generalconnection.com/

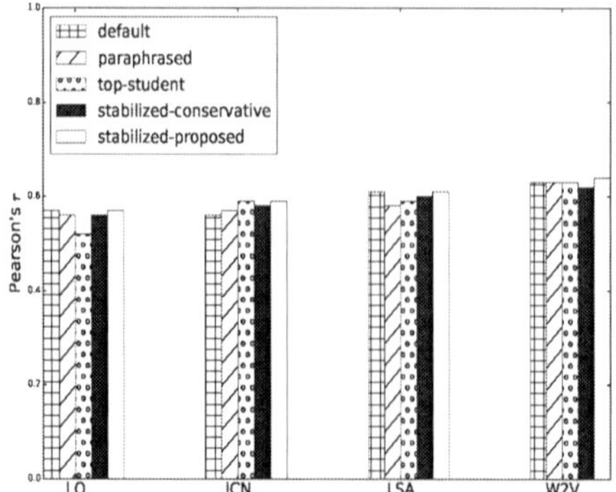

Figure 1: Aggregate Pearson's r for CSD.

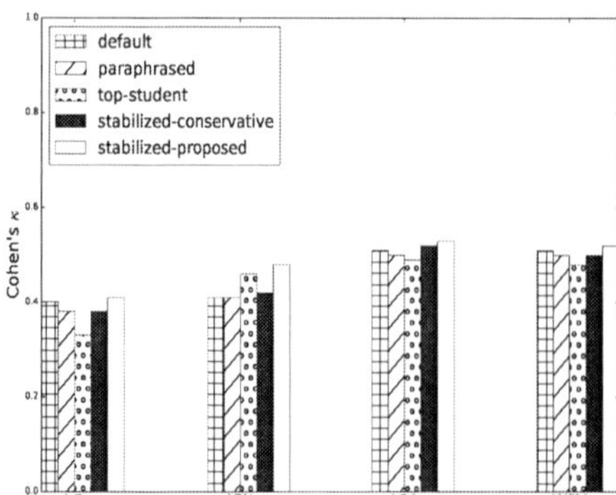

Figure 2: Aggregate Cohen's κ for CSD.

		Pearson's r			Quadratic κ		
		CSD	XCSD	RCD	CSD	XCSD	RCD
LO	no smoothing	0.11	0.11	0.10	0.12	0.14	0.06
	all students - cons	0.11	0.11	0.10	0.12	0.14	0.06
	all students	0.05	0.05	0.06	0.07	0.09	0.04
JCN	no smoothing	0.10	0.10	0.12	0.09	0.10	0.07
	all students - cons	0.09	0.09	0.11	0.09	0.10	0.06
	all students	0.05	0.04	0.06	**0.05**	0.05	0.02
LSA	no smoothing	0.11	0.08	0.09	0.12	0.12	0.03
	all students - cons	0.09	0.06	0.09	0.10	0.09	0.02
	all students	**0.04**	**0.03**	**0.05**	**0.05**	**0.04**	**0.01**
W2V	no smoothing	0.11	0.10	0.09	0.13	0.14	0.04
	all students - cons	0.09	0.08	0.08	0.10	0.11	0.04
	all students	0.05	0.04	**0.05**	0.06	0.06	**0.01**

Table 3: Aggregate standard deviation (SD) in performance (lower the better) of all techniques under the proposed smoothing technique (*all students*), its conservative variant (*all students-cons*) against the default *no smoothing* option. Best performances for each (metric, dataset) combination are emphasized (**bold**).

well as extent of human supervision needed. In this section, we cover relevant unsupervised ASAG techniques (e.g. lexical, knowledge-based, vector space etc.). Among the **lexical** measures, Evaluating Responses with BLEU (ERB) due to Perez et al. (2004) adapted a popular evaluation measure for machine translation, BLEU (Papineni et al., 2001) for ASAG with a set of NLP techniques such as stemming, closed-class word removal, etc. This work initially appeared as part of an ASAG system, *Atenea* (Alfonseca and Pérez, 2004) and later as *Willow* (Pérez-Marín and Pascual-Nieto, 2011). Mohler and Mihalcea (2009) conducted a comparative study of different semantic similarity measures for ASAG including **knowledge-based** measures using Wordnet as well as **vector space-based** measures such as LSA (Landauer et al., 1998) and Explicit Semantic Analysis (ESA) (Gabrilovich and Markovitch, 2006). LSA has remained a popular approach for ASAG and been applied in many variations (Graesser et al., 2000; Kanejiya et al., 2003; Klein et al., 2011). Lexical and semantic measures have been combined to validate natural complementarity of syntax and semantics for ASAG tasks (Perez et al., 2005). A combination of different string matching and overlap techniques were studied by Guetl on a small scale dataset (2008). Gomaa and Fahmy compared several lexical and corpus-based similarity algorithms and their combinations for grading answers in 0-5 scale (2012). This central reliance on instructor provided model answer of all these techniques leads to significant variation in performances even when it is replaced by another equivalent model answer.

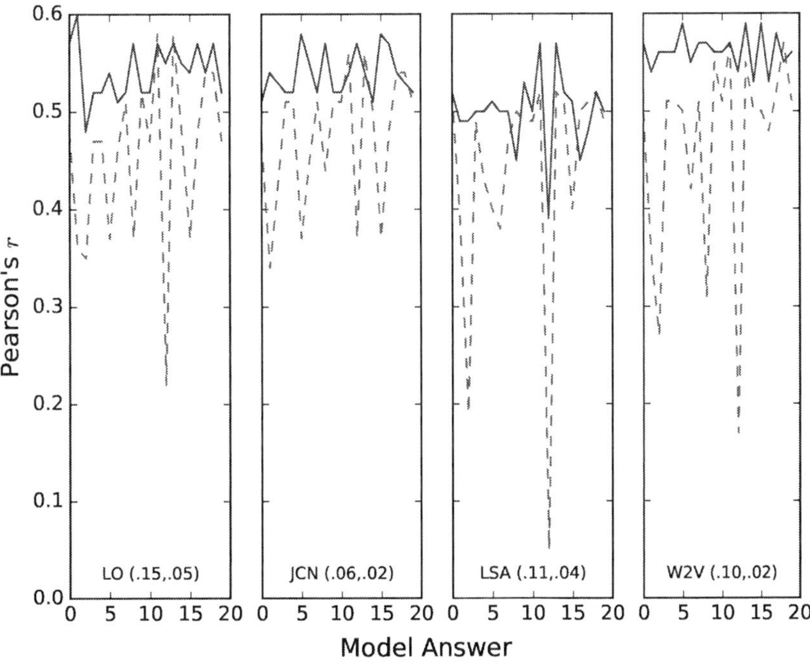

Figure 3: Fluctuation in Pearson'r of unsupervised ASAG techniques. It can be seen that unsupervised ASAG techniques with proposed fluctuation smoothing (blue solid lines) are significantly flatter than without smoothing (red dotted lines). Values within parenthesis are standard deviation (SD) value without and with smoothing respectively.

Dzikovska et al. conducted a 5-way Student Response Analysis challenge as a part of SemEval-2013 (2013). However, the task had more emphasis on giving feedback on student answers possibly using textual entailment techniques. ASAG can be seen as related to the task of textual entailment (Levy et al., 2013) especially when the elements of a model answer are compared against student answers. Textual entailment has seen a notable amount of work with a variety of shared tasks (Marelli et al., 2014; Xu et al., 2015) and vector space models have been considered as well (Zhao et al., 2015). Although the techniques are mostly supervised, the tasks and features used in such systems are relevant for consideration.

5 Conclusion and Future Work

In this paper, we introduced a fluctuation smoothing computational approach for unsupervised ASAG techniques in educational ecosystem. It addressed a major drawback - the significant effect that variations in model answers could have on the performance of these techniques. We empirically demonstrated with experimentation that the proposed approach at least retains (and in most cases, improves) the overall performance and significantly reduces the variation in performance of unsupervised ASAG techniques. We introduced additional benchmarks such as (a) paraphrasing of model answers and (b) using top-k best answers by students as model answers for comparing against the proposed approach. We intend to contribute a new dataset on high-school English reading comprehension task in a Central Board of Secondary Education (CBSE) school in India. In future, we would like to evaluate the proposed technique on other standard datasets such as SemEval-2013 dataset and Kaggle ASAP dataset (Kaggle, 2015).

6 Acknowledgment

We thank Oliver Adams and Ajay Nagesh for helpful discussions during ideation and early implementation of parts of this work.

References

Rakesh Agrawal and Ramakrishnan Srikant. 1995. Mining sequential patterns. In *Proceedings of the Eleventh International Conference on Data Engineering*, pages 3–14, Washington, DC, USA. IEEE Computer Society.

Enrique Alfonseca and Diana Pérez. 2004. Automatic assessment of open ended questions with a bleu-inspired algorithm and shallow nlp. In *EsTAL*, volume 3230 of *Lecture Notes in Computer Science*, pages 25–35. Springer.

Steven Burrows, Iryna Gurevych, and Benno Stein. 2015. The eras and trends of automatic short answer grading. *International Journal of Artificial Intelligence in Education*, 25(1):60–117.

Jill Burstein, Susanne Wolff, and Chi Lu. 1999. Using lexical semantic techniques to classify free-responses. In *Breadth and depth of semantic lexicons*, pages 227–244. Springer.

Myroslava O Dzikovska, Rodney D Nielsen, Chris Brew, Claudia Leacock, Danilo Giampiccolo, Luisa Bentivogli, Peter Clark, Ido Dagan, and Hoa T Dang. 2013. Semeval-2013 task 7: The joint student response analysis and 8th recognizing textual entailment challenge. Technical report, DTIC Document.

Evgeniy Gabrilovich and Shaul Markovitch. 2006. Overcoming the brittleness bottleneck using wikipedia: Enhancing text categorization with encyclopedic knowledge. In *AAAI*, pages 1301–1306. AAAI Press.

Wael H Gomaa and Aly A Fahmy. 2012. Short answer grading using string similarity and corpus-based similarity. *International Journal of Advanced Computer Science and Applications (IJACSA)*, 3(11).

Arthur C. Graesser, Peter M. Wiemer-Hastings, Katja Wiemer-Hastings, Derek Harter, and Natalie K. Person. 2000. Using latent semantic analysis to evaluate the contributions of students in autotutor. *Interactive Learning Environments*, 8(2):129–147.

Christian Guetl. 2008. Moving towards a fully automatic knowledge assessment tool. *iJET*, 3(1).

Zellig Harris. 1968. *Mathematical Structures of Language*. John Wiley and Son, New York.

Simon Jaillet, Anne Laurent, and Maguelonne Teisseire. 2006. Sequential patterns for text categorization. *Intelligent Data Analysis*, 10(3):199–214.

J.J. Jiang and D.W. Conrath. 1997. Semantic similarity based on corpus statistics and lexical taxonomy. In *Proc. of the Int'l. Conf. on Research in Computational Linguistics*, pages 19–33.

Kaggle. 2015. The hewlett foundation: Short answer scoring. http://www.kaggle.com/c/asap-sas. Online; accessed July 16, 2016.

Dharmendra Kanejiya, Arun Kumar, and Surendra Prasad. 2003. Automatic evaluation of students' answers using syntactically enhanced lsa. In *Proceedings of the HLT-NAACL 03 workshop on Building educational applications using natural language processing - Volume 2*, pages 53–60.

Richard Klein, Angelo Kyrilov, and Mayya Tokman. 2011. Automated assessment of short free-text responses in computer science using latent semantic analysis. In *ITiCSE*, pages 158–162. ACM.

T. K. Landauer, P. W. Foltz, and D. Laham. 1998. An Introduction to Latent Semantic Analysis. *Discourse Processes*, 25:259–284.

Claudia Leacock and Martin Chodorow. 2003. C-rater: Automated scoring of short-answer questions. *Computers and the Humanities*, 37(4):389–405.

Omer Levy, Torsten Zesch, Ido Dagan, and Iryna Gurevych. 2013. Recognizing partial textual entailment. In *ACL (2)*, pages 451–455. The Association for Computer Linguistics.

Nitin Madnani, Jill Burstein, John Sabatini, and Tenaha OReilly. 2013. Automated scoring of a summary writing task designed to measure reading comprehension. In *Proceedings of the 8th workshop on innovative use of nlp for building educational applications*, pages 163–168. Citeseer.

Marco Marelli, Luisa Bentivogli, Marco Baroni, Raffaella Bernardi, Stefano Menini, and Roberto Zamparelli. 2014. Semeval-2014 task 1: Evaluation of compositional distributional semantic models on full sentences through semantic relatedness and textual entailment. *SemEval-2014*.

Tomas Mikolov, Kai Chen, Greg Corrado, and Jeffrey Dean. 2013. Efficient estimation of word representations in vector space. *arXiv preprint arXiv:1301.3781*.

George A Miller. 1995. Wordnet: a lexical database for english. *Communications of the ACM*, 38(11):39–41.

Michael Mohler and Rada Mihalcea. 2009. Text-to-text semantic similarity for automatic short answer grading. In *Proceedings of the 12th Conference of the European Chapter of the Association for Computational Linguistics*, EACL '09, pages 567–575.

Michael Mohler, Razvan C. Bunescu, and Rada Mihalcea. 2011. Learning to grade short answer questions using semantic similarity measures and dependency graph alignments. In *ACL*, pages 752–762.

Kishore Papineni, Salim Roukos, Todd Ward, and Wei-Jing Zhu. 2001. Bleu: a method for automatic evaluation of machine translation. Technical report, IBM Research Report.

Diana Perez, Enrique Alfonseca, and Pilar Rodríguez. 2004. Application of the bleu method for evaluating free-text answers in an e-learning environment. In *LREC*. European Language Resources Association.

Diana Perez, Alfio Gliozzo, Carlo Strapparava, Enrique Alfonseca, Pilar Rodriguez, and Bernardo Magnini. 2005. Automatic assessment of students' free-text answers underpinned by the combination of a BLEU-inspired algorithm and latent semantic analysis. In *Proceedings of the Eighteenth International Florida Artificial Intelligence Research Society Conference, FLAIRS*, Clearwater Beach, FL, United states.

Diana Pérez-Marín and Ismael Pascual-Nieto. 2011. Willow: a system to automatically assess students free-text answers by using a combination of shallow nlp techniques. *International Journal of Continuing Engineering Education and Life Long Learning*, 21(2-3):155–169.

Lakshmi Ramachandran, Jian Cheng, and Peter Foltz. 2015. Identifying patterns for short answer scoring using graph-based lexico-semantic text matching. In *Proceedings of the Tenth Workshop on Innovative Use of NLP for Building Educational Applications*, pages 97–106.

Shourya Roy, Y. Narahari, and Om D. Deshmukh. 2015. A perspective on computer assisted assessment techniques for short free-text answers. In *Computer Assisted Assessment. Research into E-Assessment*, pages 96–109. Springer.

Fabrizio Sebastiani. 2002. Machine learning in automated text categorization. *ACM computing surveys (CSUR)*, 34(1):1–47.

Jana Z Sukkarieh, Ali Mohammad-Djafari, Jean-François Bercher, and Pierre Bessie´ re. 2011. Using a maxent classifier for the automatic content scoring of free-text responses. In *AIP Conference Proceedings-American Institute of Physics*, volume 1305, page 41.

Wei Xu, Chris Callison-Burch, and William B Dolan. 2015. Semeval-2015 task 1: Paraphrase and semantic similarity in twitter (pit). *Proceedings of SemEval*.

Jiang Zhao, Man Lan, Zheng-Yu Niu, and Yue Lu. 2015. Integrating word embeddings and traditional nlp features to measure textual entailment and semantic relatedness of sentence pairs. In *IJCNN*, pages 1–7. IEEE.

Japanese Lexical Simplification for Non-Native Speakers

Muhaimin Hading, Yuji Matsumoto,
Graduate School of Information Science
Nara Institute of Science and Technology
{muhaimin.hading.mc, matsu}@is.naist.jp

Maki Sakamoto
Graduate School of Informatics and Engineering
The University of Electro-Communications
maki.sakamoto@uec.ac.jp

Abstract

This paper introduces Japanese lexical simplification. Japanese lexical simplification is the task of replacing complex words in a given sentence with simple words to produce a new sentence without changing the original meaning of the sentence. We propose a method of supervised regression learning to estimate complexity ordering of words with statistical features obtained from two types of Japanese corpora. For the similarity of words, we use a Japanese thesaurus and dependency-based word embeddings. Evaluation of the proposed method is performed by comparing the complexity ordering of the words.

1 Introduction

According to the statistical data collected by Ministry of Justice, there are about two million foreigners living in Japan today. Around half of them do not have Japanese proficiency. It has been a problem for foreigners since most of information is provided in Japanese. Lexical simplification is a process to make a sentence more readable for non-native speakers by replacing complex words to simpler ones that retain the same meaning. A number of studies on lexical simplification have been conducted in recent years. Since the task of lexical simplifications is related with development of other tasks in natural language processing such as words similarity or paraphrasing words. Most of studies in simplification are conducted in English. Since there are much larger data and many tools available for English compared with other languages. In this paper, we tackle the sentence simplification problem in Japanese. We propose a method for estimating complexity of Japanese words and for obtaining semantically similar words for the replacement of complex words.

2 Related Work

Dominant approaches of previous work in simplification are hybrid approaches, which combine deep semantic and monolingual machine translation (Narayan and Gardent, 2014), word alignment approach (Coster and Kauchak, 2011; Paetzold and Specia 2013; Horn, et al., 2014) or language modeling approach (Kauchak, 2013). The main limitation of these methods is that they depend on parallel corpus between simple and complex sentences such as English Wikipedia, Simple English Wikipedia or Newsela corpus (Xu et al., 2015).

Another approach is to implement the simplification task of complex words by replacing them with the extract synonym words obtained from databases such as thesaurus (Devlin and Tait, 1998; De Belder and Moens, 2010), from dictionary definition or from WordNet (Kajiwara et al.,2013). Thesauri can provide good synonyms while their coverage is limited. Recent work (Glavas˘and Stajner, 2015; Paetzold and Specia, 2016) approached the word embedding model (Mikolov et al., 2013) to estimate word similarity and aims to mitigate the limitation of thesauri and parallel corpora.

The next approach is to identify complex words and choose simpler words for replacing them, while keeping the same meaning of the original complex words. Identifying complex words is

Proceedings of the 3rd Workshop on Natural Language Processing Techniques for Educational Applications,
pages 92–96, Osaka, Japan, December 12 2016.

common work before doing the simplification task (Carroll et al., 1998; Baustista et al., 2009; Paetzold and Specia, 2016). Estimation of word complexity is mostly based on their frequencies (Devlin and Tait, 1998; De Belder and Moens, 2010; Kauchak et al., 2014, Kajiwara et al., 2015), their length (Bautista et al.,2009), judgment by user study (Paetzold and Specia, 2016), technical words in specific domains (Kauchak et al., 2014), basic vocabularies for children (Kajiwara et. al, 2013), Japanese Language Proficiency Test levels, or Easy Japanese corpus (Moku et al.,2012). The recent work of (Kodaira et al., 2016) used crowdsourcing to for collecting simplification candidates of words.

Our approach uses more than one resource. We first use a thesaurus since thesauri produce the best candidates of synonyms. For addressing the limitation of a thesaurus, we utilize dependency-based word embedding (Levy and Goldberg, 2014) since it is shown that dependency-based embedding highlights less topical and more functional similarity than the skip-gram models. For identification of complexity of words, we use existing approaches like frequency, words used by children, technical words, and Japanese Language Proficiency Test levels.

3   Data

In our experiments, we use Japanese raw corpora. We combine Balanced Corpus of Contemporary Written Japanese (BCCWJ)[1] and Mainichi Newspaper Corpus to estimate word similarity, Japanese Language Proficiency Test vocabularies list, a corpus of compositions written by Japanese Elementary and Junior High School students (Miyagi, 2015), a corpus of compositions written by Japanese Elementary School Children (Sakamoto, 2010), and Bunrui Goi Hyo Database Japanese thesaurus[2].

4   Proposed Method

4.1   Grouping Similar Words

The purpose of this task is to find groups of words that have similar meaning. In our experiment we use Bunrui-Goi-Hyo (BGH for short), a Japanese thesaurus. This thesaurus is manually constructed. It comprises about 100K words. In BGH, all the words are arranged by their meaning. We extract all the groups of words at the bottom level as similar words. Since the number of words are limited, some words do not appear in BGH. As we mentioned in Section 2, we propose to use dependency-based embedding approach (Levy and Goldberg, 2014) to improve the grouping of words especially for those words that do not appear in BGH.

4.2   Level of Word Complexity

The purpose of this task is to predict the complexity level of words based on Japanese Language Proficiency Test (JLPT) level (Hmeljak. 2009). JLPT is the standard test of Japanese for foreign learners and classifies words into five levels: N1 is the most advanced level, N2 is the high level, N3 is the intermediate level, N4 is the lower level, N5 is the beginner level. In the JLPT list, there are approximately 800 N5 level words, 1,500 N2 level words, 3,750 N3 level words, 6,000 N2 level words, and 10,000 N1 level words.

Vocabulary lists always have limited coverage of lexical entries. To cope with this limitation, we use a machine-learning approach to predict the complexity levels of words that are not included in the JLPT vocabulary list. We choose a linear regression model in this task. We examined several features for the linear regression model to predict the JLPT level of a given word. The features we use are:

1. Unigram frequency: Most of research in simplification uses frequency of words to determine the complexity of words. Sentences that are simple to understand mostly use high frequency words or well-known words (Kauchack et al., 2014; Glavas˘and Stajner, 2015).
2. Words in children's corpora: Children basically use simple words, kanjis, and expressions. Words used by children are considered as easy words.
3. Technical Words: Technical words are in many cases complex words and commonly used in specific domains. To measure specificity, we use Jensen–Shannon divergence of words over domains. The frequency distribution of a target word over domains is compared with the

---

[1] http://pj.ninjal.ac.jp/corpus_center/bccwj/en/
[2] https://www.ninjal.ac.jp/archives/goihyo/

average distribution of all words over domains. Those words that have low scores have similar distributions over domains, meaning they appear various domains and are considered as general words. In contrast, those that have high scores are considered as technical and complex words because they tend to appear in specific domains.

$$SD(P||Q) = \frac{\sum P \log \frac{P}{Q} + \sum Q \log \frac{Q}{P}}{2}$$

In this formula of Jensen-Shannon divergence, P is the normalized frequency distribution of target word over all domains and Q is averaged normalized distribution of all words in the corpus. We used the genres defined in the BCCWJ corpus as different domains.

All these features can be the measurement of word complexity levels and we use them in our linear regression model.

5   Experiment

We divide our experiment into four steps. We start with pre-experiment, words similarity, complex words identification, and word replacement.

5.1   Pre-Experiment

This section describes preparation of the data. We use the Japanese morphological analyser MeCab to word segmentation and POS tagging of Mainichi Newspaper, BCCWJ, and the children's corpora. Since some words do not need to be the target of simplification, we make rules based on POS tags of words. In the following rules, we changed all words sharing the same POS as one word:

1. All words with POS '記号' (symbol) such as "、, 。, 「, 」" are changed to 'Symbol'.
2. All words with POS '数' (number) such as "十(ten), 四(four), 5" are changed to 'Number'.
3. All words with POS '人名' (people name) such as "山田(Yamada) are changed 'People'.
4. All words with POS '組織'(organization) such as 東芝(Toshiba) are change to 'Organization'.
5. All words with POS '地域'(Region) such as "奈良(Nara) are change to 'Place'.
6. All names of day, month and year such as "月曜日(Monday), 9月(September), 九月 (September), 2016年 (2016), 28平成 (2016)" are change to 'Date'.

All of those words are not simplified. The result of this step is used in other steps.

5.2   Words Similarity

Using the BCCWJ and Mainishi corpora, we calculate the similarity of words by using the available tools of dependency-based word embeddings (Levy and Goldberg, 2014). We prepare the training data using Japanese dependency parser CaboCha for finding the dependency relation of words in sentences. Then we calculate the similarity of words as we showed in Section 4.1. This task is to augment the groups of similar words that do not appear in BGH. The following is an example of grouped words by the dependency-based word embedding: {処分, 認定, 申請, 給付, 承認, 決議, 届出, 登記, 規制, 譲渡}

5.3   Word Complexity Order

We counted all unigram frequency of words in Children's corpus, and combination of BCCWJ-Mainichi Newspaper. Then we divided the BCCWJ and Mainichi corpora into 19 categories. Then we calculate the frequency of each word in each category to know the distribution of the word over the categories. Based on the distribution of words over the categories, we calculated the Jensen-Shannon divergence values of words. This task is to know the technicality of words.

About 10,000 words in the JLPT vocabulary list are already divided into 5 levels. For each word in JLPT level, we calculated its log frequency in the BCCWJ-Mainichi corpus, log frequency in the children's corpus, and J-S divergence value, and use them for the features of linear regression.

After training, we apply the regression function to the other words that are not in the JLPT list to predict their complexity levels. Since the level of the easiest words is 5 and that of the most complex words is 1, higher values on test data indicate easier and lower value indicate more complex words.

5.4 Word Replacement

We already have groups of similar words (Section 5.2) and complexity ordering of words (Section 5.3). In this section, we combine these results. In order to replace a complexity word with a simpler synonym, we first start an experiment with words of POS 名詞 (Noun) tag.

When we input a sentence, first thing to do is morphological analysis of the sentence using MeCab, then select all words with POS 名詞 (Noun). For each selected word, we check it in the same group of similar words and compare the complexity of the selected word with other candidates, then choose the one with the highest complexity value. Table 1 shows the result of replacement of complex words with simpler synonyms so as to make it more readable for foreigners. From Table 1, we see that '人情本'(Novel) is a complex word that has similar meaning with 小説 (Novel). While 人情本 has meaning of old novels that were written in the Edo era, learners do not need to know that kind of words, the important information is that that word means a kind of novels.

Original Sentence	Simplified sentences
私は**人情本**より詩の方が好きです	私は**小説**より詩の方が好きです
芸の**秘奥**をきわめる	芸の**秘伝**をきわめる
代数は僕の得意な学科だ	**数学**は僕の得意な学科だ
ご**尊名**はよく承っております	ご**名前**はよく承っております

Table 1 : Result of word replacement

6 Evaluation

We evaluate word complexity orders provided by the trained liner regression model. We use another JLPT data collected from JLPT books, summing up to 20,000 words. We divide this data into training and test data. Then we test how the complexity levels of pairwise test words are correctly predicted. We experimented the comparison as shown in Table 2. From the table, we can see that in one different level, the average of accuracy is about 61.89%, that in two different levels is 72.13%, that in three different levels is 79.8%, and that in four different levels is 87%. We did not do the evaluation of group of similarity in BGH since it is a thesaurus constructed by human.

Categories	Compared Levels	Accuracy	Average
One different level	N1 and N2	61.14%	61.89 %
	N2 and N3	61.61%	
	N3 and N4	58.92%	
	N4 and N5	65.90%	
Two different level	N1 and N3	70.90%	72.13 %
	N2 and N4	69.23%	
	N3 and N5	74.28%	
Three different level	N1 and N4	76.91%	79. 8 %
	N2 and N5	82.69	
Four different level	N1 and N5	87.81%	87.81%

Table 2: Results of word difficulty level comparison

7 Conclusion and Future Work

We proposed an approach for Japanese lexical simplification. Our main task is divided into two parts. The first is word similarity estimation and the second is word complexity ordering. We used combination of several Japanese corpora to implement word embedding and linear regression models. Our experiments showed the order of word complexity is usable to select simpler similar words. Because of limited space, we did not discuss problems caused by lexical replacement. The last row in Table 1 shows a problem caused by word replacement from "尊名" to "名前". The prefix existing in the original sentence "ご" fits with the former word but not with the latter word. This type of problem caused by word combination is one of the important problem to be tackled by our future work.

Reference

Colby Horn, Cathryn Manduca and David Kauchak. 2014. Learning a Lexical Simplifier Using Wikipedia. *In Proceedings of the 52nd Annual Meeting of the Association for Computational Linguistics (Short Papers)*, pages 458–463.

David Kauchak. 2013. Improving Text Simplification Language Modeling Using Unsimplified Text Data. *In Proceedings of the 51st Annual Meeting of the Association for Computational Linguistics*, pages 1537–154.

David Kauchak, Obay Mouradi, Christopher Pentoney, Gondy Leroy, PhD. 2014. Text Simplification Tools: Using Machine Learning to Discover Features that Identify Difficult Text. *47th Hawaii International Conference on System Science*, pages 2616-2625.

Goran Glavasˇ, Sanja Stajner. 2015. Simplifying Lexical Simplification: Do We Need Simplified Corpora?. *In Proceedings of the 53rd Annual Meeting of the Association for Computational Linguistics and the 7th International Joint Conference on Natural Language Processing (Short Papers)*, pages 63–68.

Gustavo H. Paetzold and Lucia Specia. 2016. Unsupervised Lexical Simplification for Non-Native Speakers. *In Proceedings of the Thirtieth AAAI Conference on Artificial Intelligence*, pages 3761-3767.

John Carroll, Guido Minnen, Yvonne Canning, Siobhan Devlin, and John Tait. 1998. Practical simplification of english newspaper text to assist aphasic readers. *In Proceedings of AAAI-98 Workshop on Integrating Artificial Intelligence and Assistive Technology*, pages 7–10.

Jan De Belder and Marie-Francine Moens. 2010. Text simplification for children. *In Proceedings of the SIGIR Workshop on Accessible Search Systems*, pages 19–26.

Kristina Hmeljak Sangawa. 2009. A corpus for Readability Measurement for Non-Native Learners of Japanese. *IEICE Technical Report*, pages 19-23

Manami Moku, Kazuhide Yamamoto, Ai Makabi. 2012. Automatic Easy Japanese Translation for Information accessibility of foreigners. *In proceedings of the workshop on speech and language processing tools in education*, pages 85-90.

Maki Sakamoto. 2010. Corpus of Texts Composed by Japanese Elementary School Children and its Application in Linguistics and Sociology. *Journal of Natural Language Processing Vol. 17 No. 5*, pages 75-98 (In Japanese).

Omer Levy and Yoav Golfberg. 2014. Dependecy-Based Word Embeddings. *In Proceedings of the 52nd Annual Meeting of the Association for Computational Linguistics (Short Papers)*, pages 302–308

Shin Miyagi and Mizuho Imada. 2015. Design of a Written Composition Corpus of Japanese Elementary and Junior High School Students. *第7回コーパス日本語学ワークショップ予稿集*, pages 223-232 (In Japanese).

Shashi Narayan and Claire Gardent. 2014. Hybrid Simplification using Deep Semantics and Machine Translation. In Proceedings of the 52nd Annual Meeting of the Association for Computational Linguistics, pages 435–445.

Susana Bautista, Pablo Gervas, and R. Ignacio Madrid. 2009. Feasibility analysis for semi-automatic conversion of text to improve readability. *In Proceedings of the Second International Conference on Information and Communication Technology and Accessibility (ICTA)*, pages 33–40.

Siobhan Devlin and John Tait. 1998. The use of a psycholinguistic database in the simplification of text for aphasic readers. *Linguistic Databases*, pages 161–173.

Tomoyuki Kajiwara, Hiroshi Matsumoto, Kazuhide Yamamoto. 2013 Selecting Proper Lexical Paraphrase for Children. *In Proceedings of the Twenty-Fifth Conference on Computational Linguistics and Speech Processing (ROCLING)*, pages 59-73.

Tomoyuki Kajiwara and Kazuhide Yamamoto. 2015. Evaluation Dataset and System for Japanese Lexical Simplification. *In Proceedings of the ACL-IJCNLP 2015 Student Research Workshop*, pages 35–40.

Tomas Mikolov, Ilya Sutskever, Kai Chen, Greg Corrado and Jeffrey Dean. 2013. Distributed Representations of Words and Phrases and their Compositionality. *In Advances in Neural Information Processing Systems 26 .Curran Associates, Inc.* pages 3111–3119.

Tomonori Kodaira, Tomoyuki Kajiwara, Mamoru Komachi. 2016. Controlled and Balanced Dataset for Japanese Lexical Simplification. In *Proceedings of the ACL 2016 Student Research Workshop*, pp.1-7.

Wei Xu, Chris Callison-Burch, Courtney Napoles. 2015. Problems in Current Text Simplification Research : New Data Can Help. *Transactions of the Association for Computational Linguistics, vol. 3*, pp. 283–297

William Coster and David Kauchak. 2011. Learning to simplify sentences using wikipedia. In Proceedings of the Workshop on Monolingual Text-To-Text Generation, pages 1–9.

A Corpus-based Approach for Spanish-Chinese Language Learning

Shuyuan Cao
Universitat Pompeu Fabra
(UPF)
shuyuan.cao@hotmail.com

Iria da Cunha
Universidad Nacional de
Educación a
Distancia (UNED)
iriad@flog.uned.es

Mikel Iruskieta
University of Basque Country
(UPV/EHU)
mikel.iruskieta@ehu.eus

Abstract

Due to the huge population that speaks Spanish and Chinese, these languages occupy an important position in the language learning studies. Although there are some automatic translation systems that benefit the learning of both languages, there is enough space to create resources in order to help language learners. As a quick and effective resource that can give large amount language information, corpus-based learning is becoming more and more popular. In this paper we enrich a Spanish-Chinese parallel corpus automatically with part of-speech (POS) information and manually with discourse segmentation (following the Rhetorical Structure Theory (RST) (Mann and Thompson, 1988)). Two search tools allow the Spanish-Chinese language learners to carry out different queries based on tokens and lemmas. The parallel corpus and the research tools are available to the academic community. We propose some examples to illustrate how learners can use the corpus to learn Spanish and Chinese.

1 Introduction[1]

As the most spoken two languages in the world, Spanish and Chinese are very important in the language learning field. Because of the different phonetics and written characters and extensive grammatical rules, syntactic structure and discourse elements between this language pair, it is not easy to carry out the Spanish-Chinese language learning tasks. Here we give some examples in order to show some morphological, syntactic and discourse similarities and differences between Spanish and Chinese that a language learner has to know and practice.

Among other issues, Chinese students that are learning Spanish as L2 need to know that Spanish language is not a gender neutral language, so the distinction of grammatical gender is crucial between masculine and feminine (among irregular constructions). There are some adjectives with a particular ending for feminine ('JJ+a'[2] such as *pública* 'feminine_public', *extranjera* 'feminine_foreigner', *china* 'feminine_chinese') and for masculine ('JJ+o' such as *moderno* 'masculine_modern', *chino* 'masculine_chinese', *rico* 'masculine_rich'). In Chinese, for example, the masculine *chino* and feminine *china* are translated as "zhongguo" (中国) ('China').

Ex.1[3]:
1.1.1 Sp: Aunque aún no contamos con resultados, intuimos que el modelo será más amplio que el del sintagma nominal.
[Aunque aún no contamos con resultados,]Unit₁ [intuimos que el modelo será más amplio que el del sintagma nominal.]Unit₂
[DM still no get results,] [we consider that the model will more extensive than the sentence group nominal.]

---

[1] This work has been supported by a Ramón y Cajal contract (RYC-2014-16935) to Iria da Cunha and it has been partially financed by TUNER (TIN2015-65308-C5-1-R) to Mikel Iruskieta.
[2] In the Stanford parser JJ means adjective.
[3] All the examples have been extracted from the corpus.

Proceedings of the 3rd Workshop on Natural Language Processing Techniques for Educational Applications,
pages 97–106, Osaka, Japan, December 12 2016.

[Aunque aún no contamos con resultados,]Unit₁ [intuimos que el modelo será más amplio que
el del sintagma nominal.]Unit₂

[DM⁴ still no get results,] [we consider that the model will more extensive than the sentence
group nominal.]⁵

1.1.2 Sp: Intuimos que el modelo será más amplio que el del sintagma nominal, aunque aún no contamos con resultados.

[Intuimos que el modelo será más amplio que el del sintagma nominal,]Unit₁ [aunque aún no
contamos con resultados.]Unit₂

[We consider that the model will more extensive than the sentence group nominal,] [DM still
no get results.]

1.2 Ch: 尽管还没有取得最终结果，但是我们认为该模型已囊括了语段模型涉及的内容。

[尽管还没有取得最终结果，]Unit₁ [但是我们认为该模型已囊括了语段模型涉及的内
容。]Unit₂

[DM1 still no get results,] [DM2 we consider that the model contains the sentence group
nominal.]

1.3 Eng: Although we haven't got the results yet, we consider that the model will be more extensive
than the nominal sentence group.

In Example 1, we can see that the Spanish passage has a similar discourse structure to the Chinese
passage. Both passages start the text with a discourse marker in the first unit. However, the usage of
discourse markers in both languages is different. To show same meaning, in Chinese, it is mandatory
to include two discourse markers: one marker is "*jinguan*" (尽管), at the beginning of the first unit,
and another marker is "*danshi*" (但是), at the beginning of the second unit. These two discourse markers are equivalent to the English discourse marker 'although'. By contrast, in Spanish, just one discourse marker "*aunque*" is being used at the beginning of the first unit, and this discourse marker is
also equivalent to the English discourse marker *although*. Moreover, the order of the discourse units in
the Spanish passage can be changed and it makes sense syntactically, but the order cannot be changed
in the Chinese passage, because neither syntactically nor grammatically makes sense.

Ex.2:

2.1 Sp: La automatización de la gestión terminológica no es una mera cuestión de producir progra-
mas informáticos, aunque ésta sea una labor de por sí costosa.

[La automatización de la gestión terminológica no es una mera cuestión de producir progra-
mas informáticos,]Unit₁ [aunque ésta sea una labor de por sí costosa.]Unit₂

[The automation of the management terminological no is a merely question of producing
programs informatics, DM this is a work which costly.]

2.2 Ch: 术语管理自动化不仅仅是建立开销巨大的信息系统的问题。

[术语管理自动化不仅仅是建立开销巨大的信息系统的问题。]Unit₁

[Terminology management automation is not only produce costly program informatics.]

2.3 Eng: Although this is a work which costly, the automation of the terminological management is
not only a merely question of producing programs informatics.

In Example 2, there are two units in the Spanish passage meanwhile in the Chinese passage there is
just one unit to show the same meaning. In the Spanish passage, the DM *aunque* 'although' is at the
beginning of the second unit; in contrast, there is no corresponding DM in the Chinese passage and a
translation strategy has been used. The Chinese phrase "*kaixiaojuda*" (开销巨大) ('great costly') includes the same meaning of the second Spanish unit and is part of the whole sentence in the Chinese
passage.

---

⁴ DM means discourse marker. In this work, we use the definition of DM by Portolés (2001). DMs are invariable linguistic
units that depend on the following aspects: (a) distinct morph-syntactic properties, (b) semantics and pragmatics and (c)
inferences that made in the communication.

⁵ In this work, we give an English literal translation for both Spanish examples and Chinese examples in order to make the
readers understand the content better.

These examples show that a comparative study could provide useful discourse information for language learning. Comparative or contrastive studies of discourse structures reveal information to identify properly equivalent discourse elements in the language pair and the information helps language learning.

An important source for language learning is corpus. As a large electronic library, a corpus can provide a large amount of linguistic information (Wu, 2014). In addition, Johns (2002) indicates that a corpus-based research could help the language learners get large amount of language information easily.

This paper aims to create a Spanish-Chinese parallel corpus annotated automatically with POS and annotated manually with discourse information in order to help Spanish-Chinese language learning with a friendly online environment to perform POS-based queries, as "it has been demonstrated that discourse is a crucial aspect for L2[6] learners of a language, especially at more advanced level" (Neff-van Aertselaer, 2015: 255).

In the second section, we mention some works related to our work. In the third section, we include information about our research approach. In the fourth section, we explain how to use our corpus for Spanish-Chinese language learning. In the last section, we present the conclusions and look ahead at our future work.

2   Related Work

Corpus-based studies for different language pairs learning exist, including some works for Spanish and Chinese. On the one hand, for example, we highlight the following corpus-based language learning studies:

i) In order to help language learning and translation tasks between English and Chinese, Qian (2005) created an English-Chinese parallel corpus with functions of sentence search, calculation of words, search of texts and authors.

ii) To compare the similarities and differences between English and Chinese from different aspects, such as aspect marking, temporal adverbials, passive construction, among other interesting topics, Xiao and McEnery (2010) used the FLOB corpus (Albert-Ludwigs, 2007)[7] and The Lancaster Corpus of Mandarin Chinese (LCMC) (McEnery and Xiao, 2004)[8], which is designed as a Chinese parallel corpus for FLOB. The study offers a great amount of language information that is useful for English-Chinese language learning.

iii) To compare both languages via different language activities, such as exploration of language differences, comparative discourse analysis and semantic analysis Lavid, Arús and Zamorano (2010) developed a small online English-Spanish parallel corpus. Then, based on the activity results, they give some linguistic suggestions for English-Spanish teaching, which can also help the English-Spanish language learners to comprehend the language differences between both languages.

On the other hand, corpus-based studies for Spanish-Chinese language learning are still few:

i) Yao (2008) uses film dialogues to elaborate an annotated corpus, and compares the Spanish and Chinese discourse markers in order to give some suggestions for teaching and learning Spanish and Chinese.

ii) Yang (2008) compares the discourse structure of proverbs between Spanish and Chinese based on the novel *Don Quijote* in order to give some conclusions for the Spanish-Chinese translation works, and language teaching and learning tasks.

iii) Taking different newspapers and books as the research corpus, Chien (2012) compares the Spanish and Chinese conditional discourse markers to give some conclusions of the conditional discourse marker for foreign language teaching between Spanish and Chinese.

iv) Wang (2013) uses *Pedro Almodóvar's* films *La mala educación* and *Volver* as the corpus to analyze how the subtitled Spanish discourse markers can be translated into Chinese, so as to make a guideline for human translation and audiovisual translation between the language pair.

---

[6] L2 means second language.

[7] The FLOB Corpus: http://www.helsinki.fi/varieng/CoRD/corpora/FLOB/ [Last consulted: 27 of July of 2016].

[8] The Lancaster Corpus of Mandarin Chinese: http://www.lancaster.ac.uk/fass/projects/corpus/LCMC/ [Last consulted: 27 of July of 2016].

v) Cao, da Cunha and Bel (2016) annotate all the cases of the Spanish DM *aunque* ('although') and their corresponding Chinese translations in The United Nations Multilingual Corpus (UN) (Rafalovitch and Dale, 2009; Eisele and Yu, 2010). They analyze the used translation strategies in the translation process and give some suggestions for how to translate this Spanish DM into Chinese.

vi) Several Spanish-Chinese parallel corpus exist and have been used for different research purposes, including Spanish-Chinese language learning, these corpora are: (a) *The Holy Bible* (Resnik, Olsen and Diab, 1999), (b) The United Nations Multilingual Corpus (UN) (Rafalovitch and Dale, 2009; Eisele and Yu, 2010) and (c) Sina Weibo Parallel Corpus (Wang et al., 2013).

The above mentioned works are great achievements that offer different approaches for language learning. However, comparing to our work, none of them gives a friendly environment to consult Spanish-Chinese parallel corpus based on POS and segmented discourse information, showing how foreign language learners can apply this information to improve or learn languages.

3 Research Approach

3.1 Theoretical Framework

In this study, we use the Rhetorical Structure Theory (RST), proposed by Mann and Thmopson (1988), which a widely used theory for discourse analysis. RST offers discourse information from two approaches: linear segmentation and rhetorical annotation. Under RST, linear segmentation is compased with Elementary Discourse Units (EDUs) (Marcu, 2000). But in linear segmentation different discourse phenomena can be studied, such as the position of the DM, the number of DMs, etc.

Discourse-annotated corpus can provide valuable insights into L2 discourse aspects, problems, and solutions (Vyatkina, 2016). Thus, information and examples of discourse segmentation are useful for those language learners who have an advanced level, that is, students that should be competent to solve complicated discourse questions.

3.2 Elaboration of the Research Corpus

The previous mentioned Spanish-Chinese parallel corpora are not adequate for language learning purposes between Spanish and Chinese from discourse level. For example, the texts in the Holy Bible cannot represent the modern language; the Spanish-Chinese UN Corpus is not a direct translated corpus, which affects the discourse structure; and the texts in the Sina Weibo Parallel Corpus are tweets that do not include a complex discourse structure. In order to use formal and natural expressed texts, we decide to use the Spanish-Chinese parallel corpus by Cao, da Cunha and Iruskieta (in press), which is especially designed for discourse studies with formal texts.

In their corpus, 100 texts are included: the longest text contains 1,774 words and the shortest one includes 111 words. The genres of the texts are: (a) Abstract of research paper, (b) News, (c) Advertisement and (d) Announcement. The corpus contains seven domains: (a) Terminology, (b) Culture, (c) Language, (d) Economy, (e) Education, (f) Art and (g) International affairs.

Firstly we enriched this corpus automatically with POS information by using Freeling (Carreras et al., 2004) for Spanish and the Stanford parser (Levy and Manning, 2003) for Chinese. Then, we segmented and harmonized the Spanish and Chinese texts into EDUs to obtain a gold standard segmented corpus. Two Chinese experts and two Spanish experts carried out the segmentation work manually, by using the RSTTool (O'Donnell, 2000) following Iruskieta, da Cunha and Taboada's (2015) segmentation and harmonization criteria. Finally, we developed a free online interface that allows students of Spanish or Chinese to do different linguistic queries that can help their language learning process[9].

3.3 Level Requirement for the Spanish-Chinese Language Learning with the Corpus

In this study, for the Chinese users who learn Spanish, we adopt the language level standardizations of *Instituto Cervantes*, the official Spanish organization to check the language level for L2 Spanish learn-

---

[9] The access of the interface is the following: http://ixa2.si.ehu.es/rst/zh/.

ing[10]; for the Spanish users who learn Chinese, we adopt the language level standardizations of *Hanban* (汉办), the official organization of Chinese government for L2 Chinese learning[11].

As we have mentioned, the corpus by Cao, da Cunha and Iruskieta (in press) includes specialized texts from different sources, which include terminology from several domains. Therefore, the users of our annotated-corpus and search tool should have an intermediate or advanced level of the language. As the webpage of *Instituto Cervantes* indicates, in the Spanish initial level only some basic expressions and vocabulary are learned. Also, the webpage of *Hanban* (汉办) offers similar information about the Chinese initial level.

In order to use our annotated-corpus and search tool, the appropriate levels for Spanish foreign language learners are level B2 (intermediate level) and level C (including C1 and C2) (advanced level). Level B2 requires language users to understand complex texts with different topics. Level C1 requires understanding a wide variety of long and demanding texts, and also writing and expressing well-structured texts in Spanish. Level C2 is a more advanced level and requires Spanish learners have enough linguistic competence to prove a spontaneous capacity of adaptation to any context, with a great deal of semantic and grammatical precision.

The appropriate level for Chinese foreign language learners is level 4 (intermediate level) and advanced level (level 5 and level 6). Level 4 requires language learners to know a certain amount of words and produce texts related to a wide range of topics, in order to maintain a fluent communication with native speakers. Level 5 requires learners to read magazines, newspapers, and films and give a full-length speech. Level 6 language learners should easily comprehend written and spoken information in Chinese.

4 Spanish-Chinese Language Learning with the Corpus

As we have mentioned, the aim of the annotated-corpus and the search tool is to help language learners of both languages by providing them with real examples that can be extracted by means of different linguistic queries including linguistic information: morpho-syntactic information and discourse-segmentation information.

On the one hand, regarding morpho-syntactic information, a Chinese foreign language-learning student can search any wanted Chinese tokens or lemmas, and a Spanish foreign language-learning student can carry out the search in an inverse way. Here we give a real example by using the search tool for Spanish. The word that we use is the Spanish word *profesor* ('teacher'). By using the search tool, we can search the token of profesor or the lemma of this word. We give some lemma search results of profesor as the example. The results are presented in Figure 1[12].

	Document	Sent Id	Word(s)	Sentence	
1	BMCS_ESP2.txt	sent1	PROFESORES	PROFESORES Y MÉTODOS Todos nuestros profesores son nativos , han recibido una formación específica en la enseñanza de español como lengua extranjera (ELE) y tienen experiencia docente en China .	View context
2	BMCS_ESP2.txt	sent4	profesor	El profesor no impone conocimientos : ayuda a sus alumnos a comunicarse en español desde el primer día , animándolos a que participen activamente en el aula .	View context
3	BMCS_ESP2.txt	sent5	profesores	Los profesores cuentan siempre con el punto de vista de sus alumnos en la toma de decisiones de la clase , fomentando la autonomía del estudiante mediante el uso de las estrategias de aprendizaje más adecuadas para cada uno .	View context
4	BMCS_ESP2.txt	sent8	profesores	El aprendizaje del léxico y de la gramática está acompañado del valor del uso comunicativo que los profesores nativos pueden y saben transmitir .	View context

Figure 1: Search result of the Spanish lemma *profesor* with the result of two different forms *profesores* 'teachers' and *profesor* '(masculine) teacher'

A Chinese learner can find different POS structures in our corpus, for example, all the words which end with '*a*' that are adjectives (*española* 'feminine_Spanish', *pública* 'feminine_public', *his-*

---

[10] A detailed explanation of the Spanish level for L2 learners can be consulted:
http://dele.cervantes.es/en/information/levels/spanish_levels.html [Last consulted: 17 of September of 2016]
[11] The detailed explanation of the Chinese level for L2 learners can be consulted: http://english.hanban.org/node_8002.htm [Last consulted: 17 of September of 2016]
[12] Due to the limitation of the required pages, here the space doesn't allow us to show the whole lemma research result of the Spanish word *profesor*. Also, we only give the partial results in the following figures.

panoamericana 'feminine_hispanicamerican', etc.) or feminine words ended with '*ora*' that are nouns (*directora* 'feminine_director', *coordinadora* 'feminine_coordinator', *editora* 'feminine_editor' etc.) to learn how feminine is used in real texts.

Also, a language learner can search the wanted token with "exact match", "start with" or "ends with". This function can help students of Chinese to learn different phrases by searching just one character. We use the Chinese word *fa* (发)[13] to explain how to search those phrases related with the character *fa* (发). Figure 2 shows some of the search results: the words starting with *fa* (发) are *fasong* (发送) ('to send'), *fayangguangda* (发扬光大) ('to flourish'), and *fazhan* (发展) ('to develop'). With different match functions, a Spanish student can learn different words including a specific character, in this case *fa* (发).

	Document	Sent Id	Word(s)	Sentence	
1	BMCS_CHN5.txt	18	发送	如有 任何 查询 请 发送 邮件 至 prof1sha@cervantes.es	View context
2	ICEG_CHN1.txt	2	发扬光大	格拉纳达 大学 的 汉语 教学 始自 1987年， 二十多 年 来 已 开设 了 各种 与 中国 历史 、 文学 、 思想 相关 的 课程， 而 格 大孔 院 要 将 这种 深厚 的 汉学 研究 传统 继续 发扬光大， 与 格拉纳达 大学 中 像 亚洲 研究会 这 样 的 学术 组织， 以及 其它 国内外 个 相关 机构 精诚 合作， 努力 开展 各 种 活动， 以 满足 社会 各界 不断 增 长 的 需求 。	View context
3	EEP_CHN4.txt	1	发展	第二 届 " 丝路 国际 论坛 2015年 会 " 在 马德里 召开 10月 28日 和 29日， 由 国务院 发展 研究 中心 、 国际 关 系 和 可持续 发展 中心 、 中国 驻 西班牙 大使馆 和 和 托雷 多 国际 和平 中心 共同 主办 的 第二 届 " 丝路 国际 论坛 2015年 会 " 在 马德里 召开 。	View context
4	EEP_CHN5.txt	1	发展	第一 届 中 西 交流 发展 论坛 西班牙 工业 、 能源 与 旅游 大臣 索里亚 与 中国 驻 西班牙 大使 吕凡于 10月 27日 在 马德里 共同 出席 了 第一 届 中 西 交流 发展 论坛 的 开幕式 。	View context

Figure 2: Chinese words starting with the word *fa* (发)

Moreover, language learners can also search by POS information for both Spanish and Chinese. Based on the character *fa* (发), we give another real example in the corpus. A Spanish student can search the Chinese lemma that start with *fa* (发) but play as verb. Figure 3 shows partial results that match the search requirement.

	Document	Sent Id	Word(s)	Sentence	
1	BMCS_CHN5.txt	18	发送	如有 任何 查询 请 发送 邮件 至 prof1sha@cervantes.es	View context
2	ICEG_CHN1.txt	2	发扬光大	格拉纳达 大学 的 汉语 教学 始自 1987年， 二十多 年 来 已 开设 了 各种 与 中国 历史 、 文学 、 思想 相关 的 课程， 而 格 大孔 院 要 将 这种 深厚 的 汉学 研究 传统 继续 发扬光大， 与 格拉纳达 大学 中 像 亚洲 研究会 这 样 的 学术 组织， 以及 其它 国内外 个 相关 机构 精诚 合作， 努力 开展 各 种 活动， 以 满足 社会 各界 不断 增 长 的 需求 。	View context
3	CCICE_CHN3.txt	1	发布	西班牙 财政部 拟 拍卖 高达 50亿 欧元 短期 国债 经济 学家 报 11月 17日 消息： 据 西班牙 财政部 在 官网 发布 的 消息 显示， 该 机构 将 在 本 周二 拍卖 6 至 12月 到期 的 短期 国债， 预期 拍卖 40亿 至 50亿 欧元 。	View context
4	CCICE_CHN3.txt	2	发行	此 次 为 财政部 从 10月 以来 首次 发行 该 类型 国债， 当时 拍卖 金额 41.21亿 欧元， 而 本次 使用 的 利率 将 比 上 次 更低 。	View context

Figure 3: Search result of verbs that start with *fa* (发)

The partial results in Figure 3 gives us four different Chinese verbs starting with *fa* (发): (a) *fasong* (发送) ('to send'), (b) *fayangguangda* (发扬光大) ('to flourish'), (c) *fabu* (发布) ('to publish') and (d) *faxing* (发行) ('to issue').

The POS information also has another function in our corpus. In Chinese, some words have two categories; the category can be a verb and a noun at the same time (Yu, Duan and Zhu, 2005). Hence, under this circumstance, it is hard to choose the category of a word for L2 students of Chinese. POS information helps to distinguish the category of a word. For example, the Chinese noun *xuyao* (需要) ('requirement') can also be the verb 'to need to'. In the corpus, when including *xuyao* (需要) in the

---

[13] In Chinese, the verb *fa* (发) has various meanings, such as "to have over", "to express", "to expand", "to begin to", among others. [Consulted from: *Xiandai hanyu cidian* (现代汉语词典)]

lemma column and choosing "VV"[14] as a POS, seven results are obtained, as Figure 3 shows. Meanwhile, there is one result of *xuyao* (需要) as a noun in Figure 4.

	Document	Sent Id	Word(s)	Sentence	
1	TERM29_CN.txt	9	需要	我们需要找到一个能够在实际情况中有效应用的解决方案，这也促使我们在进行专项研究时，不仅要兼顾上述理论原则，还应考虑在术语和信息学方面采用不同的方法论。	View context
2	TERM34_CN.txt	2	需要	在很多情况下，要找到巴斯克语对应临近语种的关系形容词，需要经过多个步骤（Ensunza，1989；Loinaz，1995）。	View context
3	TERM38_CN.txt	2	需要	各种语言中与互联网相关的术语在以很快的速度诞生和传播，影响范围广，如同建造了一条需要与时间赛跑的跑道。	View context
4	TERM38_CN.txt	4	需要	对于科技进步来说，这种现象的产生并不稀奇，但需要注意的是，介于术语新词的特点，各领域的专业性要求又赋予了新词一定的特殊性。	View context
5	TERM31_CN.txt	2	需要	简介近年来，各语种都在开发科技类文章术语的自动构建工具，尽管如此，对于自动选出的术语条目还是需要人工进行最后一步筛选。	View context
6	TERM51_CN.txt	9	需要	例如安伯托（Anboto）山、拉蒙-卡哈尔（Ramón y Cajal）大街、伊拜萨巴（Ibaizabal）河、奥尔加山丘（Alto de la Horca）等，地名自身的定义引导我们判断地理术语的重要性，同时我们也注意到在进行地名标准化时需要提出两个版本（巴斯克语和西班牙语）。	View context
7	TERM51_CN.txt	10	需要	概括地讲，这意味着共有元素可通过翻译而来，而特定元素需要保持不变。	View context

Figure 3: Search results of *xuyao* (需要) as verb

	Document	Sent Id	Word(s)	Sentence	
1	ICP_CHN8.txt	12	需要	证书分以下几个级别：·西班牙语水平证书A1级别级别证明拥有者的语言水平足以应对简单的交流、即时性需要和非常日常性的话题·西班牙语水平证书A2级别证明拥有者能够理解日常表达和其所涉及领域相关的习惯用法，尤其是一些与自身相关的基本信息，比如自己、家庭、购物、景点、职业等等。	View context

Figure 4: Search result of *xuyao* (需要) as noun

A Spanish student who uses the corpus to learn Chinese can distinguish the words that have more than one category easily by using the combination of lemma and POS, and also check their contexts of use.

The interface we created allows the search of maximum four tokens/lemmas at the same time, that is, it is possible to do complex queries. This is useful to obtain different language information, such as the use of adjectives in a phrase. For example, if a Spanish student knows the phrase *xibanyayu ketang* (西班牙语课堂), 'Spanish class' in Chinese, and wants to search for more adjectives associated to the word *ketang* (课堂) ('class'), which could be inserted in the middle of the two units of the phrase, he could do the following complex query: i) lemma *xibanyayu* (西班牙语) ('Spanish'), ii) POS information "JJ"[15], and iii) lemma *ketang* (课堂) ('class') (see Figure 5).

Figure 5: Example of the search for an adjective in a phrase

Figure 6 includes the search results of the example. Two results are obtained, including the same adjective related to the noun *ketang* (课堂) ('class'): *xuni* (虚拟) ('virtual').

	Document	Sent Id	Word(s)	Sentence	
1	BMCS_CHN3.txt	4	西班牙语/虚拟/课堂	该课程适合学生在课堂学习之外同时积极的开展自主学习，在每周不上课的日子里学生可以在家完成许多教材中的课外活动，此外也可以使用我们网络学习平台的资源西班牙语虚拟课堂。	View context
2	BMCS_CHN5.txt	1	西班牙语/虚拟/课堂	西班牙语远程课程：西班牙语虚拟课堂（AVE）西班牙语虚拟课堂（AVE）是塞万提斯学院专门为对外西班牙语教学和学习设计的，以互联网为媒介的虚拟环境。	View context

Figure 6: Result of the search for an adjective between *xibanyayu* (西班牙语) and *ketang* (课堂)

---

[14] In the Stanford parser VV means verb and NN means noun.

[15] In parsing research, J means adjective.

Another similar search function is illustrated in Figure 9. The Chinese word *kecheng* (课程) ('course') is a noun and, by using the search of POS information, different adjectives related with *kecheng* (课程) are extracted. Figure 9 shows three results of the adjective that can be combined with *kecheng* (课程): *changgui* (常规), *yiban* (一般) and *putong* (普通). All of them mean 'regular' in English. In this case, three different words with the same meaning are extracted.

	Document	Sent Id	Word(s)	Sentence	
1	BMCS_CHN3.txt	3	常规 / 课程	常规 课程 常规 课程 时 长 3 个 月， 每周 5 小时 课时 分为 2 节 课， 每节 课 2.5 小时， 一般 是 周一 、 周三 或 者 周二 、 周四 各 上 一 课 。	View context
2	BMCS_CHN3.txt	6	常规 / 课程	和 常规 课程 一样， 每周 5 小时 课时， 不同 的 是 这 5 小时 集中 在 同 一 天： 周六 或者 周日 。	View context
3	BMCS_CHN5.txt	3	一般 / 课程	在 米 盖尔·德·塞万提斯 图书馆 的 多媒体 教室 你 可以 免费 试用 AVE 各 类 课程：一般 课程： 包含 欧洲 共同 语 言 参考 标准 制定 的 A1 , A2 , B1 , B2 及 C1 级别 课程 。	View context
4	ICP_CHN5.txt	4	普通 / 课程	北京 塞万提斯 学院 提供 丰富 多样 的 西班牙语 学习 课程·普通 课程 2600 元·紧凑 课程 2600 元·周末 课程 2600 元（2015年 8月 更新 信息）我们 所有 的 老师 都 是 以 西班牙语 为 母语， 受过 对外 西班牙语 教学 培训 并 且 拥有 对 外 西班牙语 教学 经验 的 老师 。	View context

Figure 9: Search result of the category adjective with the noun *kecheng* (课程)

The search tools and the POS information are important for Spanish-Chinese language learning but, on the other hand, discourse segmentation information is also relevant to support Spanish-Chinese language learning. The Spanish-Chinese language learners can compare the similarities and differences by using the segmentation of the parallel texts. Table 1 includes an example of discourse segmentation difference in our corpus.

Spanish	**Chinese**	**English translation of the Spanish text**
[La empresa española Aritex ha colaborado con la Corporación de Aeronaves Comerciales de China (COMAC) en la fabricación del C919, primer avión comercial diseñado y fabricado por China.] EDU₁	[西班牙 Aritex 公司与中国商飞（COMAC）合作，]EDU₁ [参与了中国首架国产 C 919 大型客机的制造过程。]EDU₂	[The Spanish company Aritex has collaborated with Commercial Aircraft Corporation of China (COMAC) in making the C919, the first commercial aircraft designed and manufactured by China.]EDU₁

Table 1: The segmentation difference between a parallel Spanish-Chinese

In this Spanish-Chinese parallel example, the whole Spanish sentence is an EDU, while the Chinese sentence is divided into two coordinated EDUs. This happens because of a translation strategy: in the Chinese translation, the Spanish phrase *en la fabricación* ('in the production') has been translated into *canyule* ('have participated in the production'), which has an elliptical subject "Aritex Company" and forms a coordinated part of EDU1 in Chinese passage.

Other useful information that foreign language learners can obtain from this parallel annotated-corpus is related with DMs. For example, they can compare the different DMs used in both languages. Taking the Chinese DMs *ruo* (若) ('if') and *ze* (则) ('then'), Table 2 shows two Spanish-Chinese parallel passages from the corpus.

Table 2 shows that in Spanish there are two sentences while in Chinese there is only 1 sentece. EDU1 and EDU2 in the Spanish passage correspond to EDU1 in the Chinese passage, and EDU3 in the Spanish passage corresponds to EDU2 in the Chinese passage. The number of different EDUs in Spanish and Chinese passages is due to the Spanish DM *para* ('for' or 'in order to') in the first sentence and the used translation strategy. The Spanish DM *para* is the signal of a PURPOSE relation. Therefore, the first sentence is segmented into two EDUs. The translation strategy causes the Chinese translation as one sentence. In the Spanish passage, there is no DM for holding a discourse relation between the two complete sentences. Instead, in the Chinese passage, there are two DMs at the beginning of each EDU, one DM is *ruo* (若), which means 'if' in English, and another DM is *ze* (则),

which means 'then'. The two DMs represent a CONDITION relation. In Chinese, it is necessary to use two DMs (*ruo* and *ze*) at the same time at the beginning of each EDU.

Spanish	Chinese	English translation of the Spanish text
[Los resultados que se obtie-nen no son aún los que se precisarían]EDU₁ [para efectuar un vaciado absolutamen-te automático.]EDU₂ [Se ha de encontrar el equilibrio en-tre la cobertura (recall) y la precisión (precision).]EDU₃	[若上述过程中获得的结果仍无法完全自动构建一个精确的术语条目，]EDU₁ [则必须在覆盖度（召回率）和精确度（精确性）之间达到平衡。]EDU₂	[The obtained results are still cannot be completely required to make a precisely term automatically.]EDU₁ [It must find a balance between coverage (recall) and accuracy (precision).]EDU₂

Table 2: The difference of DMs between a Spanish-Chinese parallel sentence

The Spanish-Chinese language learners can consult any segmentation case in the corpus by using the "Bilingual EDUs" column, which is manually aligned. The different search functions are adequate for different learning tasks carried out by Spanish-Chinese language learners.

Besides of the discourse segmentation information, in the future we will annotate and align the discourse structure for the whole corpus. Spanish and Chinese learners will obtain aligned relational discourse information for language learning related to the following aspects: nuclearity, discourse relation, discourse structure and central discourse unit.

5   Conclusion and Future Work

As a complementary methodology, the use of corpora is a very adequate and useful strategy for language learning in comparison with the traditional methods (Baker, 2007). In this work, we introduce the first online POS-tagged, discourse-based segmented and manually aligned Spanish-Chinese parallel corpus for foreign language learning purposes between this language pair. This corpus offers several search possibilities for different Spanish-Chinese language learning needs. For Spanish L2 learners and Chinese L2 learners, their level must be intermediate or advanced to use the research corpus.

In the future, we will annotate the discourse structure of the whole corpus under RST. This parallel Spanish-Chinese discourse treebank will be available online, together with the search tool. It will be possible to search for parallel passages including a specific RST relation.

References

Albert-Ludwigs Christian Mair. 2007. *The FLOB Corpus* (online). http://www.helsinki.fi/varieng/CoRD/corpora/FLOB/index.html [Last consulted: 27 of July of 2016].

Asher Nicholas and Alex Lascarides. 2003. *Logics of conversation*. Cambridge: Cambridge University Press.

Baker Mona. 2007. Corpus-Based Translation Studies in the Academy. *Journal of Foreign Languages*, 171:50.

Cao Shuyuan, da Cunha Iria, and Iruskieta Mikel (in press). Toward the Elaboration of a Spanish-Chinese Parallel Annotated Corpus. *The EPiC Series in Language and Linguistics*, 2, ISSBN 2398-5283.

Cao Shuyuan, da Cunha Iria, and Bel Nuria. 2016. An analysis of the Concession relation based on the discourse marker aunque in a Spanish-Chinese parallel corpus. *Procesamiento del Lenguaje Natural*, 56: 81-88.

Carreras Xavier, Chao Isacc, Padró Lluís, and Padró Muntsa. 2004. FreeLing: An Open-Source Suite of Language Analyzers. In *Proceedings of the 4th International Conference on Language Resources and Evaluation (LREC' 2004)*, 239-242.

Chien Yi-Shan. 2012. *Análisis contrastivo de los marcadores condicionales del español y del chino*. PhD thesis. Salamanca: Universidad de Salamanca.

Eisele Andreas, and Chen Yu. 2010. A Multilingual Corpus form United Nations Documents. In *Proceedings of Language Resource and Evaluation Conference (LREC 2010)*, 2868-2872.

Iruskieta Mikel, da Cunha Iria, and Taboada Maite. 2015. A Qualitative Comparison Method for Rhetorical Structures: Identifying different discourse structures in multilingual corpora. *Language Resources and Evaluation*, 49: *263-309.*

Johns Tim. 2002. Data-Driven learning: The perpetual challenge. *Language and Computers*, 1: 107-117.

Lavid Julia, Arús Jorge, and Zamorano Juan Rafael. 2010. Desiging and exploiting a small online English-Spanish parallel corpus for language teaching purposes. Corpus-Based Approach to English Language Teaching, 138-148.

Levy Roger and Manning Christopher. 2003. Is it harder to parse Chinese, or the Chinese Treebank? In *Proceedings of the 41st Annual Meeting of the Association for Computational Linguistics* (*ACL' 2003*), 439-446.

Mann William C. and Thompson Sandra A. 1988. Rhetorical Structure Theory: Toward a functional theory of text organization. *Text&Talk*, 8(3): 243-281.

Marcu Daniel. 2000. The rhetorical parsing of unrestricted texts: A surface-based approach. *Computational Linguistics*, 26(3): 395-448.

McEnery Tony, and Xiao Richard. 2004. *The Lancaster Corpus of Mandarin Chinese* [online]. http://www.lancaster.ac.uk/fass/projects/corpus/LCMC/ [Last consulted: 27 of July of 2016].

Neff-van Aertselaer JoAnne. 2015. *Learner Corpora and Discourse*. Cambridge: Cambridge University Press.

O'Donnell Michael. 2000. RSTTool 2.4 – A Markup Tool For Rhetorical Structure Theory. In *Proceedings of First International Conference on Natural Language Generation*, 253-256.

Pórtoles José. 2001. *Marcadores del discursivo*. 4th edition. Barcelona: Ariel.

Rafalovitch Alexandre, and Dale Robert. 2009. United Nations general assembly resolutions: A six-languages parallel corpus, In *Proceedings of Machine Translation Summit XII*, 292-299.

Resnik Philip, Olsen Mari Broman, and Diab Mona. 1999. The Bible as a Parallel Corpus: Annotating the 'Book of 2000 Tongues'. *Computers and the Humanities*, 33(1-2): 129-153.

Qian Zhiying. 2005. *Yinghan/Hanying pingxingfanyi yuliaoku de sheji jiqi zai fanyi zhong de yingyong* (汉英/汉英平行翻译语料库的设计及其在翻译中的应用 *[*The Design of Chinese-English/English-Chinese Parallel Translation Corpus and its Application in Translation Studies*]*). Master thesis. Shanghai: East China Normal University.

Vyatkina Nina. 2016. What can multilingual discourse-annotated corpora do for language learning and teaching? In *Proceedings of TextLink – Structure Discourse in Multilingual Europe Second Action Conference*, 21-24.

Wang Ling, Guang Xiang, Dyer Chris, Black Alan, and Trancoso Isabel. 2013. Mircoblogs as Parallel Corpora. In *Proceedings of the 51st Annual Meeting of the Association for Computational Linguistics* (*ACL' 2013*), 176-186.

Wang Yi-Chen. 2013. *Los marcadores conversacionales en el subtitulado del español al chino: análisis de La mala educación y Volver de Pedro Almodóvar*. PhD thesis. Barcelona: Universitat Autònoma de Barcelona.

Wu Shangyi. 2014. On Application of computer-based corpora in translation. In *Proceedings of 2nd International Conference on Computer, Electrical, and Systems Sciences, and Engineering* (*CESSE' 2014*), 173-178.

Xiao Richard, and McEnery Tony. 2010. *Corpus-Based Contrastive Studies of English and Chinese*. New York: Routledge

Yang Yunmei. 2008. *Hanxi yanyu duibi yanjiu---Yi Tangjikede weili* (汉西谚语对比研究----以《唐吉坷德》为例 *[*Comparative study of Spanish and Chinese proverbs --- case study of *Don Quijote]*). Master thesis. Shandong: Shandong University.

Yao Junming. 2008. *Estudio comparativo de los marcadores del discurso en español y en chino a través de diálogos cinematográficos*. PhD thesis. Valladolid: Universidad de Valladolid.

Yu Shiwen, Duan Huiming, and Zhu Xuefeng. 2005. *Ciyujianlei ji dongci xiang mingci piaoyi xianxiang de jiliang fenxi* (词语兼类暨动词向名词飘移现象的计量分析 *[*A Quantitative Analysis on Multi-class Words and Shift from Verbs to Nouns in Chinese*]*). *Natural language understanding and large-scale computing content* (自然语言理解与大规模内容计算), 70-76.

Syntactic Well-Formedness Diagnosis and Error-Based Coaching in Computer Assisted Language Learning using Machine Translation

Luis Morgado da Costa,♠ **Francis Bond**♠   **He Xiaoling**◇
♠Linguistics and Multilingual Studies   ◇Centre for Modern Languages
Nanyang Technological University, Singapore
<luis.passos.morgado@gmail.com,bond@ieee.org,xlhe@ntu.edu.sg>

Abstract

We present a novel approach to Computer Assisted Language Learning (CALL), using deep syntactic parsers and semantic based machine translation (MT) in diagnosing and providing explicit feedback on language learners' errors. We are currently developing a proof of concept system showing how semantic-based machine translation can, in conjunction with robust computational grammars, be used to interact with students, better understand their language errors, and help students correct their grammar through a series of useful feedback messages and guided language drills. Ultimately, we aim to prove the viability of a new integrated rule-based MT approach to disambiguate students' intended meaning in a CALL system. This is a necessary step to provide accurate coaching on how to correct ungrammatical input, and it will allow us to overcome a current bottleneck in the field — an exponential burst of ambiguity caused by ambiguous lexical items (Flickinger, 2010). From the users' interaction with the system, we will also produce a richly annotated Learner Corpus, annotated automatically with both syntactic and semantic information.

1   Introduction

Asserting if a sentence is grammatical or ungrammatical is, nowadays, a fairly easy task. The real challenge lies in answering questions like: *where is the error?*, *what is its correct form?*, or *what is its intended meaning?*. But especially in language learning environments (e.g. classrooms), where context is often poor, and students are requested to make up random sentences, context alone is usually not enough to answer the questions above. In fact, the pool of possible corrections of an ungrammatical sentence that arises from ambiguity (i.e. possible intended meanings) has been identified as the bottleneck of CALL systems (Flickinger, 2010), mainly because each possible meaning may trigger a different correction and explanation. Inside a traditional classroom, there is less of a problem since a human instructor can interact with the student to find the intended meaning. We propose to take advantage of high-quality machine translation (MT) and dialog-based computer-student interactions to similarly disambiguate learners' intended meaning and use this information to provide accurate and personalized grammar corrections and coaching. Consider the example below:

1. **That dog like the cat happy.*

The fact that (1) is ungrammatical is easy to determine. Existing computational grammars have been doing so for many years. The real challenge is answering questions like: *what is wrong with (1)?* or, *what is the correct form of (1)?*

Many systems struggle with these same questions. In a real life situation, context could possibly suffice to understand the utterance's intended meaning. But let us consider a situation where students were asked to make up a sentence that would make use of the words *dog* and *cat*. In this case, there is no context from which to extract clues about the intended meaning. It only seems natural that, should the teacher share another language with the student, they would make use of it to ask: *What did you mean?*

Proceedings of the 3rd Workshop on Natural Language Processing Techniques for Educational Applications,
pages 107–116, Osaka, Japan, December 12 2016.

Student:	That dog like the cat happy.
	Hmm... something is wrong with your sentence. Did you mean any of these? A. 那只狗和猫一样高兴。 [That dog, like the cat, is happy.]* B. 那只狗喜欢猫高兴。 [That dog likes the cat happy.]* C. 那只狗喜欢高兴的猫。 [That dog likes the happy cat.]*
Student:	C. 那只狗喜欢高兴的猫。
	Ok! Then I believe you forgot to conjugate the verb 'to like'. Also, remember that an adjective must come before the noun it's modifying. Please try again!

* The English translation is what the system thinks is correct, but it is not shown.

Figure 1: Semantic disambiguation example (Chinese speaker learning English)

We propose a new design of language tutoring systems that leverages on state-of-the-art NLP technology to provide explicit feedback on users' language errors. Figure 1 exemplifies the practical reach of the system we are building. The existence of many possible corrections of an ungrammatical sentence will trigger interaction between the system and the student. If there are multiple possible intended meanings, then it uses MT technology to ask what was meant, using the student's first language. After this, it can accurately provide hints about the errors. The use of MT in meaning disambiguation in CALL is, to the best of our knowledge, completely unprecedented, and it will enable systems to detect and provide feedback on many classes of grammatical errors with great confidence. In other words, our system leverages information across languages to find the exact intended meaning before correcting the student, helping push for a new state-of-the-art in CALL research. Venturing guesses, as is customary in these kinds of systems, can lead students into confusion, especially if the proposed correction had a different meaning than the one initially intended by the student.

The MT-Enabled Bilingual Online Language Tutor prototype we are developing focuses on entry level Mandarin as Second Language (L2) learners using English as their source language. At the end of the project, it will be evaluated, in a blended learning environment, by a large cohort of undergraduate students of the first level of Mandarin L2 at Nanyang Technological University. And while the goal of this project is to build a proof of concept system usable for early Mandarin learners, we are also catering for extensibility to further levels, bidirectionality, and even adding new languages in the future.

More technically, our system integrates precise syntactic parsers and semantics-based MT (Bond et al., 2005, 2011) to leverage information across languages. We are also integrating results from surveying word meanings and syntactic structures used by different levels of Mandarin L2, and the most common writing mistakes made by Mandarin L2 learners. This survey is guiding our design and implementation of mal-rules ('error-production rules'), a type of grammar rule that selectively accepts ungrammatical sentences (Schneider and McCoy, 1998), but marking them as ungrammatical. These rules can then be used both to identify grammar errors and to reconstruct the semantics of ungrammatical inputs (Bender et al., 2004), which can then be used by the MT component to enable source-language interaction and feedback.

In the following section of this paper (2) we will discuss the motivation and significance of our system, followed by a survey of previous works in section (3). Section (4) will describe, in detail, the system implementation and our current implementation stage. Finally, we conclude and outline some future work.

2 New Learning Trends and Language Education

It is well known that Learning Sciences are rapidly entering a new era of online mediated education. A proof of this is the fact that many of the main players in the worldwide education system have identified the need of belonging to these new virtual learning spaces — joining existing or developing their own online learning platforms.

Concepts like Massive Open Online Courses (MOOCs) have only been around for a few years, and still this new learning paradigm has already caused an unprecedented change in worldwide education (Yuan et al., 2013). Unfortunately, the number of Massive Open Online Language Courses (MOOLC) available is proportionately very small — e.g. Perifanou and Economides (2014) report having found only 30 such courses in 2013. There is, easily arguable, not a lack of demand for such language courses, but a lack of technological infrastructure to support them.

And even though a considerable amount of research has been conducted in the last decades with regard to distance language learning, designing an efficient language learning course or developing a language learning platform is a very complex process. Perifanou and Economides (2014) states the ideas of **pedagogy** and **assessment** as being central challenges of these types of courses.

Our project was designed improve pedagogy — how the students learn a second language, based on improved feedback. It is targeted at university-level language learners, and will provide a scalable pedagogical infrastructure for online language learning. It can both be used in a blended learning environment, accompanying normal classroom style lectures, or it could eventually be further developed into a fully self-contained, self-paced online language course.

3   CALL: An overview

Artificial Intelligence (AI)'s contributions to CALL systems have, up to date, been mainly focused on problems like error classification, user modeling, expert systems, and Intelligent Tutoring Systems (Schulze, 2008; Gamper and Knapp, 2002). Following Gamper and Knapp (2002)'s survey on CALL systems, we known CALL systems differ mainly in the features they possess. Many of these systems have some domain knowledge, allowing detailed feedback to the learner, while others just guide students through a virtually designed course. Some present adaptive user models incorporating automated speech synthesis and recognition. Most systems use NLP techniques for analysis, but only a few also have generation capability. Some systems focus on one basic language skill (e.g. reading, writing, listening, or speaking), while others look for broader coverage. Some systems have a larger focus on grammar, others on vocabulary, and some even specialize in dialog interaction.

But ultimately, CALL systems are only a medium for language teaching. A study conducted by Nagata (1996) showed that it is not the medium itself (e.g. a computer, a book, etc.) that determines success in learning, it is the quality of the feedback produced by that medium that affects the results. This is why a language teacher is likely to be a better medium than a book, and the same reason why a properly designed CALL system can also be a better medium than a workbook, assuming that such systems can give valuable interactive feedback to the learner.

One of the main issues pointed out by Gamper and Knapp (2002) was that most CALL systems concentrate mainly on syntax and give less attention to semantic components, and only very few try to address the problem of pragmatics. At the same time, the integration of MT technology is also quite rare, and when is used, it mainly tries to give support to the training of translation skills.

More recently, a few CALL systems have started to use semantics to empower their precision and performance. An example of this is the adaptation of two high precision descriptive grammars (English and Norwegian) with semantic generation capacity into full-fledged CALL systems (Hellan et al., 2013; Flickinger and Yu, 2013; Flickinger, 2010; Bender et al., 2004). Both systems identify generation as crucial to their coaching feature. They apply the idea of semantically robust mal-rules, where the semantics of ungrammatical input is reconstructed by carefully designed rules that try to mimic common mistakes made by language learners.

The problem arises with the fact that each sentence allows a number of possible semantic representations (depending on the ambiguity of the lexicon and the strictness of the grammar rules). And while it is, in many cases, impossible to predict the intended meaning of the user's sentence, one solution is to make an educated guess with some statistical analysis (Hellan et al., 2013).

Still, previous systems (Hellan et al., 2013; Flickinger, 2010; Bender et al., 2004) report ambiguity as one of their central challenges. Balancing between the flexibility of the grammar and a high accuracy in disambiguating the intended analysis for each student sentence is essential to make the right diagnoses of errors (Flickinger, 2010). Even though statistical analysis may be tempting to solve this ambiguity, picking the incorrect intended meaning may mislead learners into thinking that they made an error that they did not. Up until today, the solution has been to reduce and control the lexicon in order to avoid ambiguity. The unfortunate consequence of this is that not all lexical entries can be equally represented in these systems.

4 Approach and Implementation

In this section we will describe the infrastructure and previous research grounding this project. We will also motivate and explain the concepts of graded lexical semantics and syntax, along with the choice of using the Open Multilingual Wordnet as a lexical ontology. We will finish by briefly introducing the relation between Learner Corpora and mal-rules, and their usage in CALL systems.

4.1 Integration of Descriptive Syntax and Semantics

The effort of creating a large-coverage, high-precision descriptive grammar is very time consuming (Copestake and Flickinger, 2000). For this reason, we chose to adapt existing grammars instead of creating new systems from scratch. Furthermore, we also needed the grammars to share some kind of semantic representation to be used for both parsing and generating across languages (i.e. to translate across languages using these grammars). We therefore selected grammars from the Deep Linguistic Processing with HPSG Initiative (DELPH-IN: Uszkoreit, 2002). DELPH-IN partners have agreed to and dedicated many years towards open-source multilingual parallel grammar development using Head Driven Phrase Structure Grammar theory (Sag et al., 2003) integrated with a computational semantics representation based on Minimal Recursion Semantics (MRS: Copestake et al., 2005; Copestake, 2007).

Concerning our specific languages of interest, for English we used the English Resource Grammar (ERG: Flickinger, 2000; Copestake and Flickinger, 2000), a grammar with a very large lexicon and wide coverage of syntactic phenomena; and for Mandarin Chinese ZHONG (Fan et al., 2015) [1] a more recent grammar with a solid coverage of core phenomena.

DELPH-IN grammars have been used in machine translation (Bond et al., 2005, 2011). DELPH-IN's MT work flow is based on semantic transfer systems — a source language is parsed by an HPSG grammar and a collection of underspecified semantic representations (i.e. MRSs) are generated and transferred to the target language's grammar — these then generate sentences encoding the same semantics in the target language.

4.2 Graded Lexical Semantics and Graded Parsers

Any CALL system must model some lexical semantics. Let us consider the example word *present*. Any mid or large sized dictionary of English would include multiple senses for this word. In the Princeton English Wordnet (Fellbaum, 1998), for example, there are 18 possible senses. Here is a selection of seven of those senses:

> 1. (noun) *something presented as a gift;* 2. (noun) *a verb tense that expresses actions or states at the time of speaking;* 3. (adjective) *being or existing in a specified place;* 4. (verb) *to give an exhibition of to an interested audience;* 5. (verb) *to introduce;* 6. (verb) *to give as a present; to make a gift of;* 7. (verb) *to recognise with a gesture prescribed by a military regulation;*

Considering the examples above, it is easy to acknowledge that lexical ambiguity is real. In real life situations, context is usually enough to disambiguate the intended sense. However, some of these senses are not commonly used in everyday situations, and can perhaps be ignored in the context of foreign language learning. Not even native speakers ever have full control of the lexical inventory of their language. So it is unreasonable to expect that an average user of English as a Foreign Language would be proficient using the word *present* as the verbal form *to recognise with a gesture prescribed by a military regulation*.

When considering many of the other common senses of *present*, it is important to note that language learners acquire different senses distributed in time (or language levels), either by necessity or by curricular requirement. Dewaele and Ip (2013) present a conclusive study that strongly relates Foreign Language Classroom Anxiety (FLCA) with Second Language Tolerance of Ambiguity (SLTA). Dealing with second language ambiguity is an important source of language use anxiety. This is also evident in the way most language courses are structured, as it is common practice to protect language learners from all the possible senses of a word until the language complexity so demands. Gradually learning to cope with

---

[1] http://moin.delph-in.net/ZhongTop

ambiguity is directly correlated with proficiency in any given language: the incremental aspect of this
process is a very important notion to take into consideration.

Exploiting this incremental increase in ambiguity can be effectively used to minimize syntactic ambiguity. Descriptive grammars can be adapted to exploit this notion of natural gradual complexity of the
learning process. Constraining the available lexicon by language levels, or even to the specific lexicon a
user is known to possess, can help reduce ambiguity, by ignoring what the student could not have intended
because it was out of their current knowledge.

We are building a model of language level based on a survey of the following resources: the first and
second level of the Hanyu Shuiping Kaoshi (HSK) official language examinations, the first volume of
the textbook New Practical Chinese Reader (Xun, 2010), Chinese Link: Beginning Chinese, Simplified
Character Version, Level 1/Part 1 (Wu et al., 2010) and supplementary materials presented to the first
level of Mandarin Chinese, as taught at our home institution.

These materials are being currently surveyed for their natural increment of lexical senses introduced
to students. In addition, these same sources also contain information concerning syntactic complexity.
In principle, the more complex syntactic structures are, the greater the likelihood that these would be
introduced at later stages of language curricula. Following the same idea of gradually introducing lexical
items into the descriptive grammars, we also argue that the same can be done with syntactic rules and
constructions (e.g. minimize syntactic ambiguity by removing grammatical rules to which the student
has not yet been introduced).

Both lexical and syntactic information is stored in a graded fashion in a database, relating statistical
information about the syntactic structures' distribution across language levels, exams and curricula. This
information will allow us to simplify descriptive grammars to a level of strictly necessary syntactic complexity to any surveyed language level — a system we named Graded Parser. By limiting the number of
rules necessary to describe a specific language level, graded parsers can help avoid unnecessary ambiguity.

The surveyed lexical information will also be integrated in the Open Multilingual Wordnet (OMW)
(Bond and Foster, 2013), a very large union of free wordnets. The OMW tightly integrates the English
Princeton Wordnet (Fellbaum, 1998) and the Chinese Open Wordnet (Wang and Bond, 2013), allowing
us to leverage on its structure to aid in the MT components.

4.3 Learner Corpora

First language transfer is widely accepted to play an important role in foreign language learning (Gass,
1988). Because of this, many CALL systems have been implemented for pairs of languages (i.e. a specific
source language is considered in the development process) (Gamper and Knapp, 2002). CALL systems
should be aware of the most common mistakes its users are known to make. For instance, missing the
copula *to be* is a common mistake made by native Chinese speakers learning English (Schneider and
McCoy, 1998). And, along the same lines, using an unnecessary copula (是 *shi*) in adjectival predication
constructions is a common mistake made by native English speakers learning Mandarin.

The study of learner corpora focuses on the collection and analysis of language learner data. This data
is especially of interest to CALL research if it has been error-tagged (i.e. all the errors in the corpus have
been described with a set of tags: Granger, 2003). Before one can hope to design error detection and
correction systems, it is necessary to survey errors contained in some learner corpora (Granger, 2003).
Also, the appropriateness of the error correction in CALL systems is often measured against these kind
of corpora (Schulze, 2008).

Even though producing an error-tagged corpus is very time-consuming, the huge return on invested
resources is undeniable (Granger, 2003). For instance, documented and organized data can be used to
customize the exercises in accordance with the learners' proficiency level and/or mother tongue background (Granger, 2003). Semantically annotated Learner Corpora are a good resource to predict the
intended meaning of students (Hellan et al., 2013). And finally, the ungrammatical inputs collected by
learner corpora can also be useful by providing examples of unparseable sentences for descriptive grammarians.

Many learner corpora are available for English learners coming from a Mandarin language background. Unfortunately, there seems to be an absence of readily available learner corpora made from Mandarin Chinese language learners. For this reason we are collecting and are currently annotating a learner corpus of Mandarin learners, using English as their source language. This learner corpus and the example sentences from the textbooks surveyed in Section 4.2 are being annotated using IMI (Bond et al., 2015), a multilingual semantic annotation environment that has been adapted to our needs.

4.4 Mal-rules

Mal-rules (also called 'error-production rules') (Schneider and McCoy, 1998) are a specific kind of rules that extend a descriptive grammar to make it accept (parse) ungrammatical phenomena. These mal-rules can be used to identify specific language errors, often triggering helpful messages to language learners. Consider the examples (2) and (3), below:

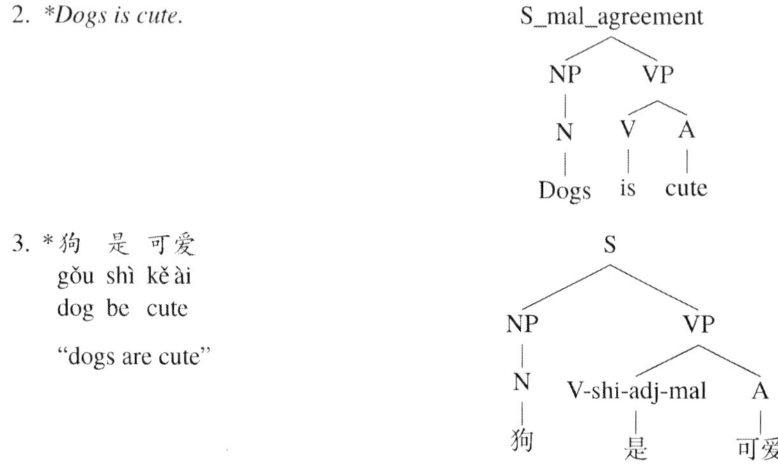

A descriptive grammar of English should reject (2) as a proper sentence. But if the intention were to capture the agreement error (between the subject NP and the VP), then expanding the English grammar with a mal-rule will serve this purpose perfectly. The node identified by *S_mal_agreement*, is a simple example of a mal-rule that was designed to explicitly allow a disagreement between the subject and the main clause. Similarly, a prescriptive grammar of Mandarin should reject (3) as a proper sentence, since the use of copula with adjectival predicates is not recommended (except in rare cases where pragmatics take a more prominent role). But as seen in (3), we can easily catch this error by adding a mal-lexical-entry, in this case named *V-shi-adj-mal* to flag the use of a copula that takes an adjectival complement. (3) is the first of many such mal-constructions to be implemented in our system, many more will follow.

The names of these rules are important, since checking the nodes of a parse tree can easily identify that the sentence was not grammatical because there is a *mal* (or any another tag) in the name of one of the nodes. The full rule name or lexical entry can be used to identify the specific kind of error and hence allow a system to say, for example, "there is something wrong with the agreement in that sentence", for (2), or "you should not use 是 before an adjective" for (3).

The mal-rules can be applied selectively. They can, for example, be used for parsing but not for generation (Bender et al., 2004), or to allow one type of error but not other. Also, because the grammars we are working with produce a semantic representation, these mal-rules are being designed to reconstruct the semantics of ungrammatical sentences, in a way that allows the generation of corrected counterparts (Bender et al., 2004). In some cases, the same error triggers multiple different mal-rules, each one reconstructing different semantics, so as to mimic different possible intended meanings by the student.

4.5 Our System's Architecture

In this section we will bring together all the previously presented details to elaborate on the design of our CALL system. Figure 2 presents a flowchart view of the coming description.

The final system will be web-based (accessible from any computer, tablet or phone with an internet connection). At the top of this system we have an authentication module. This ID will allow the system to retrieve all the necessary information to launch the tutoring system. The Student Model is the center of information. There we can find the vocabulary known by each student, the grammatical complexity the student is expected to work with, and the entire history of the student's interaction with the system (e.g. previous completed exercises, previous mistakes, time spent with each exercise, etc.).

Once the student is identified, the system allows two main tasks: Vocabulary Introduction and Exercise Randomiser. The Vocabulary Introduction module is

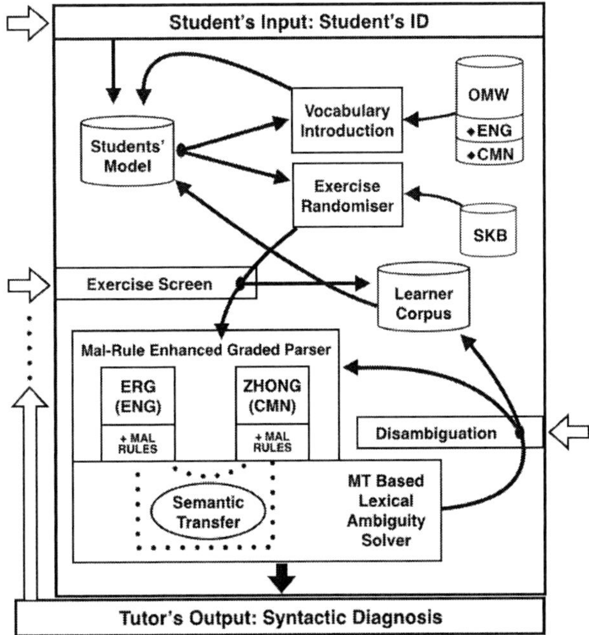

Figure 2: CALL system flowchart

directly linked to the new OMW extensions previously described (i.e. identifying individual lexical senses to specific language levels), allowing the student to preview necessary vocabulary in the target language. All the previously previewed vocabulary is stored in the Student Model and it feeds the Exercise Randomiser module.

The Exercise Randomiser module makes use of the previously known lexicon and the Syntactic Knowledge Base (SKB) to generate a one-sentence composition exercise, where learners must select words out of a randomly generated pool of words to compose a grammatical sentence. The number and type of spurious words that will be generated will be taken into account to determine its difficulty. The students inputted sentences will be stored in a Learner Corpus and sent to the Parser module. The Mal-Rule Enhanced Graded Parser module comprises the mal-rule enhanced grammars and a Semantic Transfer Machine Translation system.

The basic workflow of this module is as follows: if a parse is possible without activating mal-rules, then the solution is considered grammatical, the student is congratulated and the system returns to the beginning. If, on the other hand, one or more mal-rules are necessary to parse the student's solution, then there are two possible scenarios:

- there is no ambiguity about what errors were made: in this case the system can output a message prompting the student about the error made. The error tags will be added to the Learner Corpus, and the student will be asked to submit a new solution to the same problem until he/she can solve it; or

- there is ambiguity in the student's intended meaning, and different mal-rules that convey different meanings were triggered: in this case the system can't immediately output where the student made a mistake without first finding the intended meaning. In this case the solution of the student will enter the Ambiguity Solver module.

The MT Based Ambiguity Solver is a basic dialog system (similar to Figure 1) that will request help from the student to decide what the intended meaning was, and thus which errors were made. This module assumes that mal-rules have been constructed with robust semantics (i.e. reconstructing the right semantics for each particular error encoded in the rule). This will allow the system to use the reconstructed semantic representation to generate correct sentences. If there is a huge amount of ambiguity to solve, then parse ranking algorithms can help select the most probable set of intended meanings. This set of probable meanings is translated from target to source languages, and the student will be prompted to choose his/her intended meaning, between a set of translations.

Having found the student's intended meaning, a simple backwards analysis can be made to check which mal-rules were used to generate the selected choice. The ungrammatical solution will be stored in the learner corpus tagged with its intended meaning. The system will use the mal-rules used to generate the student's intended meaning in order to trigger an appropriate coaching message.

Finally, the system also has to account for completely unexpected sentences. Assuming the grammar will only be enhanced with common errors made by language learners, the system is likely to find inputs that it neither considers a grammatical input, nor does it have mal-rules that can help parse it. Also, students may still use a perfectly grammatical structure that the system is not expecting the student to use (given its graded architecture). In these cases, the system cannot say that the input is ungrammatical. Instead, a sentence that cannot be parsed can generate some general comments like: "You should not try to create sentences with structures you haven't learned yet. Try to make simpler sentences!". This is both uncommitted to the grammaticality of the input, and pedagogical in the sense that it tries to focus the student on his/her curriculum. These sentences should be flagged for the instructor to examine and give feedback on.

We hope to employ a few tricks to make the system friendlier to the students. For example, it can make intelligent use of ambiguous and unambiguous lexical entries to spare the student from having to take this disambiguation step too often. Also, when considering ambiguous input, it can automatically take the most probable intended meaning by default and output something like "If you mean A, then you need to be careful about mistake X. If you did not mean A, then help me understand what you meant by selecting from B, C or D."

The learner corpus compiled from this process will have very rich information when compared to other similar corpora. This system will not only collect statistics of common syntactic errors made by learners, but will also link these mistakes with the semantic annotation concerning the intended meaning. Also, when students are prompted to help the system disambiguate their solutions, an implicit parallel bilingual corpus is being created. The system will constantly be feeding itself information that makes it more intelligent, allowing interesting expansion over time.

5   Conclusions and Future Work

In this paper we have described a system that will hopefully help push for a new state-of-the-art on-line learning environments, by closely integrating semantics-based MT with computational grammars. Though still in an early stage of development, we have shown how we can use cutting-edge grammatical and semantic research research to build a system focused on reinforcing grammatical knowledge to Mandarin Chinese L2 learners.

Expandability (within the same language), adaptability to other languages and a component based architecture is at the core of our research agenda. So we expect not only that this system will be a useful resource for Mandarin L2 students, but that it can also help CALL research to further explore the integration of semantics, MT and other NLP field into its field.

At a pedagogical level, our approach empowers language educators, allowing them to focus their lectures on other major language skills (e.g. listening and speaking) rather than drilling. Educators can rely on CALL systems to provide personalized grammatical feedback to each individual student, and better attend to their individual struggles. At the same time, our system is designed for the students, providing them autonomy in self-paced study, and allowing them to spend more time practicing parts of the curriculum where they struggle the most.

We intend to evaluate this tool both with an intrinsic evaluation (how many errors can be correctly identified in a learner corpus) and an extrinsic one (in a classroom, does using this improve students test scores).

References

Bender, E. M., Flickinger, D., Oepen, S., Walsh, A., and Baldwin, T. (2004). Arboretum: Using a precision grammar for grammar checking in CALL. In *InSTIL/ICALL Symposium 2004*.

Bond, F. and Foster, R. (2013). Linking and extending an Open Multilingual Wordnet. In *51st Annual Meeting of the Association for Computational Linguistics: ACL-2013, Sofia*, pages 1352–1362.

Bond, F., Morgado da Costa, L., and Lê, T. A. (2015). IMI – a multilingual semantic annotation environment. *ACL-IJCNLP 2015*, pages 7–12.

Bond, F., Oepen, S., Nichols, E., Flickinger, D., Velldal, E., and Haugereid, P. (2011). Deep open-source machine translation. *Machine Translation*, 25(2):87–105.

Bond, F., Oepen, S., Siegel, M., Copestake, A., and Flickinger, D. (2005). Open source machine translation with DELPH-IN. In *Open-Source Machine Translation: Workshop at MT Summit X*, pages 15–22, Phuket.

Copestake, A. (2007). Semantic composition with (robust) minimal recursion semantics. In *Proceedings of the Workshop on Deep Linguistic Processing*, pages 73–80. Association for Computational Linguistics.

Copestake, A. and Flickinger, D. (2000). An open source grammar development environment and broad-coverage English grammar using HPSG. In *In proceedings of LREC 2000*, pages 591–600.

Copestake, A., Flickinger, D., Pollard, C., and Sag, I. A. (2005). Minimal recursion semantics: An introduction. *Research on Language and Computation*, 3(2-3):281–332.

Dewaele, J.-M. and Ip, T. S. (2013). The link between foreign language classroom anxiety, second language tolerance of ambiguity and self-rated English proficiency among Chinese learners. *Studies in Second Language Learning and Teaching*, (1):47–66.

Fan, Z., Song, S., and Bond, F. (2015). An hpsg-based shared-grammar for the chinese languages: Zhong [[]. In *Proceedings of the Grammar Engineering Across Frameworks (GEAF) Workshop*, pages 17–24.

Fellbaum, C. (1998). *Wordnet: An electronic lexical database*. MIT Press Cambridge.

Flickinger, D. (2000). On building a more effcient grammar by exploiting types. *Natural Language Engineering*, 6(01):15–28.

Flickinger, D. (2010). Prescription and explanation–using an HPSG implementation to teach writing skills. In *Invited talk, HPSG Conference*.

Flickinger, D. and Yu, J. (2013). Toward more precision in correction of grammatical errors. In *Proceedings of the Seventeenth Conference on Computational Natural Language Learning: Shared Task, CoNLL 2013, Sofia, Bulgaria, August 8-9, 2013*, pages 68–73.

Gamper, J. and Knapp, J. (2002). A review of intelligent CALL systems. *Computer Assisted Language Learning*, 15(4):329–342.

Gass, S. M. (1988). *Second Language Acquisition and Linguistic Theory: The Role of Language Transfer*, pages 384–403. Springer Netherlands, Dordrecht.

Granger, S. (2003). The International Corpus of Learner English: a new resource for foreign language learning and teaching and second language acquisition research. *Tesol Quarterly*, 37(3):538–546.

Hellan, L., Bruland, T., Aamot, E., and Sandoy, M. H. (2013). A Grammar Sparrer for Norwegian. In *Proceedings of the 19th Nordic Conference of Computational Linguistics (NODALIDA 2013), Oslo, Norway. NEALT Proceedings Series*, volume 16.

Nagata, N. (1996). Computer vs. workbook instruction in second language acquisition. *CALICO journal*, 14(1):53–75.

Perifanou, M. and Economides, A. (2014). MOOCs for foreign language learning: an effort to explore and evaluate the first practices. *INTED2014 Proceedings*, pages 3561–3570.

Sag, I. A., Wasow, T., Bender, E. M., and Sag, I. A. (2003). *Syntactic theory: A formal introduction*, volume 2. CSLI Stanford.

Schneider, D. and McCoy, K. F. (1998). Recognizing syntactic errors in the writing of second language learners. In *Proceedings of the 17th International Conference on Computational Linguistics - Volume 2*, COLING '98, pages 1198–1204, Stroudsburg, PA, USA. Association for Computational Linguistics.

Schulze, M. (2008). AI in CALL – artificially inflated or almost imminent? *Calico Journal*, 25(3):510–527.

Uszkoreit, H. (2002). New chances for deep linguistic processing. pages XIV–XXVII, Taipei.

Wang, S. and Bond, F. (2013). Building the Chinese Open Wordnet (COW): Starting from core synsets. In *Proceedings of the 11th Workshop on Asian Language Resources, a Workshop at IJCNLP-2013*, pages 10–18, Nagoya.

Wu, S., Tian, W., and Zhang, Y. (2010). *Chinese Link: Beginning Chinese: Simplified Character Version, Level 1*. Chinese Link: Zhong Wen Tian Di. Beginning Chinese. Level 1. Prentice Hall.

Xun, L. (2010). *New Practical Chinese Reader Vol. 1 (2nd.Ed.)*. Beijing Language Culture University Press.

Yuan, L., Powell, S., and CETIS, J. (2013). MOOCs and open education: Implications for higher education. *Cetis White Paper*.

An Aligned French-Chinese corpus of 10K segments from university educational material

Ruslan Kalitvianski   **Lingxiao Wang**   **Valérie Bellynck**   **Christian Boitet**

LIG-GETALP, Bâtiment IMAG, 700 av. Centrale,
CS 40700, 38058 Grenoble cedex 9, France

`firstname.lastname@imag.fr`

Abstract

This paper describes a corpus of nearly 10K French-Chinese aligned segments, produced by post-editing machine translated computer science courseware. This corpus was built from 2013 to 2016 within the MACAU project, by native Chinese students. The quality, as judged by native speakers, is adequate for understanding (far better than by reading only the original French) and for getting better marks. This corpus is annotated at segment-level by a self-assessed quality score. It has been directly used as supplemental training data to build a statistical machine translation system dedicated to that sublanguage, and can be used to extract the specific bilingual terminology. To our knowledge, it is the first corpus of this kind to be released.

1   Introduction

The ongoing MACAU project, started in 2012 at the University of Grenoble, aims at providing multilingual access to course material taught at the university (Kalitvianski et al, 2015). It is motivated by the fact that many foreign students struggle with understanding material taught in French, and have to spend extra time in dictionary lookup and translation to fully comprehend the meaning.

The MACAU platform[1] is designed to create multilingual versions of initially monolingual course material by producing machine translations into the desired language, and by providing an interface that allows readers to post-edit these translations, segment by segment, until the desired level of quality is achieved.

A direct by-product of this activity is a bilingual corpus of post-edited sentences, constituting full courses, exercises and so on, concerning several fields of theoretical and practical computer science. Such a corpus could be employed as supplemental data for training a custom machine translation system. It can also serve for extraction of domain-specific lexicon.

In this paper we describe the data, provide corpus statistics, and delineate potential uses for the corpus.

2   The MACAU corpus

In this section we describe the MACAU project within which this corpus was constructed, and give the corpus' characteristics.

2.1   The MACAU project

The MACAU project has been ongoing since 2012. Its purpose is to help foreign students access educational material produced by the university in their native tongues, as those are the ones they understand best.

This is achieved by post-editing machine-translated documents, segment by segment. The post-edition is done via the iMAG web interface (Boitet et al, 2008). An iMAG is an interactive multilingual access gateway, which allows its users to visit a web page in the language of their choice while preserving its layout.

Pages are automatically segmented into translation units, typically sentences or titles. Segments are substituted by either a machine translation output if the segment is not found in the dedicated translation memory, or by the best post-edition available if the segment has been post-edited. Users can contribute corrections directly on the page by hovering the mouse pointer over the segment they desire to

---

[1] Currently migrating to `macau.imag.fr`

117

Proceedings of the 3rd Workshop on Natural Language Processing Techniques for Educational Applications,
pages 117–121, Osaka, Japan, December 12 2016.

correct, which makes a post-editing palette appear. The quality of a post-edition is explicitly "self-assessed" by the post-editor through a score in [0..20]. That score can later be revised, for example by other Chinese students using the Chinese version to study. Note that the interface allows to see the target (Chinese) and source (French) versions to appear side by side, so that, while learning some topic in computer science, Chinese students can also progress in French.

Post-editing through the iMAG interface is typically 3 times faster than translation from scratch (15-20 mins vs. 1 hour per standard page of 250 words). Also, for the post-editor, such an interface has the benefit of allowing post-editors to see the segment within its context.

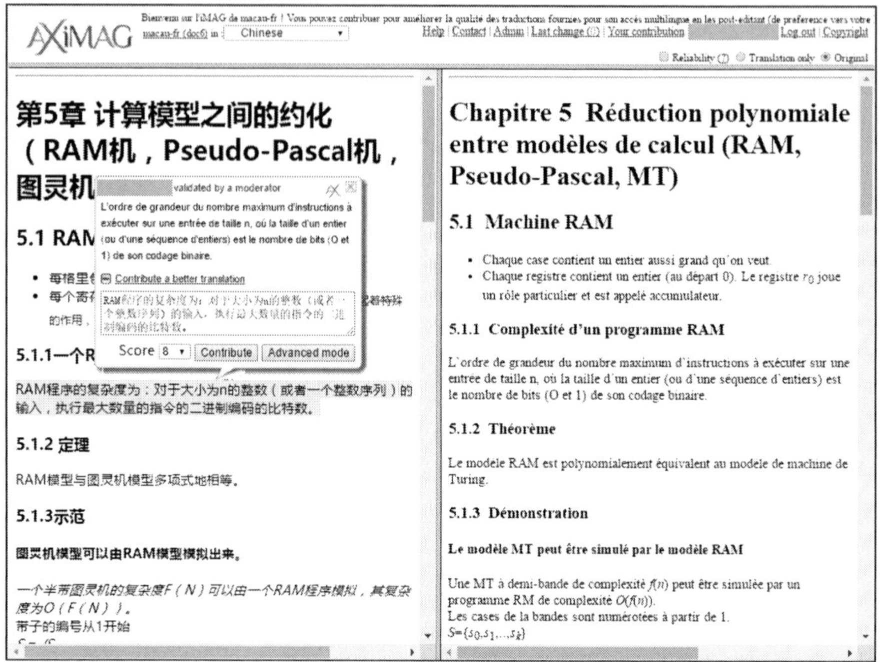

Figure 1: a chapter of a course on computational complexity, in bilingual view, with a post-editing window displayed over a segment.

For the MACAU project, the source documents are provided by teachers and also by students, and cover subjects concerning bachelor and master-level computer science. Table 1 below describes the quantity and the subject matters included in the corpus.

Subject matter	Content type	Pages (html)
Introduction to Propositional and First-Order Logic	Full book	45
C programming	Teacher lectures	14
Object-oriented programming	Teacher lectures	13
Computational Complexity	Lecture notes	13
Human-Machine interaction	Teacher lectures	7
Formal Languages and Parsing	Teacher lectures, hand-outs	5
Modelling of digital systems	Exam paper	2
AI and automatic planning	Exam paper	2
Introduction to Ergonomics	Student report	1

Table 1. Current status of the MACAU platform

Post-editing was performed by three Chinese-speaking university students, selected for their knowledge of the courses. Two were masters' students, one was a third year bachelors'. All have been taught the subject in French.

Students were selected on the basis of their knowledge of Chinese, their familiarity with the subject matters, and their interest in the task. They were explained the purpose of the task, and practiced on training documents before post-editing those that are included in the corpus. They received some monetary compensation for their work (as interns).

The students were asked to post-edit machine-generated translations segment by segment, through the iMAG interface, until an acceptable Chinese formulation of each segment was obtained. They were also told that the priority was not literary quality, but rather understandability. A group of two other native Chinese speakers subsequently verified the correctness a subset of randomly selected translations.

2.2 Corpus characteristics

The corpus is a collection of 9662 aligned French-Chinese segments, extracted from courseware in HTML. This corpus is cleaned of all HTML markup, however it does contain other non-linguistic elements, such as mathematical and logical formulas.

The segmentation was produced automatically and has not been corrected manually, therefore some segments correspond to fragments of sentences, and, more rarely, to two sentences fused together. Primary translations were obtained automatically via Google Translate.

The average source segment length is ~72 characters, or about 11 French words, and the median length is 53 characters. 25% of the source segments are less than 26 characters long and another 25% are over 100 characters long. Moreover, the corpus contains 108860 words, of which 8819 are unique French tokens.

The corpus initially contained many redundancies, but has been substantially cleaned. The remaining few source redundancies differ by their Chinese translations. The quality of the segments, as judged by bilingual readers, is considered adequate for understanding.

La complexité d'un programme pseudo-Pascal est l'ordre de grandeur du nombre d'instructions élémentaires à exécuter sur une entrée de taille n.	伪帕斯卡程序的复杂性是基本指令的数量级上的大小为 n 条输入运行。
Question: Sont-ils décidables dans le modèle de calcul déterministe?	问题：他们是能用确定性计算解决的问题吗？
(a ⇒ b)∧(b ⇒ c)∧¬(a ⇒ c) est insatisfaisable.	(a ⇒ b)∧(b ⇒ c)∧¬(a ⇒ c)是不可满足的。
Voici la référence principale, et son résumé, qui nous semble tout à fait clair.	这里是主要的参考和总结，这似乎是相当清楚的。
Ces trois formules n'ont pas de variables libres.	这三个公式没有自由变量。

Table 2. Examples of segments from the corpus

This corpus is now available on GitHub[2].

3 Building a specialized MT system for that sublanguage

One possible use of this corpus is the training of a specialized MT system for educational documents.

3.1 Motivations and method

We are interested in increasing the usage quality of machine translation systems. We measure usage quality as a function of post-edition times related to an estimate of the human translation time, which by default is assumed to be 60 minutes per standard 250 word page.

$$Q = 1 - (2/100 \times \frac{Tpe_{total}(for\ the\ task)}{Thum_{estim}(for\ the\ task)} \times Thum_{std_{page}}(mn))$$

(1)

Formula 1: A measure for the usage quality of a MT system.

For example, Q = 40% is Tpe_{total} = 30 mn/p (8/20), and Q = 90% if Tpe_{total} = 5 mn/p (18/20).

This corpus has been used by Wang (2015) as supplemental data for training a specialized Moses (Koehn et al. 2007) probabilistic machine translation system through incremental training, yielding better usage quality than a generalistic PMT system.

---

[2] https://github.com/macau-getalp/macau

3.2 Usage of Moses incremental training

When new training data is available, a way of adding it to an existing model is incremental training. It is an iterative process that avoids the time-consuming retraining of a new model from scratch[3].

The V_0 of the system was trained on 100K bilingual segments from the MultiUN corpus (Eisele et al, 2010). Batches of 5000 segments taken from several in-domain corpora were iteratively added, including a raw form of this corpus that contained 16000 unfiltered segments.

3.3 Evolution of post-editing times

After 16 iterations, results show that the incremental training method reduces post-edition times, in a short amount of time (16 iterations, about 90 hours of computation, without ever recompiling everything). This system yields a usage quality of 70%, with 15 mins/std_page, better than Google Translate.

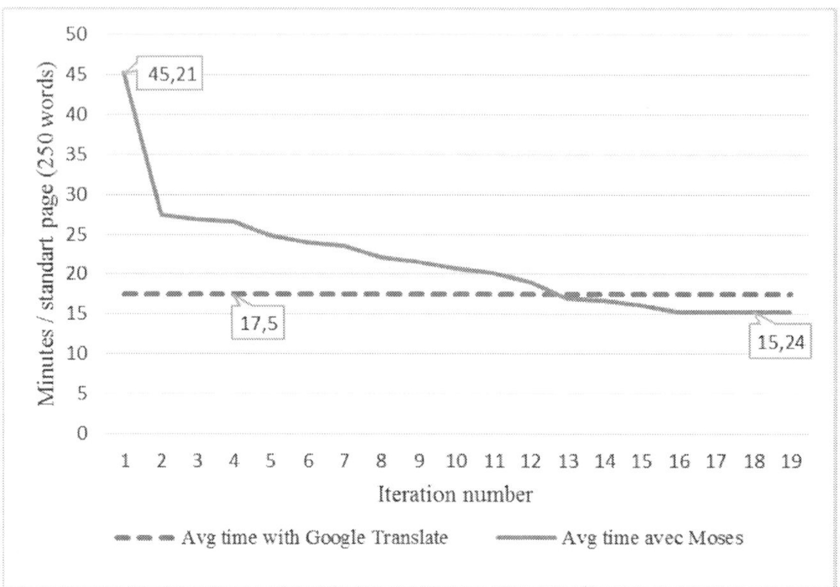

Figure 2: observed reduction in post-edition times after incremental training

The BLEU score (Papineni et al. 2002) improved as well, going from 13.8% after the first iteration to 48.3% after the last one.

Conclusion

We have presented a bilingual parallel corpus of nearly 10K aligned French-Chinese segments, produced over three years in the course of the MACAU project. This corpus is released under a free license and will be periodically updated as new post-editions become available. To our knowledge, this is the first corpus of this kind to be published

The multilingual access platform being open to everyone, this corpus can be extended by anyone by post-editing either pre-existing or newly uploaded documents, something that we encourage.

Although a large-scale evaluation of the usefulness of the platform will be carried out in the near future, we have already observed that the process of post-editing improves understanding and exam grades. An example of this is a student whose exam grade rose from 2.5/20 to 11/20 after a month of post-editing material related to the subject. Undoubtedly, several factors were at play, but this appears to be an interesting avenue of investigation.

---

[3] The details of the incremental training process are described here:
http://www.statmt.org/moses/?n=Advanced.Incremental

Acknowledgements

The authors would like to express gratitude to the *PédagoTICE* initiative, as well as to Pr. Marie-Christine Rousset, Guillaume Huard and Pascal Lafourcade for their assistance.

References

Christian Boitet, Cong-Phap Huyhn, Hong-Thai Nguyen and Valérie Bellynck. 2010. *The iMAG concept: multilingual access gateway to an elected Web sites with incremental quality increase through collaborative post-edition of MT pretranslations.* In Proceedings of TALN-2010, 8 p.

Ruslan Kalitvianski, Valérie Bellynck and Christian Boitet. 2015. *Multilingual Access to Educational Material through Contributive Post-editing of MT Pretranslations by Foreign Students*; In Proceedings of ICWL 2015, 10 p.

Philipp Koehn, Hieu Hoang, Alexandra Birch, Chris Callison-Burch, Marcello Federico, Nicola Bertoldi, Brooke Cowan, Wade Shen, Christine Moran, Richard Zens, Chris Dyer, Ondrej Bojar, Alexandra Constantin and Evan Herbst. 2007. *Moses: Open Source Toolkit for Statistical Machine Translation. Annual* Meeting of the Association for Computational Linguistics (ACL), demonstration session, Prague, Czech Republic, June 2007.

Lingxiao Wang. 2015. *Outils et environnements pour l'amélioration incrémentale, la post-édition contributive et l'évaluation continue de systèmes de TA. Application à la TA français-chinois.* PhD dissertation, Université de Grenoble.

Andreas Eisele and Yu Chen. 2010. *MultiUN: A Multilingual Corpus from United Nation Documents.* In the Proceedings of the Seventh conference on International Language Resources and Evaluation, European Language Resources Association (ELRA), Pages 2868-2872

Kishore Papineni, Salim Roukos, Todd Ward, and Wei-Jing Zhu. 2002. *BLEU: a method for automatic evaluation of machine translation.* ACL-2002: 40th Annual meeting of the Association for Computational Linguistics. pp. 311–318.

Analysis of Foreign Language Teaching Methods:
An Automatic Readability Approach

Nasser Zalmout, Hind Saddiki and Nizar Habash
Computational Approaches to Modeling Language Lab
New York University Abu Dhabi, UAE
{nasser.zalmout,hind.saddiki,nizar.habash}@nyu.edu

Abstract

Much research in education has been done on the study of different language teaching methods. However, there has been little investigation using computational analysis to compare such methods in terms of readability or complexity progression. In this paper, we make use of existing readability scoring techniques and our own classifiers to analyze the textbooks used in two very different teaching methods for English as a Second Language – the grammar-based and the communicative methods. Our analysis indicates that the grammar-based curriculum shows a more coherent readability progression compared to the communicative curriculum. This finding corroborates with the expectations about the differences between these two methods and validates our approach's value in comparing different teaching methods quantitatively.

1 Introduction

In today's highly interdependent economies and intercultural exchange, learning a second language has become increasingly valued. With over 1.5 billion speakers, including 360 million native speakers, English is the most common second language worldwide. The study of different language teaching methods has been a dominant research pillar of education literature, with numerous contributions spanning various domains (Allen and Widdowson, 1974; Richards and Renandya, 2002) However, there has been little investigation using computational analysis of various teaching methods, and how they compare against each other in terms of readability or complexity progression.

In this paper, we make use of existing readability scoring techniques to analyze the textbooks used in two very different teaching methods for English as a Second Language (ESL). The first method follows a grammar-based approach, and is represented with school textbooks spanning grades 1 through 12 of the educational system of a non-English speaking country (Palestine). The second method uses a communicative approach, and is represented with four graded textbooks from a generic ESL course called *Lane's English as a Second Language Course*. We use several commonly used readability scoring metrics, and we implement machine learning readability classifiers exploiting various syntactic and lexical features. We employ these tools to make inferences regarding the language readability progression, with increasing grade levels, for the two teaching methods and their affiliated textbooks.

In the next section, we discuss some related work. This is followed by a detailed presentation of our dataset (Section 3) and readability algorithms (Section 4). We finally present and discuss our results in Section 5.

Proceedings of the 3rd Workshop on Natural Language Processing Techniques for Educational Applications,
pages 122–130, Osaka, Japan, December 12 2016.

2 Related Work

2.1 Foreign Language Teaching Methods

Previous ESL teaching methods relied heavily on grammar-based methods, where there is more focus on sentence structure rather than sentence flow. This trend continued throughout the 60s and 70s (Richards and Renandya, 2002), and found its way into many ESL school-based curricula still in use today. Recently, more consideration is given to the actual needs and backgrounds of the learners themselves (Lane, 1978). Teaching methods have generally shifted away from grammar-based methods and have come to rely more on lexical factors such as frequency and word count. The communicative approach later emerged (Allen and Widdowson, 1974), focusing on linguistic patterns, and facilitated by audio support. However, this approach has been criticized since relying on pure communicative contexts would still require building up sufficient vocabulary and grammar knowledge beforehand (Lane, 1978). Many of the English language textbooks for non-native speakers follow a variation of this approach. These textbooks exhibit more emphasis on grammar and vocabulary in the early grade levels, then shift to a more communicative approach in subsequent grades. The school textbooks used in this paper follow this trend. Another recent variation for learning English focuses much more on the communicative approach, but with emphasis on gradual rules and patterns. When students are exposed to these, they can experience proper communication and gather the momentum to carry them through the new and unfamiliar parts. This approach is used for Lane's course.

2.2 Previous Work on Readability Analysis

In the scope of this paper, analyzing the readability of a given text involves quantifying lexical and syntactic features of the text and obtaining a measure of its difficulty or readability. Some of the early contributions for readability scoring date back to the 40s, using approximate and generic regression formulas to get an indicative score of the observed readability. These scores reflect the readability of the text in terms of grade levels or bound score tag. Such algorithms include:

- Flesch Reading Ease scores (FRE) (Flesch and others, 1949): Scores run from 0 to 100, with lower FRE scores indicating more complex, i.e. less readable text.

- The Flesch-Kincaid Grades (FKG) (Kincaid et al., 1975): Text readability is expressed through the most fitting grade tag from around 0.3 to 12, 12 being the highest.

- Dale-Chall (DC) scores (Dale and Chall, 1948): A grading scheme similar to FKG is applied (ranging from 4.9-or-lower to 9.0-9.9), but with greater emphasis placed on vocabulary by using a list of 3000 commonly used words in English.

These formulas and others were usually obtained from manual computation of regression models fitted on parameters quantifying text complexity (DuBay, 2008). The most commonly used quantifications relied on counting occurrences from vocabulary word lists considered rare or difficult, and on measuring other text attributes that were easy to compute, such as average sentence length in words, average word length in syllables, and so on. It should be noted that these traditional formulas, while lauded for their ease of computation and use, were also criticized for being too superficial to accurately capture the multiple factors that influence text readability (Redish, 2000). The issue of automatic readability scoring has also been covered extensively in more recent literature. Benjamin (2011) presented a survey of text readability methods within various contexts,(Crossley et al., 2007; Zhang et al., 2013) further discuss how to extract the best readability features selection and readability performance. These papers present and compare several readability calculation methods and text cohesion issues, some of which are extensions to the more traditional scores involving more elaborate feature analysis. As computational methods for natural language processing and machine learning matured, researchers began addressing the readability issue from this new angle, with increasingly promising results (Francois and Miltsakaki, 2012). More recent attempts at readability scoring, including (Collins-Thompson, 2014; Pilán et al., 2014; Pilán et al., 2016), discuss utilizing machine learning and Support Vector Machines (SVM), among other classifiers, to predict readability levels. Collins-Thompson (2014) discusses feature set selection, and classification algorithm choices, among other implementation details. Existing work analyzing second languages mostly treats the foreign language as a single coherent entity, without looking into different methods or resources for the learning process (Collins-Thompson, 2014), and without delving into the various factors that might affect the learning process such as contexts, teaching methods, teaching resources, or the students' first language. Our work investigates readability progression spanning several grade levels of two sets of textbooks, each of which follows a different ESL teaching method. We apply established formulaic algorithms and build our own machine learning classifier to assess readability.

3 Dataset

The grammar-based textbooks we use in this paper pertain to the English language curriculum of a non-English speaking country (Palestine), henceforth referred to as the *Palestinian Curriculum Textbooks* (PCT). The communicative textbooks are from *Lane's English as a Second Language Course*, henceforth referred to as *Lane's Course Textbooks* (LCT). The textbooks are divided into 12 grades for PCT (spanning grades 1 through 12) and four consecutive levels for LCT (beginner, advanced beginner, intermediate, advanced intermediate). The PCT textbooks are grouped into four parts, as shown in Table 1, and detailed in the following section.

In some of the experiments, we also include a control corpus comprised of four excerpts from literature used for teaching various school grades in the State of New York, henceforth referred to as *New York Curriculum Textbooks* (NYCT).

We perform a number of pre-processing steps for all the textbooks, including eliminating irrelevant fragments, such as repeated instructions or text intended for instructors rather than students.

	PCT	LCT
Level 1	Grades 1-3	Part 1 (Beginner)
Level 2	Grades 4-6	Part 2 (Advanced Beginner)
Level 2	Grades 7-9	Part 3 (Intermediate)
Level 4	Grades 10-12	Part 4 (Advanced Intermediate)

Table 1: Restructuring the curricula into four parts.

3.1 PCT: Grammar-Based Method

In the Palestinian educational system, English is taught as a second language from first grade, all through high school and the first year of university. Softcopies of the textbooks were acquired through direct communication with the Palestinian ministry of education.

The PCT textbooks, originally distributed across 12 grades, were restructured into four levels, each one covering three consecutive grades, as shown in Table 1. The purpose of this restructuring is twofold. Firstly, grade-level granularity does not provide sufficient tokens/types for reliable analysis, whereas a more coarse-grained structure would remedy that. Additionally, sectioning the corpus into four parts makes it comparable in structure to the LCT corpus. Table 2 presents some statistics of the school textbooks dataset after restructuring the textbooks. The table shows the number of tokens and types for each of the designated groups.

	PCT		LCT		NYCT Samples	
	Tokens	**Types**	**Tokens**	**Types**	**Tokens**	**Types**
Level 1	13,942	1,276	17,724	1,665	902	381
Level 2	51,385	3,049	30,839	1,721	1,209	434
Level 3	126,149	6,042	52,316	2,862	993	411
Level 4	215,527	11,400	47,107	3,086	1,175	494

Table 2: Dataset statistics: Palestinian Curriculum Textbooks (PCT), Lane's Course Textbooks (LCT), and New York Curriculum Textbooks (NYCT) samples

3.2 LCT: Communicative Method

Lane's course, LCT, is a generic English learning textbook with four different levels: Beginner, Advanced Beginner, Intermediate and Advanced Intermediate. The textbooks are designed per the communicative teaching method. It also uses a controlled vocabulary set that is gradually augmented with new words that can be put together and inflected in various ways. Table 2 provides statistics about LCT, grouped by the different parts.

In addition to difference in teaching method between PCT and LCT, we observe other factors that could affect the readability evaluation. PCT targets learners with a specific first language (L1), which might influence the structure and language of the corresponding textbooks. LCT, on the other hand, is not tailored to a specific type of learner. PCT is also designed to be taught over a 12-year period, spanning the Palestinian educational system, while LCT is not restricted to any specific duration. In fact, LCT is most likely be taught at a much accelerated pace.

Another major difference between the two curricula is the age range of the intended target audience. PCT's target learners fall within the 6-18 age bracket, whereas LCT likely caters to an older target audience, although no explicit mention of that was found in the textbooks.

3.3 NYCT Samples

For samples of English learning as L1, we use excerpts of English literature recommended for various grades within the educational system of the State of New York. The full text for the works of literature were difficult to get ahold of. We used excerpts of each piece instead, which was sufficient for our purposes. Table 2 presents some details and statistics of the used texts.

4 Readability Algorithms

In this section, we present the different readability algorithms we employ in this paper. We group them in two sets. First are conventional readability algorithms that have been extensively used for English. And second are two Support Vector Machine (SVM) readability classifiers that we train on the specific datasets – PCT and LCT. All readability algorithms are applied to all the datasets discussed above. The results are discussed in Section 5.

4.1 Conventional Readability Analysis Algorithms

We use three traditional readability analysis tools: Flesch Reading Ease scores (FRE), Flesch-Kincaid Grades (FKG) and Dale-Chall (DC) scores. Both FRE and FKG rely on the same text features to quantify readability: word length and sentence length, but they vary in relative weights attributed to these factors, as well as the interpretation of their respective scores. While FRE increasing scores indicate decreasing reading difficulty, FKG results of increasing grade levels correlate with increasing reading difficulty.

The DC formula also considers average sentence length; however, it differs from the previous two tools by relying on reader comprehension of familiar vs. difficult words. In DC, familiar words are defined by a set of 3,000 words considered accessible to 4th grade level US students and above. Any words outside that list are considered difficult.

4.2 Readability Classification Using Machine Learning

The traditional readability algorithms discussed above provide a generic view of text. To create a more domain and context-specific readability analysis, we build our own machine learning classifiers trained on the specific datasets we study in this paper (PCT and LCT). In designing our classifiers, we build on previous contributions that study relevant features for readability analysis using SVM (Heilman et al., 2008; Petersen and Ostendorf, 2009; Feng et al., 2010).[1] We use a number of lexical and syntactic features, which we discuss next.

Lexical features The lexical features reflect the significance of the words and vocabulary of the analyzed text towards the overall readability of the text, capturing word and phrase-level (as bigrams) attributes. The following lexical features are used in the classifier learning: unigrams, bigrams, syllable counts, types-to-tokens ratio (TTR), and ratio of function words, such as articles, particles and pronouns, among others. Pre-processing includes lowercasing and punctuation removal.

Syntactic features We use the Stanford Parser (De Marneffe et al., 2006) to obtain dependency parses for the sentences. The Stanford Parser produces syntactic structures in the form of triplets, containing the relation name, governor (and its POS) and dependent (and its POS). We only use the POS tags of the governor and dependent words and their relation name. The idea is to use the de-lexicalized syntactic patterns that are observed in the document.

We measure the accuracy of the classifiers using 10-fold cross-validation on the training datasets. The cross-validation accuracy scores for PCT are noticeably higher than those of LCT, with around 83% and 72% respectively. We cannot draw any concrete readability conclusions based on the classifier accuracy since the training used different training datasets with different sizes.

5 Results and Analysis

We first present an overview of the vocabulary sizes in Section 5.1, and the results for the readability algorithms in Section 5.2. Then we discuss the results for the readability classifier in Section 5.3.

5.1 Vocabulary Size and Growth Rate

	Coverage Growth		Coverage Intersection	
	PCT	**LCT**	**PCT**	**LCT**
Level 1	9.6%	29.4%	29.9%	23.9%
Level 2	25.5%	46.9%	27.3%	36.6%
Level 3	53.4%	74.67%	24.2%	42.7%
Level 4	100.0%	100.0%	21.3%	52.4%
Total Vocabulary	13,388	5,442	13,388	5,442

Table 3: The *Coverage Growth* presents ratios of PCT and LCT cumulative vocabularies over their respective total vocabularies. The *Coverage Intersection* presents ratios of intersections of PCT and LCT cumulative vocabularies over their respective total vocabularies.

---

[1] We use the SVM Scikit-learn API (Pedregosa et al., 2011) provided in the NLTK package (Loper and Bird, 2002).

	PCT			LCT			NYCT Samples		
	DC	FRE	FKG	DC	FRE	FKG	DC	FRE	FKG
Level 1	5.43	84.85	3.06	7.08	72.03	5.16	6.69	78.13	2.93
Level 2	7.53	75.17	3.87	6.43	77.14	3.95	8.36	70.21	6.10
Level 3	7.72	71.35	4.65	7.43	65.02	5.03	8.13	68.30	5.93
Level 4	9.02	61.37	6.32	7.24	71.40	4.47	9.68	58.46	7.09

Table 4: Readability scores of all datasets: Palestinian Curriculum Textbooks (PCT), Lane's Course Textbooks (LCT), and New York Curriculum Textbooks (NYCT) samples

In Table 3, we present two sets of results comparing the vocabulary progression at different levels for PCT and LCT – *Coverage Growth* and *Coverage Intersection*.

Coverage Growth   Coverage Growth is defined as the ratio of PCT and LCT cumulative vocabularies over their respective total vocabularies:

$$Coverage\,Growth(PCT) = \frac{|PCT_{1,i}|}{|PCT_{1,4}|} \quad Coverage\,Growth(LCT) = \frac{|LCT_{1,i}|}{|LCT_{1,4}|}$$

Where $PCT_{1,i}$ and $LCT_{1,i}$ represent the cumulative vocabulary for Level 1 up to Level i of PCT and LCT, respectively. The actual counts of total vocabularies are indicated in the last row of Table 3. The difference between PCT and LCT is stark. LCT introduces a relatively bigger portion of the overall vocabulary at Level 1, and maintains a smaller growth rate than PCT. PCT, on the other hand, starts with a relatively small percentage of the vocabulary at Level 1, but maintains a much higher growth rate. This difference in vocabulary growth rates is consistent with the expected vocabulary use in the grammar-based and communicative methods.

Coverage Intersection   *Coverage Intersection* is defined as the ratio of the **intersection** of PCT and LCT cumulative vocabularies over their respective total vocabularies. The Coverage Intersection formula below is for PCT, to calculate the metric for LCT replace the denumerator with the corresponding LCT values.

$$Coverage\,Intersection(PCT) = \frac{|PCT_{1,i} \cap LCT_{1,i}|}{|PCT_{1,4}|}$$

While the total vocabulary of PCT is over twice as large as LCT, the intersection between the two only accounts for half of LCT and one-fifth of PCT. Furthermore, while the intersection ratio of PCT in Level 1 is higher than that for LCT in Level 1, the intersection ratios for PCT drop slowly, while those for LCT grow at a higher rate. These observations indicate that in addition to the difference in vocabulary coverage growth discussed above, the choice of vocabulary is rather different. This is likely to affect how readability algorithms will perform on these two textbook collections.

5.2   Conventional Readability Analysis Algorithms

Table 4 shows the various readability scores (DC, FRE, FKG) of the different textbook sets (PCT, LCT, NYCT) for Levels 1 through 4.

For PCT, the figures indicate that the overall complexity tends to increase with higher levels, as seen with the higher grade values for the DC and FKG, and the decreasing FRE values (indicating less ease, higher complexity). To examine the consistency across the different metrics, we calculated the correlation coefficient R (Pearson) scores for the three pairs. The R value for FKG and DC is 0.93, FKG and FRE is -0.983 and DC and FRE is -0.981. The high R values indicate a significant correlation between the readability scores, and hence show consistency of

Input text (PCT)	Classifier result (LCT)
Grades 1-3	Part 2
Grades 4-6	Part 3
Grades 7-9	Part 1
Grades 10-12	Part 1

Input text (LCT)	Classifier result (PCT)
Part 1	Grade 10 -12
Part 2	Grades 4 - 6
Part 3	Grades 7 - 9
Part 4	Grades 10-12

Table 5: Classifying the texts of each set by the classifier of the other.

Input text (NYCT)	Classifier result (PCT)	Classifier result (LCT)
The Stupid Smelly Bus (2nd grade)	Grades 1 - 3	Part 2
The Giver (6th grade)	Grades 7 - 9	Part 4
A House on Mango Street (8th grade)	Grades 10 - 12	Part 1
Things Fall Apart (12th grade)	Grades 10 - 12	Part 4

Table 6: Classifying the US excerpts (NYCT Samples) by each of the classifiers.

the readability behavior. It is worth noting here is that the negative correlation is the result of the FRE score indicating the ease, rather than the complexity, of the readability.

For LCT, the readability scores show no clear pattern with the course levels they indicate as they progress. Level 1 shows noticeable high scores across all metrics for a beginner's course, for example. FRE, DC and FKG values show clear fluctuations in the overall complexity values they reflect. The fluctuations in all these metrics, however, seem to correlate with each other as shown at the table, indicating that the fluctuating behavior is not a result of bias at certain metrics. The correlation coefficient R scores for the three pairs also show consistency here as well. The R value for FKG and DC is 0.773, FKG and FRE is -0.737 and DC and FRE is -0.92. The high R values indicate a correlation between the readability scores, and hence show consistency of the readability behavior

Finally, for NYCT Samples, the results match the actual grade designation of the texts. This also agrees with the pattern of the L2 school textbooks (PCT) in following an incremental grade growth.

5.3 Domain-Specific Readability: Machine Learning Classification

Table 5 presents the results for the text of each level of each collection (PCT or LCT) as an input to the classifier trained on the other textbook collection (LCT or PCT, respectively). The results for LCT show that the tags do not follow a clear readability progression pattern. The results for PCT, on the other hand, fit the original grade progression pattern of the educational system well.

Table 6 shows the results for classifying the NYCT Samples by both classifiers. The results show a more structured readability progression pattern for the PCT classifier, similar to the patterns we have seen before for this set. The results for LCT classifier, however, do not follow the original levels progression of the NYCT Samples. This indicates no clear pattern of the readability progression of LCT, as seen for the previous results. Finally, the NYCT Samples have higher readability levels than both PCT and LCT, which matches the intuition of studying English as an L1 versus L2 language.

5.4 Discussion

The major observation throughout the different experiments conducted in this paper indicate that LCT, as an example of an ESL textbook using the communicative-based teaching method, shows lack of coherent readability/complexity progression with the various teaching levels. PCT, on the other hand, used as an example of the grammar-based teaching method, showed a clear complexity progression with increasing grades. More samples of both approaches need to be analyzed before making a generalization, but this should serve as a cue. Moreover, results indicate that the complexity of both sets is relatively lower than that of the US text samples, as an L1. The lack/presence of the progression structure may indicate higher/lower dependency on the textbooks themselves in the learning process, where the lack of structure in LCT might potentially be compensated by more effort from the teacher's side. The domain-specific readability classifier, implemented using machine learning approaches, served well in supporting the vocabulary progression claim also by showing clear progression complexity for the PCT classifier when classifying the NYCT texts, compared to the LCT classifier.

6 Conclusions and Future Work

We presented a computational approach for analyzing ESL teaching methods. We did so by performing readability progression analysis on textbooks following two different methods (grammar-based and communicative). Our experiments indicated that the grammar-based curriculum showed a more coherent readability progression compared to the communicative curriculum. This finding corroborates with the expectations about the differences between these two methods and validates our approach's value in comparing different teaching methods quantitatively.

Future work includes analyzing more textbooks that follow each of the covered teaching methods, along with other methods. It will also be interesting to consider L2 language teaching for varied L1 languages. The two curricula we studied were differently paced. It will also be interesting to consider other curricula targeting different initial age-groups and with different planned durations. Finally, we will extend the classifier to be able to classify other texts to the most relevant teaching method and level, which may be of great value to education research.

Acknowledgement

We would like to thank the Palestinian Ministry of Education and Higher Education for providing us with the Palestinian English curriculum textbooks.

References

John PB Allen and Henry G Widdowson. 1974. Teaching the communicative use of english. *IRAL-International Review of Applied Linguistics in Language Teaching*, 12(1-4):1–22.

Rebekah George Benjamin. 2011. Reconstructing readability: Recent developments and recommendations in the analysis of text difficulty. *Educational Psychology Review*, 24(1):63–88.

Kevyn Collins-Thompson. 2014. Computational assessment of text readability: A survey of current and future research. *ITL-International Journal of Applied Linguistics*, 165(2):97–135.

Scott A Crossley, David F Dufty, Philip M McCarthy, and Danielle S McNamara. 2007. Toward a new readability: A mixed model approach. In *Proceedings of the 29th annual conference of the Cognitive Science Society*, pages 197–202.

Edgar Dale and Jeanne S Chall. 1948. A formula for predicting readability: Instructions. *Educational research bulletin*, pages 37–54.

Marie-Catherine De Marneffe, Bill MacCartney, Christopher D Manning, et al. 2006. Generating typed dependency parses from phrase structure parses. In *Proceedings of LREC*, volume 6, pages 449–454.

William H DuBay. 2008. Unlocking language: The classic readability studies. *IEEE Transactions on Professional Communication*, 4(51):416–417.

Lijun Feng, Martin Jansche, Matt Huenerfauth, and Noémie Elhadad. 2010. A comparison of features for automatic readability assessment. In *Proceedings of the 23rd International Conference on Computational Linguistics: Posters*, pages 276–284. Association for Computational Linguistics.

Rudolf Franz Flesch et al. 1949. Art of readable writing.

Thomas Francois and Eleni Miltsakaki, 2012. *Do NLP and machine learning improve traditional readability formulas?*, pages 49–57. Association for Computational Linguistics.

Michael Heilman, Kevyn Collins-Thompson, and Maxine Eskenazi. 2008. An analysis of statistical models and features for reading difficulty prediction. In *Proceedings of the Third Workshop on Innovative Use of NLP for Building Educational Applications*, pages 71–79. Association for Computational Linguistics.

J Peter Kincaid, Robert P Fishburne Jr, Richard L Rogers, and Brad S Chissom. 1975. Derivation of new readability formulas (automated readability index, fog count and flesch reading ease formula) for navy enlisted personnel. Technical report, DTIC Document.

Richard R Lane. 1978. *English as a second language*. EIC.

Edward Loper and Steven Bird. 2002. Nltk: The natural language toolkit. In *Proceedings of the ACL-02 Workshop on Effective Tools and Methodologies for Teaching Natural Language Processing and Computational Linguistics - Volume 1*, ETMTNLP '02, pages 63–70, Stroudsburg, PA, USA. Association for Computational Linguistics.

Fabian Pedregosa, Gaël Varoquaux, Alexandre Gramfort, Vincent Michel, Bertrand Thirion, Olivier Grisel, Mathieu Blondel, Peter Prettenhofer, Ron Weiss, Vincent Dubourg, Jake Vanderplas, Alexandre Passos, David Cournapeau, Matthieu Brucher, Matthieu Perrot, and Édouard Duchesnay. 2011. Scikit-learn: Machine learning in python. *J. Mach. Learn. Res.*, 12:2825–2830, November.

Sarah E Petersen and Mari Ostendorf. 2009. A machine learning approach to reading level assessment. *Computer speech & language*, 23(1):89–106.

Ildikó Pilán, Elena Volodina, and Richard Johansson. 2014. Rule-based and machine learning approaches for second language sentence-level readability. In *Proceedings of the Ninth Workshop on Innovative Use of NLP for Building Educational Applications*, pages 174–184.

Ildikó Pilán, Sowmya Vajjala, and Elena Volodina. 2016. A readable read: Automatic assessment of language learning materials based on linguistic complexity. *arXiv preprint arXiv:1603.08868*.

Janice Redish. 2000. Readability formulas have even more limitations than klare discusses. *ACM Journal of Computer Documentation*, (3):132–137.

Jack C Richards and Willy A Renandya. 2002. *Methodology in language teaching: An anthology of current practice*. Cambridge university press.

Lixiao Zhang, Zaiying Liu, and Jun Ni. 2013. Feature-based assessment of text readability. In *2013 Seventh International Conference on Internet Computing for Engineering and Science*, pages 51–54. IEEE.

Generating and Scoring Correction Candidates in Chinese Grammatical Error Diagnosis

Shao-Heng Chen, Yu-Lin Tsai, and Chuan-Jie Lin
Department of Computer Science and Engineering
National Taiwan Ocean University
No 2, Pei-Ning Road, Keelung, Taiwan ROC
{shchen.cse, yltsai.cse, cjlin}@ntou.edu.tw

Abstract

Grammatical error diagnosis is an essential part in a language-learning tutoring system. Based on the data sets of Chinese grammar error detection tasks, we proposed a system which measures the likelihood of correction candidates generated by deleting or inserting characters or words, moving substrings to different positions, substituting prepositions with other prepositions, or substituting words with their synonyms or similar strings. Sentence likelihood is measured based on the frequencies of substrings from the space-removed version of Google n-grams. The evaluation on the training set shows that Missing-related and Selection-related candidate generation methods have promising performance. Our final system achieved a precision of 30.28% and a recall of 62.85% in the identification level evaluated on the test set.

1   Introduction

Although that Chinese grammars are not defined as clearly as English, Chinese native speakers can easily identify grammatical errors in sentences. This is one of the most difficult parts for foreigners to learn Chinese. They are often uncertain about the proper grammars to make sentences. It is an interesting research topic to develop a Chinese grammar checker to give helps in Chinese learning. There have been several researches focusing on Chinese (Wu *et al.*, 2010; Chang *et al.*, 2012; Yu and Chen, 2012; Lee *et al.*, 2014).

There are 3 evaluation tasks focusing on Chinese grammatical error diagnosis. CGED 2014 (Yu *et al.*, 2014) defined four kinds of grammatical errors: redundant, missing, selection, and disorder. At most one error occurred in one sentence. The evaluation was based on error detection and error classification in sentence level. CGED 2015 (Lee *et al.*, 2015) further required the positions of the errors. CGED 2016 tested on the ability of finding multiple errors in one sentence.

This paper is organized as follows. Section 2 describes Chinese grammatical error diagnosis task. Section 3 defines the sentence likelihood scoring function. Section 4 explains how correction candidates are generated for different error types. Section 5 clarifies the details of decision making. Section 6 shows the evaluation results and Section 7 concludes this paper.

2   Task Definition

The task of Chinese grammatical error diagnosis (CGED) is defined as follows. Given a sentence, a CGED system should first decide if there is any error occurring in the sentence. If so, report its error type, starting and ending positions.

Errors are divided into four types: redundant, missing, selection, and disorder, which are shortly explained here. All examples are selected from CGED-2015 training set.

Proceedings of the 3rd Workshop on Natural Language Processing Techniques for Educational Applications,
pages 131–139, Osaka, Japan, December 12 2016.

- Redundant: some unnecessary character appears in a sentence

    [A2-0598, Redundant, 3, 3]
    (X) 他是真很好的人 (*He is a really very good man.)
    (O) 他是很好的人　　(He is a very good man.)

- Missing: some necessary character is missing in a sentence

    [B1-0046, Missing, 4, 4]
    (X) 母親節一個禮拜就要到了　　(*Mother's Day is coming in one week.)
    (O) 母親節再一個禮拜就要到了　　(Mother's Day is coming in one more week.)

- Selection: a word is misused and should be replaced by another word

    [B1-1544, Selection, 1, 2]
    (X) 還給原來的地方只花幾秒鐘而已
        (*It only takes a few seconds to return it to its original place.)
    (O) 放回原來的地方只花幾秒鐘而已
        (It only takes a few seconds to put it back to its original place.)

  Note that sometimes a SELECTION error looks like a missing or redundant case rather than a misused word. It is because there are many one-character words in Chinese. An example is given as follows.

    [B1-1546, Selection, 5, 5]
    (X) 關於跟你見的事　　(*About the seeing with you...)
    (O) 關於跟你見面的事　(About the meeting with you...)

- Disorder: some words' locations should be changed

    [B1-2099, Disorder, 4, 6]
    (X) 當然我會一定開心　(*Of course I will be certainly happy.)
    (O) 當然我一定會開心　(Of course I will certainly be happy.)

CGED systems were evaluated in 3 levels: detection level for whether each sentence has errors; identification level for what type the error is; and position level for where the error appears (in terms of Chinese characters). Evaluation metrics are well-known accuracy, precision, recall, and F-measure.

3 Sentence Likelihood Scoring

The systems proposed in this paper were based on our previous work of (Lin and Chen, 2015). Our contributions include proposing candidate generation for Selection-type errors (described in Section 4), and observing the effects of factors in the candidate generation methods and sentence scoring functions. We also examined how to propose multiple errors in a given sentence so that our system can be evaluated on the CGED 2016 test set.

In our previous work (Lin and Chen, 2015), we have defined a sentence likelihood scoring function to measure the likelihood of a sentence to be common and correct. This function uses frequencies provided in the Chinese Web 5-gram dataset in a way described as follows.

Chinese Web 5-gram[1] consists of real data released by Google Inc. which were collected from a large amount of webpages in the World Wide Web. Entries in the dataset are unigrams to 5-grams. Frequencies of these n-grams are also provided. Some examples from the Chinese Web 5-gram dataset are given in the left part of Table 1.

In order to avoid interference of word segmentation errors, we decided to use substrings instead of word n-grams as the scoring units of likelihood. When scoring a sentence, frequencies of all substrings in all lengths are used to measure the likelihood.

---

[1] https://catalog.ldc.upenn.edu/LDC2010T06

Gram	Text	Freq	Length	Text	Freq
Unigram	稀釋劑	17260	9	稀釋劑	17260
Bigram	蒸發量 超過	69	15	蒸發量超過	69
Trigram	能量 遠 低於	113	15	能量遠低於	113
4-gram	張貼 色情 圖片 或	73	18	張貼色情圖片或	73
5-gram	幸好 我們 發現 得 早	155	24	幸好我們發現得早	155

Table 1. Examples of Google N-grams (before and after Space Removal)

Frequencies of substrings are derived by removing space between n-grams in the Chinese Web 5-gram dataset. For instances, n-grams in the left part of Table 1 will become the strings in the right part, where length of a substring is measured in bytes and a Chinese character often occupies 3 bytes in UTF-8 encoding. Note that if two or more different n-grams are transformed into the same substring after removing the space, they become one entry and its new frequency is the summation of their original frequencies. Simplified Chinese words were translated into Traditional Chinese in advanced.

Some notations are explained as follows. Given a sentence S, let $SubStr(S, n)$ be the set of all substrings in S whose lengths are n bytes, and **Google String Frequency** $gsf(u)$ be the frequency of a string u in the modified Chinese Web 5-gram dataset. If a string does not appear in that dataset, its gsf value is defined to be 1 (so that its logarithm becomes 0).

Equation 1 gives the equation of *length-weighted string log-frequency score* $SL(S)$. Each substring u in S contributes a score of the logarithm of its Google string frequency weighted by u's length n. The value of n starts from 6, because most content words are not shorter than 6 bytes (i.e. two Chinese characters).

$$SL(S) = \sum_{n=6}^{len(S)} \left(n \times \sum_{u \in SubStr(S,n)} \log(gsf(u)) \right) \qquad \text{Eq 1.}$$

This function was also explained in the work of Lin and Chu (2015). Please refer to that paper for examples of how to compute the sentence generation likelihood scores.

4 Correction Candidate Generation

4.1 Character or Word Deletion (Case of Redundant)

Generating correction candidates in the case of Redundant type is quite straightforward: simply removing any substring in an arbitrary length. However, in order not to generate too many unnecessary candidates, we only do the removal under three special cases: removing one character, removing two-adjacent characters, and removing one word whose length is no longer than two Chinese characters. The examples are as follows, where org is the original sentence and new is a correction candidate.

[B1-0764] org: 我 很 想到 跟 你 見面

(By removing characters)
new: 很想到跟你見面 (*by removing* 我)
new: 我想到跟你見面 (*by removing* 很)

......
new: 我很想到跟你見 (*by removing* 面)
new: 想到跟你見面 (*by removing* 我很)
new: 我到跟你見面 (*by removing* 很想)

......
new: 我很想到跟你 (*by removing* 見面)
(By removing one word)
new: 很想到跟你見面 (*by removing* 我)
new: 我想到跟你見面 (*by removing* 很)
new: 我很跟你見面 (*by removing* 想到)
......
new: 我很想到跟你 (*by removing* 見面)

Given a sentence with n characters constituting m words (whose lengths are not longer than 2 Chinese characters), removing one character will generate n candidates, removing two adjacent characters will generate $n-1$ candidates, and removing one word will generate m candidates.

Obviously all candidates generated by removing one word were also generated by other two methods. We would like to see the efficiency of each method in terms of accuracy and the size of candidate set.

4.2   Character Insertion (Case of Missing)

The idea of generating correction candidates in the case of Missing type is to insert a character or a word into the given sentence. But it is impractical to enumerate candidates by inserting every known Chinese characters or words. We observed the CGED 2015 training set (Lin and Chen, 2015) and collected 34 characters which were commonly missing in the essays written by Chinese-learning foreign students. Table 2 shows some of these frequent missing characters in the training data. These 34 characters occurred at least three times and covered 73.7% of the missing errors in the CGED 2015 training set.

Char	Freq	Char	Freq	Char	Freq
的	74	有	24	要	13
了	65	會	18	在	12
是	44	就	17	過	12
都	34	很	16	讓	11

Table 2. Examples of Frequent Missing Characters

Insertion happens between characters or words as usual. Examples of insertion between characters are as follows.

[B1-0764] org: 我 很 想到 跟 你 見面
(*By inserting between characters*)
new: 的我很想到跟你見面 (*by inserting* 的 *before* 我)
new: 我的很想到跟你見面 (*by inserting* 的 *between* 我 *and* 很)
......
new: 我很想到跟你見面的 (*by inserting* 的 *after* 面)
new: 了我很想到跟你見面 (*by inserting* 了 *before* 我)
......
new: 我很想到跟你見面買 (*by inserting* 買 *after* 面)

Given a sentence with n characters constituting m words in total, insertion between characters will generate $34 \times (n+1)$ candidates and insertion between words will generate $34 \times (m+1)$ candidates.

4.3   Substring Moving (Case of Disorder)

Generating correction candidates in the case of Disorder type is also straightforward: simply moving any substring in any length to another position to its right (not to its left so that no duplication will be produced). Examples of substring moving are as follows.

[B1-0764] org: 我 很 想到 跟 你 見面
(*By moving a substring to a new position between characters*)
new: 很我想到跟你見面   (*by moving* 我 *to the position between* 很 *and* 想)
new: 很想我到跟你見面   (*by moving* 我 *to the position between* 想 *and* 到)
......
new: 很想到跟你見面我   (*by moving* 我 *to the position after* 面)
new: 想我很到跟你見面   (*by moving* 我很 *to the position between* 想 *and* 到)
......
new: 面我很想到跟你見   (*by moving* 我很想到跟你見 *to the position after* 面)

Given a sentence with n characters, there are $(n-k)$ substrings whose lengths are k ($1 \le k \le n-1$). A substring with lengths k at the position t ($1 \le t \le n-k+1$) can be moved to $(n-k-t+1)$ new positions. By summing on all k and t, there will be $(n^3-n)/6$ candidates by moving substrings to positions between characters. Similarly, there will be $(m^3-m)/6$ candidates by moving substrings to positions between words for a sentence with m words. The number will grow fast if the given sentence is long.

4.4   Preposition Substitution (Case 1 of Selection)

In our observation, some selection errors are misuse of prepositions. But unlike the case in English, it is not the most major errors in selection type.

To generate the correction candidates for preposition substitutions, we first extracted all prepositions in the Academia Sinica Balanced Corpus (ASBC for short hereafter, cf. Chen *et al.*, 1996). An input sentence is word-segmented and POS-tagged automatically before hand. Correction candidates are generated by replacing each preposition (whose POS is "P") in the given sentence by other prepositions. Examples of preposition substitution are as follows, where only the word "跟" (with) is a preposition.

[B1-0764] org: 我 很 想到 跟(P) 你 見面
(By moving a substring to a new position between characters)
new: 我很想到在你見面　　*(by replacing 跟 by 在)*
new: 我很想到為你見面　　*(by replacing 跟 by 為)*
......

There are 243 prepositions in ASBC. Given a sentence containing k prepositions, $243 \times k$ correction candidates will be generated.

4.5   Synonym Substitution (Case 2 of Selection)

In our observation, another type of selection errors is misuse of words which are synonyms. As we known, even synonyms cannot freely replace each other without considering context.

To generate the correction candidates for synonym substitutions, we consulted a Chinese thesaurus, Tongyici Cilin[2] (the extended version; Cilin for short hereafter). A given sentence is word-segmented before hand. Correction candidates are generated by replacing each word in the given sentence by its synonyms in Cilin if any. Examples of synonym substitution are as follows.

[B1-0764] org: 我 很 想到 跟 你 見面
(By moving a substring to a new position between characters)
new: 我很悟出跟你見面　　*(by replacing 想到 by its synonym 悟出)*
new: 我很想開跟你見面　　*(by replacing 想到 by its synonym 想開)*
......
new: 我很想到跟你相會　　*(by replacing 見面 by its synonym 相會)*

The number of candidates depends on the number of Cilin terms and their synonyms in a given sentence. Generally the number is not too large.

4.6   Similar String Substitution (Case 3 of Selection)

In our observation, we found a special type of selection errors that the misusing words were lexically similar to the correct ones. It should be the case when the writer tried to use a word but misused another word with similar looking, such as "仔細" (carefully) and "細節" (details).

To generate but not over-generate the correction candidates for similar string substitutions, we first collected all 2-character words in ASBC and Cilin. Correction candidates are generated by replacing each 2-character word in the given sentence by another 2-character word having at least one character in common, such as "仔細" and "細節" where "細" appears in both words, or "合適" (suitable, *adjective*) and "適合" (suiting, *verb*) where both characters appear in both words. Examples of similar string substitution are given in the next page.

The number of candidates depends on the number of 2-character words and their similar words in a given sentence. Generally the number is not small.

---

[2] http://ir.hit.edu.cn/
　http://www.ltp-cloud.com/

[B1-0764] org: 我 很 想到 跟 你 見面
(*By moving a substring to a new position between characters*)
new: 我很想出跟你見面　　(by replacing 想到 by a similar string 想出)
new: 我很思想跟你見面　　(by replacing 想到 by a similar string 思想)

......

new: 我很想到跟你面向　　(by replacing 見面 by a similar string 面向)

5　Error Detection and Classification

5.1　Error Decision

All correction candidates, as well as the original sentence, are scored by the sentence likelihood function in Eq 1. They are ranked according to their likelihood scores. If the top-1 sentence is the original sentence, report it as a "Correct" case. Otherwise, output the first top 2 candidates as errors by reporting their corresponding error types and occurring positions. If the top-2 candidate conflicts with the top-1 candidate in position (i.e. they are overlapped), discard it and take the next candidate until 2 errors are reported or the rank of the original sentence is reached. Moreover, if more than 2 candidates have the same scores, report them all (if no position confliction).

The choice of 2 is based on the average errors appearing in a sentence in the CGED 2016 training set, which are 1.314 errors in one sentence. To increase recall, we decide to propose 2 errors for each sentence. We have also done an observation by propose only 1 error for one sentence. We found that the precision was not improved but the recall was greatly harmed.

5.2　Selection Error Classification Fixing

For a correction candidate of the Redundant type, if the deleted character appears in a multi-character word in the original sentence, it should be a Selection-type error. An example is given as follows.

[B1-0764] Redundant => Selection
(X)　　我 很 想到 跟 你 見面　　(*I really want to to meet you.)
(O)　　我 很 想 跟 你 見面　　(I really want to meet you.)

In this example, the deleted character "到" appears in a 2-character word "想到" in the original sentence. This error will be classified into Selection type because the word "想到" (think-of) should be corrected into "想" (want). Our system will check the word boundary in the original sentence to fix this error type classification.

Similarly for a correction candidate of the Missing type, if the inserted character appears in a multi-character word in the new sentence, it should be a Selection-type error. An example is given as follows.

[B1-1047] Missing => Selection
(X)　　我 真 很 怕　　(*I am real scared.)
(O)　　我 真的 很 怕　　(I am really scared.)

In this example, the inserted character "的" appears in a 2-character word "真的" in the new sentence. This error will be classified into Selection type because the word "真" (real) should be corrected into "真的" (really). Our system will check the word boundary in the new sentence to fix this error type classification.

6　Experiments

6.1　Evaluating of Correction Candidates in Individual Methods

Table 3 shows the evaluation results when each candidate generation method is used individually. These methods were evaluated on the whole CGED 2016 training set. The names in the "Method" column represent the following candidate generation methods:

- RDN_char: deleting one character
- RDN_2char: deleting two adjacent characters
- RDN_word: deleting one word
- MIS_char: inserting frequent missing characters between characters
- MIS_word: inserting frequent missing characters between words
- WDO_char: moving substrings based on characters
- WDO_word: moving substrings based on words
- SEL_P: substituting prepositions
- SEL_CLN: substituting with synonyms in Cilin
- SEL_SIM: substituting with similar 2-character words
- SEL_R1C: fixed Selection type from RDN_char cases
- SEL_R2C: fixed Selection type from RDN_2char cases
- SEL_M1C: fixed Selection type from MIS_char cases
- SEL_M1W: fixed Selection type from MIS_word cases

Method	#Cands	P	R	F1	Method	#Cands	P	R	F1
RDN_char	433613	13.72	3.03	4.97	SEL_P	6433812	10.03	9.88	9.95
RDN_2char	390096	6.92	0.40	0.75	SEL_CLN	10862488	8.22	25.68	12.46
RDN_word	281069	13.62	3.21	5.20	SEL_SIM	49465905	5.00	9.67	6.60
MIS_char	16215314	6.48	15.56	9.15	SEL_R1C	(206825)	8.03	0.13	0.26
MIS_word	11337266	6.54	15.41	9.18	SEL_R2C	(140564)	0.60	0.01	0.02
WDO_char	14247107	1.47	2.16	1.75	SEL_M1C	(152175)	8.28	14.49	10.53
WDO_word	4278827	1.36	1.91	1.59	SEL_M1W	(151986)	8.33	14.47	10.58

Table 3. Evaluation Results of Individual Candidate Generation Methods

In Table 3, the "#Cands" columns show the number of correction candidates generated by different methods. Note that the numbers of candidates of the fixed Selection types are included in the Redundant and Missing sets. Moreover, only those candidates whose scores are higher than the original sentences can have the chance to fix their error types. P, R, and F1 stand for precision, recall, and F1 measure, respectively. All evaluations were done in position level (cf. Section 2).

As we can see in Table 3, Selection-related methods achieved better performance. Maybe it is because Selection is the major error type in the dataset. The missing-related methods achieved good recalls while the Redundant-related methods achieved good precisions, but recall dominates the experimental results in this observation. The missing-related methods also provided many correct candidates for Selection type.

The Disorder-related methods were surprisingly poor. Although a correct answer in this type could be generated, too many incorrect candidates were also generated and lowered the rank of the correct candidate. The performance of RDN_2char was also poor. We will discard these two methods in the final system.

6.2 Evaluating of Correction Candidates by All Methods on the Training Data

We have tried every combination of generation methods and evaluated their performances when proposing top-2 candidates. Table 4 shows the performance of the best system and its comparisons evaluated in position level. P, R, and F1 stand for precision, recall, and F1 measure, respectively.

The best system used only Missing-related and Selection-related candidate generation methods. By comparing S2 with S1, adding candidates from Redundant-related method did not affect the performance at all. But by removing Missing-related candidates (S3 and S4), the performance would drop in a certain degree.

To see the effect of 3 different Selection-related methods, each method was discarded from the best system. As we can see, synonym substitution was the best because its absence (S6) decreased the performance the most.

However, if we chose the best system as our final system, we would never be able to capture the Redundant-type and Disorder-type errors. We still used them in the final systems.

#	Systems	P	R	F
S1	MIS_char, SEL_M1C, SEL_M1W, SEL_P, SEL_CLN, SEL_SIM	9.11	30.95	14.08
S2	MIS_char, SEL_M1C, SEL_M1W, SEL_P, SEL_CLN, SEL_SIM, RDN_char	9.11	30.95	14.08
S3	MIS_char, SEL_P, SEL_CLN, SEL_SIM	8.64	29.03	13.32
S4	SEL_P, SEL_CLN, SEL_SIM	8.40	27.53	12.87
S5	MIS_char, SEL_M1C, SEL_M1W, SEL_CLN, SEL_SIM	8.91	30.26	13.76
S6	MIS_char, SEL_M1C, SEL_M1W, SEL_P, SEL_SIM	7.66	23.05	11.50
S7	MIS_char, SEL_M1C, SEL_M1W, SEL_P, SEL_CLN	9.07	30.81	14.02

Table 4. Evaluation Results of Overall Systems on the Training Data

	Detection Level			Identification Level			Position Level		
	P	R	F	P	R	F	P	R	F
S8	51.73	100.00	68.19	30.28	62.17	40.73	2.03	13.55	3.53
S9	51.73	100.00	68.19	29.78	62.85	40.41	2.02	13.50	3.52

Table 5. Evaluation Results of Final Systems on the Test Data

6.3   Evaluating on the Test Data

Two final systems S8 and S9 were evaluated on the CGED 2016 test set. Table 5 shows the evaluation results. The definitions of S8 and S9 are as follows:

- S8: RDN_char, RDN_word, MIS_char, SEL_*
- S9: RDN_char, RDN_word, MIS_char, SEL_*, WDO_word

As we can see in Table 5, the two systems have similar performance. It means that the candidates from Missing-related and Selection-related methods dominate the systems. But the system with the Disorder-related method WDO_word is a little worse than the system without using it, which is consistent to our previous observation.

7   Conclusion

This paper describes the design of our Chinese grammatical error diagnosis system. Correction candidates corresponding to 4 error types are first generated. The sentence likelihood scores of these candidates are measured based on web frequencies provided in the space-removed version of Google n-grams. Top-2 candidates are reported as errors.

Redundant correction candidates are generated by deleting characters or words; Missing candidates are generated by inserting frequently missed characters into position between characters or words; Disorder candidates are generated by moving sequences of characters or words to different positions; Selection candidates are generated by substituting prepositions with other prepositions and substituting words with their synonyms in Tongyici Cilin.

The best system uses the candidates generated for Missing and Selection types. Adding candidates for Redundant type does not affect the performance, but adding candidates for Disorder type harms the performance.

When evaluating on CGED 2016 test set, our final system achieved a precision of 30.28% and a recall of 62.85% in the identification level, which is better than our system in 2015. The final system proposed in this paper used candidates for Redundant, Missing, and Selection types.

The performance looks not good enough, which means that the task is very hard. We need to find out the reason why Redundant and Disorder candidates cannot improve the performance. More rules or features should be discovered in the future.

Acknowledgement

This research was funded by the Taiwan Ministry of Science and Technology (grant MOST 105-2221-E-019-071-).

Reference

Ru-Yng Chang, Chung-Hsien Wu, and Philips Kokoh Prasetyo (2012) "Error Diagnosis of Chinese Sentences Using Inductive Learning Algorithm and Decomposition-Based Testing Mechanism," *ACM Transactions on Asian Language Information Processing*, Vol. 11, No. 1, article 3.

Keh-Jiann Chen, Chu-Ren Huang, Li-ping Chang, and Hui-Li Hsu (1996) "Sinica Corpus: Design Methodology for Balanced Corpora," *Proceeding of the 11th Pacific Asia Conference on Language, Information and Computation*, pp. 167-176.

Lung-Hao Lee, Liang-Chih Yu, Kuei-Ching Lee, Yuen-Hsien Tseng, Li-Ping Chang, and Hsin-Hsi Chen (2014) "A Sentence Judgment System for Grammatical Error Detection," *Proceedings of the 25th International Conference on Computational Linguistics (COLING '14)*, pp. 67-70.

Lung-Hao Lee, Liang-Chih Yu, and Li-Ping Chang (2015) "Overview of the NLP-TEA 2015 Shared Task for Chinese Grammatical Error Diagnosis," *Proceedings of The 2nd Workshop on Natural Language Processing Techniques for Educational Applications (NLP-TEA 2), the 53rd Annual Meeting of the Association for Computational Linguistics and the 7th International Joint Conference on Natural Language Processing of the Asian Federation of Natural Language Processing (ACL-IJCNLP 2015)*, pp. 1-6.

Chuan-Jie Lin and Shao-Heng Chen (2015) "NTOU Chinese Grammar Checker for CGED Shared Task," *Proceedings of The 2nd Workshop on Natural Language Processing Techniques for Educational Applications (NLP-TEA 2), the 53rd Annual Meeting of the Association for Computational Linguistics and the 7th International Joint Conference on Natural Language Processing of the Asian Federation of Natural Language Processing (ACL-IJCNLP 2015)*, pp. 15-19.

Chuan-Jie Lin and Wei-Cheng Chu (2015) "A Study on Chinese Spelling Check Using Confusion Sets and N-gram Statistics," *International Journal of Computational Linguistics and Chinese Language Processing (IJCLCLP)*, Vol. 20, No. 1, pp. 23-48.

Chung-Hsien Wu, Chao-Hong Liu, Matthew Harris, and Liang-Chih Yu (2010) "Sentence Correction Incorporating Relative Position and Parse Template Language Models," *IEEE Transactions on Audio, Speech, and Language Processing*, Vol. 18, No. 6, pp. 1170-1181.

Chi-Hsin Yu and Hsin-Hsi Chen (2012) "Detecting Word Ordering Errors in Chinese Sentences for Learning Chinese as a Foreign Language," *Proceedings of the 24th International Conference on Computational Linguistics (COLING '12)*, pp. 3003-3017.

Liang-Chih Yu, Lung-Hao Lee, and Li-Ping Chang (2014) "Overview of Grammatical Error Diagnosis for Learning Chinese as a Foreign Language," *Proceedings of the 1st Workshop on Natural Language Processing Techniques for Educational Applications (NLPTEA '14)*, pp. 42-47.

Grammatical Error Detection Based on Machine Learning for Mandarin as Second Language Learning

Jui-Feng Yeh*
Department of Computer and
information Science
National Chia-Yi University
Chiayi, Taiwan (R.O.C.)
raiph@mail.ncyu.edu.tw

Tsung-Wei Hsu
Department of Computer and
information Science
National Chia-Yi University
Chiayi, Taiwan (R.O.C.)
s1050480@mail.ncyu.edu.tw

Chan-Kun Yeh
Department of Computer and
information Science
National Chia-Yi University
Chiayi, Taiwan (R.O.C.)
s1030484@mail.ncyu.edu.tw

Abstract

Mandarin is not simple language for foreigner. Even using Mandarin as the mother tongue, they have to spend more time to learn when they were child. The following issues are the reason why causes learning problem. First, the word is envolved by Hieroglyphic. So a character can express meanings independently, but become a word has another semantic. Second, the Mandarin's grammars have flexible rule and special usage. Therefore, the common grammatical errors can classify to missing, redundant, selection and disorder. In this paper, we proposed the structure of the Recurrent Neural Networks using Long Short-term memory (RNN-LSTM). It can detect the error type from the foreign learner writing. The features based on the word vector and part-of-speech vector. In the test data found that our method in the detection level of recall better than the others, even as high as 0.9755. That is because we give the possibility of greater choice in detecting errors.

1   Introduction

In recent years, the rapid development of communication between countries. Especially the Chinese region, more and more foreign people came to traveling or working. So the Mandarin become the option as second language learner. But it is not easy to learn because its grammars are very complexity.

To research Mandarin as second language, we can distinguish two parts: word level and sentence level. In word level, there have two main aspects are Word Segmentation and Part-of-Speech (POS) Tagging. We want to segment the sentence to the basic semantic units and give the correct tagging. About the research of word segmentation and POS tagging, (Ye, J. et al., 2011) the authors proposed using the prefix and suffix query of Chinese word segmentation algorithm for maximum matching. This structure can choose the best structure of words as the dictionary. (Li, Zhenghua et al., 2014) the authors proposed joint algorithm to optimize the POS tagging and dependency parsing. They use the parsing tree to find the relationship between words and sentence. (Ma, Wei-Yun and Chen, Keh-Jiann, 2005) the authors proposed the system to word segmentation and POS tagging about Chinese. They define the 47 class of POS in Chinese and this system is now using in Taiwan Academia Sinica. And we employ this POS classification in our research.

In the word level, the Chinese common grammar error can classify the four parts: Missing, Redundant, Selection, Disorder (see example in Table 1). In the grammar and word order, (Xiao Sun and Xiaoli Nan, 2010) proposed using latent semi-CRF model on the Chinese phrase classifications. (Jinjin Zhu and Yangsen Zhang, 2010) the authors proposed auto-detect the Chinese errors by using hybrid algorithm. They are looking for word, syntax and semantic. (B. Zhang et al., 2010) the authors proposed extracting opinion sentence by SVM and syntax template. Then in the grammar error detection, (H. H. Feng et al., 2016) the authors proposed Automated Error Detection of ESL (English as a Second Language) Learners. And (Chung-Hsien Wu et al., 2010) the authors proposed sentence correction incorporating relative position and parse template language models. They are looking for the English errors. Then in Chinese error detection, (Lung-Hao Lee et al., 2013) proposed the linguistic rules of Chinese error detection for CFL (Chinese as a For-

Proceedings of the 3rd Workshop on Natural Language Processing Techniques for Educational Applications,
pages 140–147, Osaka, Japan, December 12 2016.

eign Language). And (Chi-Hsin Yu et al., 2012) the authors proposed detect the errors of word order by training the HSK corpus. The HSK corpus is simplified Chinese data. Then (Shuk-Man Cheng et al., 2014) they also using HSK corpus to proposed word ordering errors detection and correction by SVM to ranking the optimal sentences.

Table 1: Common grammatical error type

Grammatical error types	Examples of erroneous sentences	Examples of correct sentences
漏字錯誤(Missing)	我送你家 (I take you home.)	我送你回家
冗詞錯誤(Redundant)	他是我**的**最重要的朋友 (He is my important friend.)	他是我最重要的朋友
詞彙誤用(Selection)	我是騎腳踏車的**拿手**	我是騎腳踏車的**好手**
語序運用不當(Disorder)	我**去學校早上** (I go to school in the morning.)	我**早上去學校**

In our research, we proposed the architecture for grammatical error detection by recurrent neural network using long-short term memory (RNN-LSTM) as a second language learner. We use this architecture to generate the language model and error rule patterns are made based on parsing tree.

2   Method

In this section, The processing flow is illustrated here. There are distinguish two phases: training phase and testing phase. In training phase, we were doing word segmentation and part-of-speech (POS) by CKIP (Chinese Knowledge and Information Processing) Autotag. Then classify words to several class and transform the sentence to the word vector. We will explain how to classify words in section 2.1. And we will describe how to generate the language model by RNN-LSTM in the section 2.2. Final, we show some parsing tree examples to explain the error pattern model in the section 2.3. In section 2.4, we explain the testing phase in our system how to detect the grammatical error.

2.1 Word Clustering

How to express the meaning of a word in the computer? In traditional methods, we could research the semantic dictionary. Such as WordNet for English or E-HowNet for Chinese. They have to spend a lot of time to tagging by people.

In our method to clustering word is based on probability from (Franz J. O., 1999) proposed model. $P(w_1^N)$ represent a sentence sequence. $w_1^N = w_1 \ldots w_N$ represent the set of the words. The probability of the context of words in sentence is

$$P(w_1^N) = \prod_{t=1}^{N} p(w_t \mid w_{t-1}) \tag{1}$$

We made the close probability of the words to C classes. So we can represent the relationship of sentence correspond to classes:

$$P(w_1^N \mid C) = \prod_{t=1}^{N} p(w_t \mid C(w_t)) \cdot p(C(w_t) \mid C(w_{t-1})) \tag{2}$$

Where $P(w_t | C(w_t))$ represent the relationship of words correspond to classes. $P(C(w_t) | C(w_{t-1}))$ represent the relationship of context of classes.

Then choose the best classification from all class. It can represent by

$$\hat{C} = \underset{c}{\arg\max}\ p(w_1^N | C) \tag{3}$$

If the word's probability is use formula (2) and combine the maximum likelihood algorithm from (Kneser, 1999) proposed to get optimal likelihood. It can represent by

$$ML(C,n) = -\sum_{C,C'} n(C,C')\ln n(C,C') + 2\sum_C n(C)\ln(C) \tag{4}$$

$$\hat{C} = \underset{c}{\arg\max}\ ML(C,\ n) \tag{5}$$

Where n(.) represent the probability in the training corpus. In this paper, we use the classification model to classify the words in the training corpus and build the codebook for query.

2.2 RNN-LSTM

In this section, the depth of learning architecture and why the use of recurrent neural network (RNN) to training model. And analyse the sentence structure with the concept of the parsing tree. Then replace hidden units to long-short term memory (LSTM) units in RNN hidden layer. RNN's horizontal nodes of the hidden layer are connected. So this structure suitable for train the length of different sentences with represent the contextual relationship.

The Figure 1 is the structure of RNN and it has three parts: input layer, hidden layer, and output layer. The hidden layer can have many layer in this structure so we assume the 30 layer in hidden layer to train the optimum parameters. And it shows that the training process is carried out by x_0 to x_t. So the cost function in the time t is

$$J = -y_t \log(n_t) - (1 - y_t)\log(1 - n_t) \tag{6}$$

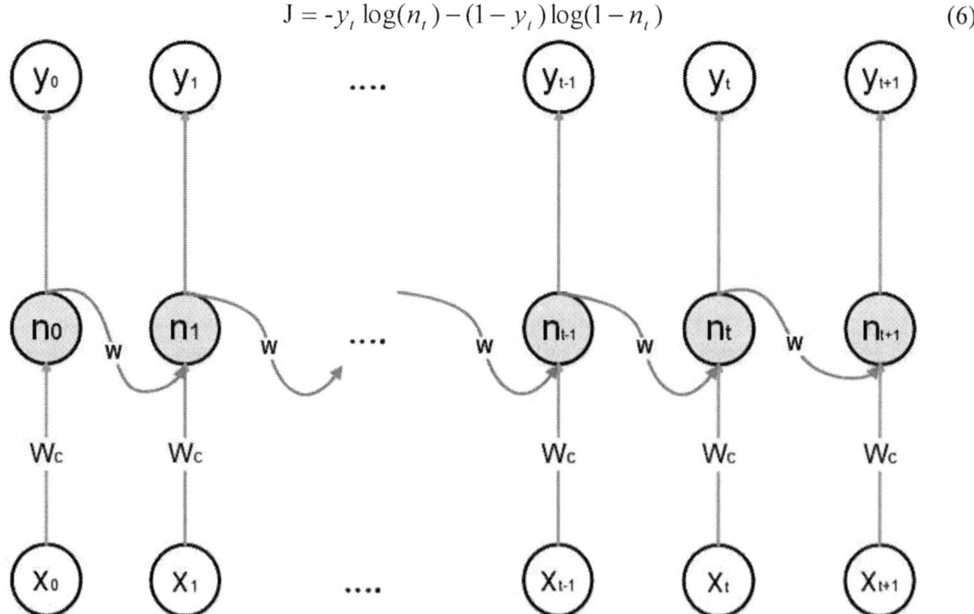

Figure 1: The sentence input in RNN-LSTM

The figure 2 shows the RNN traditional unit and LSTM unit in the hidden layer. In figure 2(a), we could find the unit input then using the sigmoid function to normalize. The sigmoid is shown $\sigma(x) = 1/1 + \exp(-x)$. So the hidden unit n_t is

$$n_t = \sigma(\omega_c x_t + \omega_p n_{t-1}) \tag{7}$$

Where ω_c and ω_p is the weights of the current input and previous output. And the output y_t is

$$y_t = \varphi(\omega_t x_t) \tag{8}$$

In figure 2(b), we could see the three gates in the LSTM unit: input gate, forget gate, and output gate. First, the input gate IG controlled whether cells in the input layer can enter. Second, the forget gate FG controlled whether cells in the hidden layer can enter and output to next node. Final, the output gate OG controlled the current cell output. Then the formula (9) ~ (11) represent IG, FG, OG:

$$IG = \sigma(\omega_i x_t + \omega_p x_{t\text{-}1}) \tag{9}$$

$$FG = \sigma(\omega_c x_t + \omega_p n_{t\text{-}1}) \tag{10}$$

$$OG = \sigma(\omega_o x_t + \omega_p x_{t\text{-}1}) \tag{11}$$

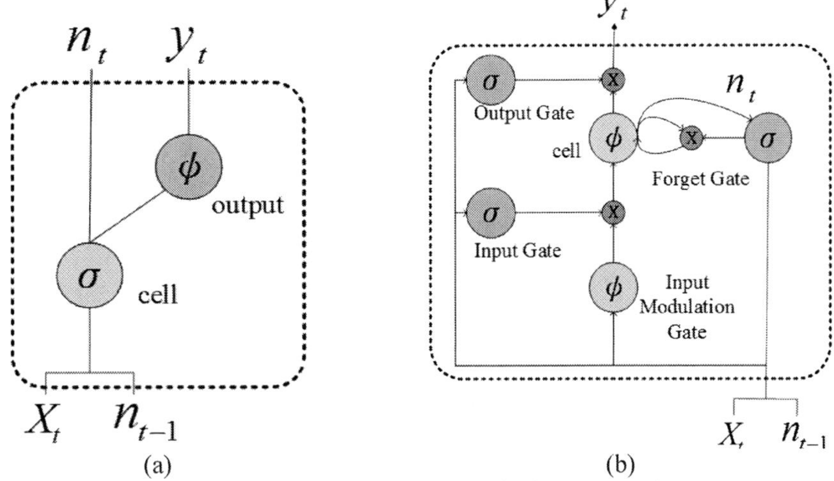

Figure 2: (a) RNN traditional unit (b) LSTM unit

Where we can using (9)~(11) to get the cell result in hidden layer and the output y_t are

$$cell = FG + IG \tanh(\omega_c x_t + \omega_p n_{t-1}) \tag{12}$$

$$y_t = OG \tanh(cell) \tag{13}$$

2.3 Error Pattern Model

In this paper, we focus on the English-speaking learners who are influenced by their native language and build the error pattern model. First, we need to analysis the error pattern in the sentence which using the parsing tree. We integrated the concept of RNN-LSTM to detect the error patterns. The bottom node of parsing tree is the input node in RNN-LSTM. The parent node is the LSTM node.

2.4 Testing Phase

First, read the test data and then word segmentation and part-of-speech tagging. Then the sentence according to the codebook to vector expression, and input the training model. We could get the probabilities from every types' model. After get the probabilities, we compare four errors with the correct probability to find all possible errors. And the output format is <sentence id, start position, end position, error type>. There is not only one error type in a sentence; it maybe has two or more errors. In addition to the system detected, we also adopted the error pattern model as the final output.

3 Experiment

In this section, we analyse the performance of the proposed architecture. First, we introduced the corpus in our training model and the evaluation of testing. Final, we showed the experiment result in training model and the result of NLP-TEA 3 competition.

3.1 Data and Evaluation Criterion

We used the three datasets from NLP-TEA 1(Yu, Liang-Chih et al, 2014) to NLP-TEA 3. There are two datasets: TOCFL corpus (Traditional Chinese) and HSK corpus (Simplified Chinese), the details are showed in the table 2.

Table 2: The Training Corpus

SOURCE / SENTENCES	Missing	Redundant	Selection	Disorder	Correct
TOCFL	6328	4122	5439	1621	18483
HSK	2810	2322	3834	896	10071

In this paper, we have two evaluation criterion: perplexity (Oparin et al, 2012) and confusion matrix. Perplexity is used to evaluate the performance of language model training from RNN-LSTM. Its format can represent:

$$PPL_n = \exp(-\frac{1}{I_n} \sum_{i \in I_n} \log p(w_i \mid w_1^{i-1})) \tag{14}$$

In addition, we used three parameters based on the confusion matrix to evaluate our system. They are precision, recall, and F1-score and can represented:

$$precision = \frac{tp}{tp + fp} \tag{15}$$

$$recall = \frac{tp}{tp + fn} \tag{16}$$

$$F1 - Score = 2 * \frac{precision * recall}{precision + recall} \tag{17}$$

3.2 Experiment Result

First, we wanted to find the optimal class to our language model in the training phase. Therefore, we used the perplexity to evaluate and showed the result in table 3. In the table, we could see the 30-class is in average better than other classes. And we use internal validation and proved the 30-class is better.

Table 3: The Perplexity of language model to each type

	30 class	35 class	40 class	45 class
Missing	**167.5952**	183.9607	226.9839	179.2754
Redundant	**178.8971**	217.7797	209.461	179.3632
Selection	188.2969	206.3802	242.5115	**156.4807**
Disorder	250.8187	282.3815	262.3684	**248.5769**
Correct	130.5262	121.8946	**85.0405**	101.9611

Therefore, we chose the 30-class to training and used to the test phase. Second, we showed the result from NLP-TEA 2016.

In detection level (see the Table 4), our recall is better than other teams. It means we can find more error rate in dataset. In addition, our F1-Score is the best in this level. It means our overall is superior to the others, although our precision is less than other teams.

In identification level (see the Table 5), it show who can find most error and error type is correct. In our method, we found that our recall is better than other teams. It means we find more correct error type than other teams, although our precision is less than other teams. Nevertheless, our F1-Score is better than NCTU+NTUT.

In Position level (Table 5), our method that looking for accurate location is not illustrious in this level. We consider the reasons are our correction is not enough standard.

Table 4, Table 5, and Table 6 are the performance with the NLP-TEA 2016 TOCFL dataset and compare the others team

Table 4: Detection level

	Accuracy	Precision	Recall	F1
NCYU	0.5218	0.5202	**0.9726**	**0.6779**
NCTU+NTUT	0.5442	**0.6593**	0.246	0.3583
CYUT	**0.5955**	0.6259	0.5419	0.5809

Table 5: Identification-level

	Accuracy	Precision	Recall	F1
NCYU	0.2328	0.2265	**0.4744**	0.3066
NCTU+NTUT	0.511	**0.4892**	0.1224	0.1958
CYUT	**0.5154**	0.46	0.3021	0.3647

Table 6: Position-level

	Accuracy	Precision	Recall	F1
NCYU	0.0231	0.0129	0.0195	0.0155
NCTU+NTUT	**0.4603**	**0.2542**	0.0483	0.0811
CYUT	0.3113	0.1461	0.1089	**0.1248**

In detection level (see the Table 7), our recall is better than other teams. It means we can find more error rate in dataset. Although our precision is less than other teams, our F1-Score is better than SKY's method.

In Identification level (see the Table 8), our recall is better than SKY's method that we can find more correct error type. However, our precision is less than other teams.

In Position level (see the Table 9), our method that looking for accurate location is not illustrious in this level. We consider the reasons are our correction is not enough standard.

Table 7, Table 8, and Table 9 are the performance with the NLP-TEA 2016 HSK dataset and compare the others team

Table 7: Detection level

	Accuracy	Precision	Recall	F1
NCYU	0.5042	0.4964	**0.9755**	0.658
HIT	0.637	0.6071	0.7296	**0.6628**
SKY	0.6579	**0.8746**	0.3505	0.5005

Table 8: Identification-level

	Accuracy	Precision	Recall	F1
NCYU	0.2687	0.2588	0.5263	0.347
HIT	0.5565	0.5002	**0.5447**	**0.5215**
SKY	0.6765	**0.8821**	0.2972	0.4446

Table 9: Position-level

	Accuracy	Precision	Recall	F1
NCYU	0.0312	0.0158	0.0217	0.0183
HIT	0.4475	0.3695	**0.3697**	0.3696
SKY	0.6376	0.7054	0.2217	0.3373

Conclusion

In this paper, we present a method using conditional random field model for predicting the grammatical error diagnosis for learning Chinese. In the grammatical error diagnosis, not only do we find a single error, but we can also find a sentence with multiple errors. After observe the experiment results, our method is acceptable in NLP-TEA 2016. We believe this system is feasible. This system is useful for a foreign who learn Chinese as a second language. Even the people who use Chinese as a first language might use the wrong grammars. There are some issues should be revise. First, finding the best way to solve the problem to find the precise location. Second, increase the ranking mechanism to find the optimal words to correct the sentence. In the future, we will pay attention to improve the precision and recall rates in this system. Let it can automatic correct the error if the people input the sentences.

Reference

Ye, J., Li, S., Hao, G., Li, S., Yang, Y., & Jin, C. (2011, October). The prefix and suffix query of Chinese word segmentation algorithm for maximum matching. In 2011 International Conference on Image Analysis and Signal Processing (pp. 74-77). IEEE.

Li, Z., Zhang, M., Che, W., Liu, T., & Chen, W. (2014). Joint Optimization for Chinese POS Tagging and Dependency Parsing. Audio, Speech, and Language Processing, IEEE/ACM Transactions on, 22(1), 274-286.

Ma, W. Y., & Chen, K. J. (2005). Design of CKIP Chinese word segmentation system. Chinese and Oriental Languages Information Processing Society, 14(3), 235-249.

X. Sun, & X. Nan, "Chinese base phrases chunking based on latent semi-CRF model," In International Conference on Natural Language Processing and Knowledge Engineering (NLP-KE), pp. 1-7, IEEE, August, 2010.

Z. Jinjin, & Z. Yangsen, "Research and implementation on a hybrid algorithm for Chinese automatic error-detecting," In International Conference on Artificial Intelligence and Computational Intelligence (AICI), vol. 1, pp. 413-417, IEEE, October, 2010.

B. Zhang, Y. Zhou, & Y. Mao, "Extracting opinion sentence by combination of SVM and syntactic templates," In International Conference on Natural Language Processing and Knowledge Engineering (NLP-KE), pp. 1-7, IEEE, August, 2010.

H. H. Feng, A. Saricaoglu, & E. Chukharev-Hudilainen, "Automated Error Detection for Developing Grammar Proficiency of ESL Learners," calico journal, vol. 33, no. 1, pp. 49, 2016.

C. H. Wu, C. H. Liu, M. Harris, & L. C. Yu, "Sentence correction incorporating relative position and parse template language models," IEEE Transactions on Audio, Speech, and Language Processing, vol. 18, no. 6, pp. 1170-1181, 2010.

L. H. Lee, L. P. Chang, K. C. Lee, Y. H. Tseng, & H. H. Chen, "Linguistic rules based Chinese error detection for second language learning," In Work-in-Progress Poster Proceedings of the 21st International Conference on Computers in Education (ICCE-13), pp. 27-29, November, 2013.

C. H. Yu, & H. H. Chen, "Detecting Word Ordering Errors in Chinese Sentences for Learning Chinese as a Foreign Language," In COLING, pp. 3003-3018, 2012.

Shuk-Man Cheng, Chi-Hsin Yu, and Hsin-Hsi Chen, "Chinese Word Ordering Errors Detection and Correction for Non-Native Chinese Language Learners," Proceedings of COLING'14, pp. 279-289, 2014.

Och, F. J. (1999, June). An efficient method for determining bilingual word classes. In Proceedings of the ninth conference on European chapter of the Association for Computational Linguistics (pp. 71-76). Association for Computational Linguistics.

Kneser, R., & Ney, H. (1993, September). Improved clustering techniques for class-based statistical language modelling. In Eurospeech (Vol. 93, pp. 973-76).

Agrawal, R., & Srikant, R. (1994, September). Fast algorithms for mining association rules. In Proc. 20th int. conf. very large data bases, VLDB (Vol. 1215, pp. 487-499).

Yu, Liang-Chih, Lung-Hao Lee, and Li-Ping Chang. 2014. Overview of grammatical error diagnosis for learning Chinese as a foreign language. In Proceedings of the 1st Workshop on Natural Language Processing Techniques for Educational Applications (NLP-TEA 2014). 42-47

Lee, Lung-Hao, Liang-Chih Yu, and Li-Ping Chang. 2015. Overview of the NLP-TEA 2015 shared task for Chinese grammatical error diagnosis. In Proceedings of the 2nd Workshop on Natural Language Processing Techniques for Educational Applications (NLP-TEA 2015). 1-6.

Oparin, I., Sundermeyer, M., Ney, H., & Gauvain, J. L. (2012, March). Performance analysis of neural networks in combination with n-gram language models. In 2012 IEEE International Conference on Acoustics, Speech and Signal Processing (ICASSP) (pp. 5005-5008). IEEE.

Bi-LSTM Neural Networks for Chinese Grammatical Error Diagnosis

Shen Huang and **Houfeng Wang**[*]
Key Laboratory of Computational Linguistics, Ministry of Education
School of Electronics Engineering and Computer Science, Peking University
Beijing, P.R.China, 100871
{huangshenno1,wanghf}@pku.edu.cn

Abstract

Grammatical Error Diagnosis for Chinese has always been a challenge for both foreign learners and NLP researchers, for the variousity of grammar and the flexibility of expression. In this paper, we present a model based on Bidirectional Long Short-Term Memory(Bi-LSTM) neural networks, which treats the task as a sequence labeling problem, so as to detect Chinese grammatical errors, to identify the error types and to locate the error positions. In the corpora of this year's shared task, there can be multiple errors in a single offset of a sentence, to address which, we simutaneously train three Bi-LSTM models sharing word embeddings which label Missing, Redundant and Selection errors respectively. We regard word ordering error as a special kind of word selection error which is longer during training phase, and then separate them by length during testing phase. In NLP-TEA 3 shared task for Chinese Grammatical Error Diagnosis(CGED), Our system achieved relatively high F1 for all the three levels in the traditional Chinese track and for the detection level in the Simpified Chinese track.

1 Introduction

As China plays a more and more important role of the world, learning Chinese as a foreign language is becoming a growing trend, which brings opportunities as well as challenges. Due to the variousity of grammar and the flexibility of expression, Chinese Grammatical Error Dignosis(CGED) poses a serious challenge to both foreign learners and NLP researchers. Unlike inflectional languages such as English which follows grammatical rules strictly(i.e. subject-verb agreement, strict tenses and voices), Chinese, as an isolated language, has no morphological changes. Various characters are arranged in a sentence to represent meanings as well as the tense and the voice. These features make it easy for beginners to make mistakes in speaking or writing. Thus it is necessary to build an automatic grammatical error detection system to help them learn Chinese better and faster.

In NLP-TEA 3 shared task for Chinese Grammatical Error Diagnosis(CGED), four types of errors are defined: 'M' for missing word error, 'R' for redundant errors, 'S' for word selection error and 'W' for word ordering error. Some typical examples of the errors are shown in Table 1. Different from the two previous editions for the CGED shared task, each input sentence contains at least one of defined error types. What's more, there can be multiple errors in a single offset of a sentence, which means we can no longer treat it a simple multi-class classification problem. As a result of that, we cannot simply rely on some existing error detection systems but can only seek for a new solution.

---

[*]Corresponding author

Proceedings of the 3rd Workshop on Natural Language Processing Techniques for Educational Applications,
pages 148–154, Osaka, Japan, December 12 2016.

Error Type	**Error Sentence**	**Correct Sentence**
M(Missing word)	我一完了考試，就回家。	我一考完了考試，就回家。
R(Redundant word)	爸爸是軍人，也很想他的太太。	爸爸是軍人，很想他的太太。
S(Selection error)	一般人不可以隨意出國外。	一般人不可以隨意出國。
W(Word ordering error)	它是讓我哭其中之一的電影。	它是讓我哭的電影其中之一。

Table 1: Some typical examples for grammatical errors in Chinese

In order to address the problem, we regard it as a sequence multi-labeling problem and split it into multiple sequence labeling problems which only label 0 or 1. To avoid feature engineering, for each error type except 'W', we trained a Bi-LSTM based neural network model, sharing word embeddings and POS tag embeddings. We treat the word ordering error as a special kind of word selection error. They are trained together and separated during the testing phase. Experiments show that together training is better than separate training. More details are described in the rest of the paper.

This paper is organized as follows: Section 2 briefly introduces some previous work in this area. Section 3 describes the Bi-LSTM neural network model we proposed for this task. Section 4 demonstrates the data analysis and some interesting findings. Section 5 shows the data analysis and the evaluation results. Section 6 concludes this paper and illustrates the future work.

2 Related Work

Grammatical error detection and correction has been studied with considerable efforts in the NLP community. Compared to Chinese, the language of English attracted more attention from the researchers, especially during the CoNLL2013 and 2014 shared task (Ng et al., 2013; Ng et al., 2014). However, different from English which has various language materials and annotated corpura, the grammatical error correction related resource for Chinese is far from enough. We are glad to see the shared tasks on CGED (Yu et al., 2014; Lee et al., 2015) in last two years.

There were some previous related work for Chinese grammatical error detection or correction. Wu et al. (2010) proposed two types of language models to detect the error types of word order, omission and redundant, corresponding to three of the types in the shared task. Experimental results showed syntactic features, web corpus features and perturbation features are useful for word ordering error detection (Yu and Chen, 2012). A set of handcrafted linguistic rules with syntactic information are used to detect errors occurred in Chinese sentences (Lee et al., 2013), which are shown to achieve good results. Lee et al. (2014) introduced a sentence level judgment system which integrated several predefined rules and N-gram based statistical features.

Our submission was an exploration to a neural network model in CGED which didn't need any feature selection efforts. As a model well known for its good maintainance of both preceding and succeeding information, Bi-LSTM came to be the first choice.

3 Bi-LSTM Neural Network based Model

We regard CGED task as a word-based sequence multi-labeling problem, by labeling each word zero or more tags from {**M, R, S, W**}. For some reason described in Section 4, we treat word ordering error as a special kind of word selection error, as a result of which, we need to deal with only three kinds of error types during the training phase.

As different error types are relatively independent from each other from a single word's perspective, we can train three sequence labeling models to judge whether this kind of error ocurrs in a certain position for each error type respectively. As shown in Figure 1, the architecture of a Bi-LSTM neural network model for CGED for a single error type can be characterized by the following three specialized layers: (1) Embedding layer (2) Encoding layer (3) Decoding layer.

As the errors are judged on words instead of characters, we first segment the input sentence into individual words using the CKIP Chinese Segmentation System[1] provided by Taiwan Academia Sinica and

---

[1] http://ckipsvr.iis.sinica.edu.tw/

149

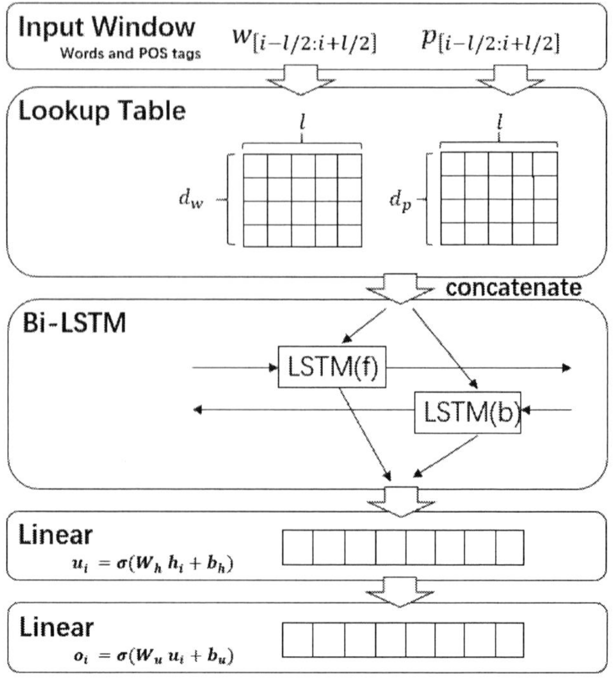

Figure 1: Architecture of Bi-LSTM neural network model for CGED for a single error type

get the simplified Part-of-Speech tag for each corresponding segmented word, which is our preprocess for the system. The words and POS tags are then embeded in the embedding layer.

The most common tagging approach is the window approach. The window approach assumes that the tag of a word largely depends on its neighboring words. For each word w_i in a given input sentence $w_{[1:n]}$, the context words $w_{[i-l/2:i+l/2]}$ and the context POS tags $p_{[i-l/2:i+l/2]}$ are chosen to be fed into the networks, where l is context window size and usually $l = 5$ or $l = 7$. Here we set $l = 7$ in our experiments. The words and POS tags exceeding the sentence boundaries are mapped to two special symbols, "<BOS>" and "<EOS>", representing *Beginning of a Sentence* and *End of a Sentence* respectively. And the out-of-character-set words will be replaced with a symbol "<UNK>" which represents *Unknown*.

Given a word set V of size $|V|$, the embedding layer will map each word $w \in V$ into a d_w-dimensional embedding space as $Embed_w(w) \in \mathbb{R}^{d_w}$ by a lookup table $\mathbf{M_w} \in \mathbb{R}^{d_w \times |V|}$. In the same way, we can map each POS tag $p \in P$ into a d_p-dimensional embedding space as $Embed_p(p) \in \mathbb{R}^{d_p}$ by a lookup table $\mathbf{M_p} \in \mathbb{R}^{d_p \times |P|}$, where P is the POS tag set whose size if $|P|$. The embeddings of the context words $w_{[i-l/2:i+l/2]}$ and The embeddings of the context POS tags $p_{[i-l/2:i+l/2]}$ are then concatenated into a single vector $x_i \in \mathbb{R}^{H_1}$, where $H_1 = l \times (d_w + d_p)$. Then this vector x_i is fed into the encoding layer.

The encoding layer is a Bi-LSTM layer followed by a full-connection layer, which can be simply expressed by the following:

$$h_i = BiLSTM_\theta(x_i) \tag{1}$$

$$u_i = \sigma(W_h h_i + b_h) \tag{2}$$

where θ is the inner parameters of the Bi-LSTM layer and σ is the logistc sigmoid function.

The Long Short-Term Memory cell(Hochreiter and Schmidhuber, 1997) is a special kind of the RNN cell which replaces the hidden layer updates by purpose-built memory cells. As a result, they can utilize long range dependencies and realize the function just like memory. A single LSTM cell is illustrates in Figure 2.

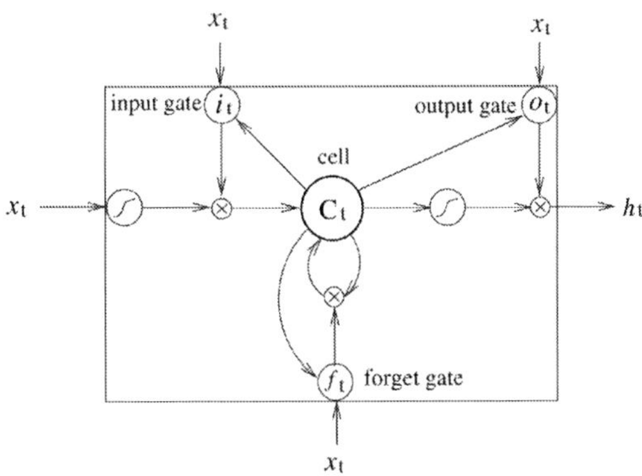

Figure 2: A LSTM cell

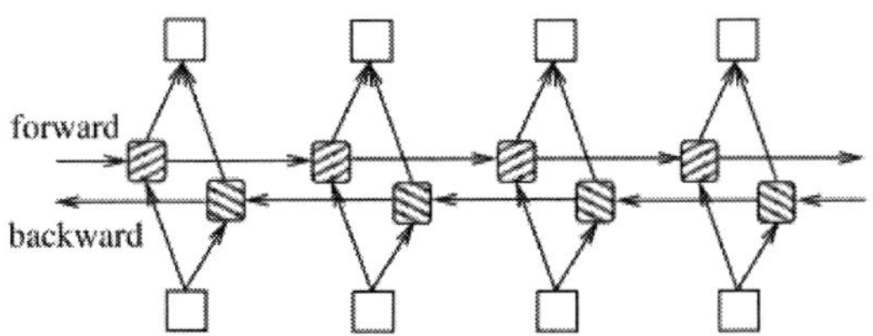

Figure 3: The structure of a Bi-LSTM layer

The LSTM cell is implemented as the following:

$$
\begin{aligned}
i_t &= \sigma(W_{xi}x_t + W_{hi}h_{t-1} + W_{ci}C_{t-1} + b_i) \\
f_t &= \sigma(W_{xf}x_t + W_{hf}h_{t-1} + W_{cf}C_{t-1} + b_f) \\
c_t &= f_t c_{t-1} + i_t tanh(W_{xc}x_t + W_{hc}h_{t-1} + b_c) \\
o_t &= \sigma(W_{xo}x_t + W_{ho}h_{t-1} + W_{co}C_t + b_o) \\
h_t &= o_t tanh(c_t)
\end{aligned}
\tag{3}
$$

where σ is the logistic sigmoid function, and i, f, o and c are the input gate, forget gate, output gate and the cell, all of which are the same size as the hidden output h. The subscripts of the weight matrix describe the meaning as the name suggests. For instance, W_{xi} is the input gate weight matrix for input x.

A single LSTM forward layer can only utilize the previous information, which is not enough for grammatical error detection, where sometimes the error can only be inferred from the following words. Therefore, a bidirectional LSTM layer is proposed (Graves, 2013), which can be regarded as a simple stack of a forward LSTM layer and a backward LSTM layer. The structure of a Bi-LSTM layer is shown in Figure 3.

The output of the encoding layer is then fed into a decoding layer, which is another full-connection layer with 1 output size. The output layer is implemented as the following:

$$
o_i = \sigma(W_u u_i + b_u) \tag{4}
$$

$$
f(w_i) = o_i > 0.5 \tag{5}
$$

where σ is still the logistic sigmoid function and $f(w_i)$ indicates whether there is an error of this type on the word w_i or not.

As there are many more non-errors than errors in a sentence from a word perspective, the model always tends to label 0, which means correct for the word, if without any balance. Thus we assigned weights for the loss function, in order to rebalance the correct and incorrect labels. The loss function without regularization is calculated as follows:

$$loss = y_i * -log(f(w_i)) * W_{pos} + (1 - y_i) * -log(1 - f(w_i)) \tag{6}$$

where W_{pos} is the coefficient on the positive examples.

We can decide if there are errors from {**M**, **R**, **S&W**} through the model described above. Then we separate the 'S' and 'W' tags according to the successive word length of the error during the testing phase. If the length is 1 the error is a word selection error, otherwise it is a word ordering error if the length is greater than 1.

4   Data Preparation and Analysis

4.1   Datasets

In the TOCFL track, the data we used for training includes training and testing data from NLP-TEA 1 (Yu et al., 2014), training data from NLP-TEA 2 (Lee et al., 2015), and training data from NLP-TEA 3. We used the testing data from NLP-TEA 2 for validation.

In the HSK track, despite of the training set provided by the organizers, we simplified the training data from TOCFL track as supplements. However, the simplified data from TOCFL track seem to be no use to the evaluation results.

Table 2 shows the statistics of our training sets.

	NLP-TEA 1	NLP-TEA 2	NLP-TEA 3 TOCFL	NLP-TEA 3 HSK
number of sentences	7389	2205	10693	10072
total errors	7389	2205	24831	24784
Missing words	2932	620	9078	6619
Redundant words	2399	430	4472	5532
Word selection errors	1087	849	9897	10942
Word ordering errors	971	306	1384	1691

Table 2: Statistics of training sets

Due to the limitation of time and resource, the word embeddings and POS tag embeddings we used are all random initialized.

4.2   Word selection error and word ordering error

Take NLP-TEA 3 TOCFL dataset as an example, as there are 1384 word ordering errors in the training set, which takes only 5.5% in all 24831 errors. It is difficult to train this kind of errors without rebalance or resampling. Thus we came up with a new method, by treating word ordering error as a special kind of word selection error. Suprisingly, in the training set, after word segmentation, most word selection errors are within one word and all word ordering errors are longer than one word, we can easily separate them by the successive error length.

5   Experiments

In the formal run of NLP-TEA 3 CGED shared task, there are 5 teams submitting 15 runs in total for the TOCFL dataset track and 8 teams submitting 21 runs in total for the HSK dataset track. Our system achieved relatively high F1 for all the three levels in the traditional Chinese track and for the detection level in the Simpified Chinese track. Since our evaluation results for HSK dataset are not good, here we only display the evaluation results compared with the average values for TOCFL dataset. The performance evaluations in detection level, identification level and position level are shown as follows:

	False Positive Rate	Accuracy	Precision	Recall	F1
PKU-Run1	0.2284	0.521	**0.5739**	0.2871	0.3828
PKU-Run2	**0.7205**	0.5258	0.5292	**0.7556**	**0.6224**
PKU-Run3	0.525	0.5349	0.5467	0.5907	0.5678
Average of all 15 runs	0.4812	**0.5442**	0.5701	0.5680	0.5456

Table 3: Performance evaluation in detection level

	Accuracy	Precision	Recall	F1
PKU-Run1	**0.4575**	**0.3418**	0.1173	0.1747
PKU-Run2	0.3242	0.2792	**0.3712**	**0.3187**
PKU-Run3	0.3705	0.2729	0.2192	0.2431
Average of all 15 runs	0.3912	0.3265	0.2732	0.2716

Table 4: Performance evaluation in identification level

6 Conclusion and Future work

In this paper, we present a Bi-LSTM neural network based model to predict the possible grammatical errors for Chinese, which needs no feature engineering and provides reasonable evaluation results in the NLP-TEA 3 CGED shared task. Different from most previous work, we didn't use any external corpus or rule-based inductions. Due to the limitation of time and resource, we didn't test our system under various experiment environments. More neural network architectures and more features can be tried. There is still space for further development.

Acknowledgements

We gratefully acknowledge the kind cooperation of Prof. Houfeng Wang in guidance of this work.

References

Ng, Hwee Tou and Wu, Siew Mei and Wu, Yuanbin and Hadiwinoto, Christian and Tetreault, Joel 2013. *The CoNLL-2013 Shared Task on Grammatical Error Correction*. Proceedings of the Seventeenth Conference on Computational Natural Language Learning: Shared Task. Sofia, Bulgaria, 1-12.

Ng, Hwee Tou and Wu, Siew Mei and Briscoe, Ted and Hadiwinoto, Christian and Susanto, Raymond Hendy and Bryant, Christopher 2014. *The CoNLL-2014 Shared Task on Grammatical Error Correction*. In Proceedings of the Eighteenth Conference on Computational Natural Language Learning: Shared Task. Baltimore, Maryland, 1-14.

Chung-Hsien Wu, Chao-Hong Liu, Harris Matthew and Liang-Chih Yu. 2010. *Sentence correction incorporating relative position and parse template language models*. IEEE Transactions on Audio, Speech, and Language Processing, 18(6), 1170-1181.

Chi-Hsin Yu and Hsin-Hsi Chen. 2012. *Detecting word ordering errors in Chinese sentences for learning Chinese as a foreign language*. In Proceedings of the 24th International Conference on Computational Linguistics (COLING'12), 3003-3017

	Accuracy	Precision	Recall	F1
PKU-Run1	**0.3844**	**0.0996**	0.0263	0.0416
PKU-Run2	0.1381	0.068	**0.0824**	**0.0745**
PKU-Run3	0.2331	0.0872	0.0651	**0.0745**
Average of all 15 runs	0.2402	0.0846	0.0460	0.0597

Table 5: Performance evaluation in position level

Lung-Hao LEE, Li-Ping CHANG, Kuei-Ching LEE, Yuen-Hsien TSENG and Hsin-Hsi CHEN 2013. *Linguistic Rules Based Chinese Error Detection for Second Language Learning*. In Proceedings of the 21st International Conference on Computers in Education (ICCE'13), 27-29,

Lung-Hao Lee, Liang-Chih Yu, Kuei-Ching Lee, Yuen-Hsien Tseng, Li-Ping Chang, Hsin-Hsi Chen 2014. *Sentence Judgment System For Grammatical Error Detection*. In Proceedings of the 25th International Conference on Computational Linguistics (COLING'14), 67-70

S. Hochreiter and J. Schmidhuber. 1997. *Long short-term memory*. Neural Computation, 9(8):1735-1780.

A. Graves, A. Mohamed, and G. Hinton. 2013. *Speech Recognition with Deep Recurrent Neural Networks*. arxiv.

Liang-Chih Yu, Lung-Hao Lee, and Li-Ping Chang 2014 *Overview of Grammatical Error Diagnosis for Learning Chinese as a Foreign Language*. Proceedings of the 1st Workshop on Natural Language Processing Techniques for Educational Applications, 42-47.

Lee, Lung-Hao and Yu, Liang-Chih and Chang, Li-Ping 2015 *Overview of the NLP-TEA 2015 Shared Task for Chinese Grammatical Error Diagnosis*. Proceedings of the 2nd Workshop on Natural Language Processing Techniques for Educational Applications, 1-6.

Chinese Grammatical Error Diagnosis Using Single Word Embedding

Jinnan Yang, Bo Peng, Jin Wang, Jixian Zhang, Xuejie Zhang
School of Information Science and Engineering
Yunnan University
Kunming, P.R. China
Contact: xjzhang@ynu.edu.cn

Abstract

Automatic grammatical error detection for Chinese has been a big challenge for NLP researchers. Due to the formal and strict grammar rules in Chinese, it is hard for foreign students to master Chinese. A computer-assisted learning tool which can automatically detect and correct Chinese grammatical errors is necessary for those foreign students. Some of the previous works have sought to identify Chinese grammatical errors using template- and learning-based methods. In contrast, this study introduced convolutional neural network (CNN) and long-short term memory (LSTM) for the shared task of Chinese Grammatical Error Diagnosis (CGED). Different from traditional word-based embedding, single word embedding was used as input of CNN and LSTM. The proposed single word embedding can capture both semantic and syntactic information to detect those four type grammatical error. In experimental evaluation, the recall and f1-score of our submitted results Run1 of the TOCFL testing data ranked the fourth place in all submissions in detection-level.

1   Introduction

The growing global influence of China has prompted a surge of interest in learning Chinese as a foreign language (CFL) (Yu et al., 2014). The number of commonly used Chinese characters are about 2000, but there are a large number of corresponding vocabulary. In this way, some same words may have different meanings because of different contexts and moods. This has caused difficulties for foreigners to learn Chinese. However, while many learning tools of computer-assisted have been developed for students of English as a Foreign Language (EFL), there is relatively little support for CFL learners. Especially, these tools cannot automatically detect and correct Chinese grammatical errors. For example, although Microsoft Word has been integrated with robust English spelling and grammar checking for many years, the tools for Chinese are still primitive (Yu et al. 2014). The aim of Chinese Grammatical Error Diagnosis (CGED) shared task is to develop computer-assisted tools to help detect four types of grammatical errors in the written Chinese, including missing word (**M**), redundant word (**R**), word ordering error (**W**) and word selection error (**S**).

The shared task is divided into three levels, including detection-, identification- and position-level. Detection-level task can be considered as a binary classification of a given sentence, i.e., correct or incorrect should be exactly as same as the gold standard. All error types will be treated as incorrect. Identification-level task could be considered as a multi-label classification task. In addition to the correct instance, all error types should be clearly identified. This level identified the error types for the wrong sentence. Besides identifying the error types, the position-level also judges the positions of erroneous range. Some of the previous works have sought to identify Chinese grammatical errors using template- and learning-based methods.

Wu et al. (2010) proposed a combination of relative position and analytic template language model to detect Chinese errors written by American learners. Yu and Chen et al. (2012) used simplified Chinese corpus to study word ordering errors (W) in Chinese and proposed syntactic features, external corpus features and perturbation features for W detection. Cheng et al. (2014) detected and corrected word

Proceedings of the 3rd Workshop on Natural Language Processing Techniques for Educational Applications,
pages 155–161, Osaka, Japan, December 12 2016.

ordering errors by using conditional random field (CRF) (Lafferty, 2010) and support vector machine (SVM) together with frequency learning from a large *n*-gram corpus. Zampieri et al. (2014) used frequent *n*-grams and news corpus as a reference corpus to detect errors in the written by CFL learners. Chen et al. (2015) used conditional random fields based on word attributes and grammar rules to detect Chinese syntax errors. However, there are several limitations of the existing methods, these methods on the one hand only consider part of the grammar rules, and the other hand only consider the order of the word or relationship. They didn't consider the semantic relationship between words and the flexible expression and irregular grammar in Chinese.

In this paper, we introduced convolutional neural network (CNN) and long-short term memory (LSTM) for the task of Chinese Grammatical Error Diagnosis. In contrast of traditional word-based embedding (Mikolov et al., 2013), single word embedding was used as input of CNN and LSTM, which is similar to character-level embedding in English. The proposed single word embedding can capture both semantic and syntactic information to detect those four type grammatical error. Then, the single word vectors were used to establish the sentence representation for detection-level and identification-level tasks. In position-level, this paper also used single word embedding as input feature to train a multi-class support vector machine (SVM) to identify the error type of each word. The recall and f1-score of the submitted results Run1 of the TOCFL testing data ranked the fourth place in all submissions in detection-level. In identification-level, the recall score also ranked in the fourth place.

The remainder of this paper is organized as follows. Section 2 describes the learning method that used for Chinese grammatical error diagnosis. Section 3 shows the experimental results. Conclusions are drawn in section 4.

2   Feature Selection and Error Detection

The procedure for using single word embedding for each level grammatical error detection is described as follow. Given a large Chinese corpus, single word embedding are first trained through word2vec and fastText tools. Then, the obtained single word representations were input to CNN, LSTM and SVM for the mentioned three level diagnosis tasks. The following sub-sections explain the details of single word embedding and the CNN, LSTM and SVM models implementation.

2.1   Single Word Embedding

We use fastText (Bojanowski et al. 2016) and word2vec (Mikolov et al. 2013) toolkits to train single word embedding on Chinese Wikipedia corpus.

Word2vec is a set of related models used to generate word embedding. These models are two-layer neural networks that are trained to reconstruct linguistic contexts of words. Word2vec toolkit takes large corpus text as its input and produces a high-dimensional null and each unique word in the corpus is assigned the corresponding vector in that space. In Chinese, a sentence may be generated to ambiguities segmentation, leading to different embedding results.

- Example 1 "乒乓球拍卖完了"
    1. "乒乓球/拍卖/完了" (The auction of table tennis is over.)
    2. "乒乓球拍/卖/完了" (The paddles of table tennis are sold out.)
- Example 2 "在这种环境下工作是太可怕了"
    1. "在/这种/环境/下工/是/太/可怕/了"
    2. "在/这种/环境/下/工作/是/太/可怕/了"(Working in such environment is horrible)

For Example 1, these two forms of segmentation are both syntactically and semantically. Even if the manual division of the sentences in Example 1 will be ambiguous. In this case, we can get correct sentence segmentation when taking the context into consideration. However, for example 2, only the second sentence segmentation is correct. Therefore, the segmented for Chinese word may produce ambiguities segmentation.

In addition, there are 696,326 words in the Chinese corpus of Chinese Wikipedia corpus. There are some uncertainties in the Chinese word segmentation, and it cannot completely cover the vocabulary of the training set. Such as "开一个" (open a), "上海"(Shanghai) did not appear directly in the corpus, but

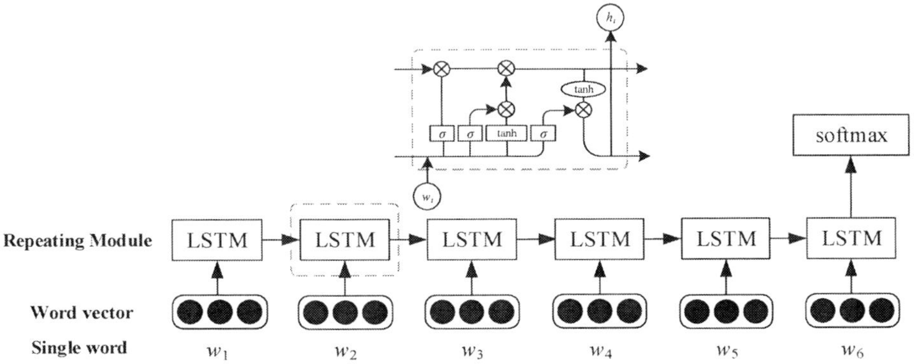

Fig. 1.   The sequential LSTM model

these was split or integrated with other words, such as "开" (open), "一个"(one), "上海医院"(Shanghai Hospital).

The grammatical rules of Chinese are different from English. The spaces between English words can be used to segment a sentence. In English, the method of word embedding acquires the characteristics of the sentence, but this method is not suitable for the Chinese sentences. Based on the characteristics of Chinese, a Chinese sentence without considering the context of the case can only use single word to segment the sentence. By using the single word embedding method, all Chinese sentences in corpus can be segmented into single words. Meanwhile, the single word embedding can be obtained by using either word2vec or fastText. Finally, we can get the text features of Chinese sentences.

All words in the document are converted into vectors by lookup table, and the results are classified by linear classifier. As same as word2vec, fastText used n-grams to train embedding. The word vector will be derived from the n-grams. This improvement enhances the effect of the model on morphology, which means that the distance of similar words will be smaller. Thus, two different single word embedding are obtained by these two models.

2.2   Grammatical Error Diagnosis Models

Taking the single word embedding as input, the convolutional neural network (CNN) (LeCun, et al., 1990), the recursive neural network (RNN) (Ronald, et al.,1989), and the long-short term memory (LSTM) (Hochreiter et al., 1997) were introduced to classify the sentences. The sequential LSTM model was shown in Fig. 1.

The obtained single word vectors (word2vec and fastText) were fed to deep neural network models, such as CNN, RNN and LSTM. To tune the best performance, 5-folder cross-validation was applied. For unbalanced problem of positive and negative training samples in identification- and position-level, e.g. the number of train samples within **R** label is smaller L times than other classes, we divided the more abundant class into L distinct clusters. Then L classifiers were trained, where each classifier is trained on only one of the distinct clusters, but on all of the data from the rare class. That is, the data from rare class was used in the training of all L classifier. Finally, the averaging output of L models was considered as the final classification result. The cross-validation results of different models are shown in Table 1. Then, the support vector machine model is applied to find the error location in each error sentence.

This paper completes the Shared Task requirement in the following three steps.

- **Determining the correctness of a sentence (detection-level).** The method adopted in this paper is to segment each sentence in the training set by every single word, e.g. "你/开/一/个/庆/祝/会/的/时/候/我/不/能/会/参/加/是/因/为/我/在/外/国/做/工/作", so that each single word in a sentence corresponds to a single word vector. By using word2vec and fastText toolkit, we train single word embedding in the Chinese Wikipedia corpus. Then, we trained neural network models, such as CNN, RNN, and LSTM, to distinguish correct sentences from wrong sentences in training set. The trained models were then used to categorize each sentence in testing set into correct or wrong class.

- **Judge the four types of errors (identification-level).** The method in this level can be considered

157

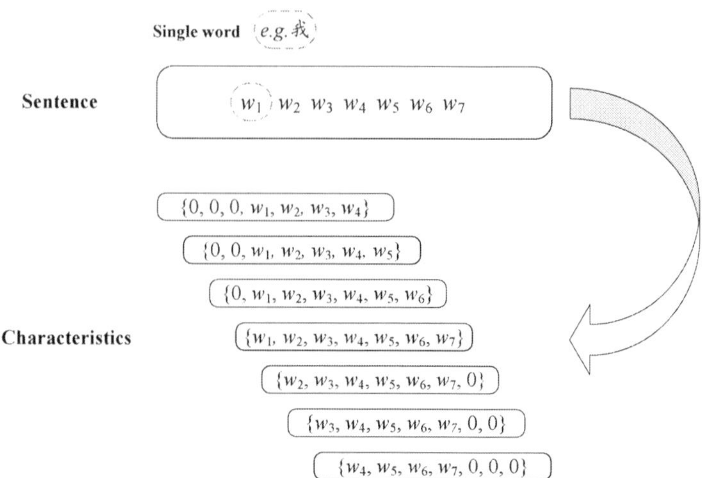

Fig. 2. Single word embedding feature extraction for SVM

as a multi-label problem, which is something different with the detect-level. Each samples in this level contain only one or more error labels. Therefore, *one-vs-all* strategy were applied. It consists in fitting one classifier per class. For each classifier, the class (**R**, **M**, **S** and **W**) is fitted against all the other classes. One advantage of this approach is its interpretability. Since each class is represented by one classifier only, it is possible to categorize each sentence with more than one labels. For each error type, we trained a neural network model, such as CNN, RNN and LSTM to determine the error type in testing dataset.

- **Locate the wrong position (position-level).** In this level, support vector machine (SVM) (Christopher, 1998) was used as classifier to locate the wrong position. As shown in Fig. 2, a single word with its context can be considered as a training sample, so that the word appeared in the middle can be judged whether the location is wrong or not. The size of slide window was set to 7 in our experiment. Then, single word embedding of 7 words were concatenated as a 1-D vector, and then fed into SVM. Since each position is assigned to one and only one label. That is, position can be either **R**, **M**, **S**, **W** or correct, but not both at the same time. Therefore, we trained a multi-class SVM to determine the error type of each word in testing sentence.

3　Experimental Results

3.1　Dataset

Two Chinese corpus are given in this shared task: TOCFL and HSK. TOCFL is the traditional Chinese training set, and HSK is the simplified Chinese training set. Apart from the difference between traditional and simplified, there is almost no difference of grammar and expression. In the training set, each id corresponds to two sentences, including a wrong sentence, and a corrected formation of this sentence. The error type, as well as the location of the error range are also provided. Each wrong sentence may have one error type, or more. These data sets were preprocessed to extract the single words, the error types and the error positions. The TOCFL corpus consists of 10693 training texts and 3528 testing texts. Similarly, the HSK corpus consists of 10072 training texts and 3011 testing texts.

3.2　Implement Details

As previously mentioned, the proposed method includes neural network and single word embedding. The two parts may have their own parameters for optimization. We use fastText and word2vec toolkits to pre-train the word vector on Chinese Wikipedia corpus.

The Chinese Wikipedia corpus is segmented by single words, we set the embedding dimension of each single word to 300. In this way, we can get 300-dimensional feature vectors for all single words in the corpus. There are 2563 single words in TOCFL training set and 2583 single words in HSK training set.

Method	Detection Level			
	Accuracy	Precision	Recall	F1
LSTM	0.3769	0.3813	0.4088	0.3923
RNN	0.4081	0.4053	0.4017	0.4013
CNN	0.480	0.486	0.660	0.560

Table 1: The cross-validation results of different methods using word2vec embedding

Results	False Positive Rate	
	TOCFL	HSK
Run1	0.6289	0.5608
Run2	0.5931	0.7122
Run3	0.3382	0.271
Average	0.5201	0.5147

Table 2: The false positive rate results of different methods.

The two training sets have already contained the most commonly used 2000 Chinese characters. Therefore, this method can obtain the text feature for each sentence in the training set.

We submitted three results for both TOCFL and HSK testing sets, the first submission (Run1) used the word representation trained by word2vec and classified by LSTM. The second submission (Run2) also used the LSTM to do the classification with word representation trained by fastText. Besides, the word representation of the third submission (Run3) was trained by word2vec and classified by CNN. The results can be obtained in three steps in Section 2.2. The sharing task has five evaluation indicators, they are false positive rate, accuracy (**Acc**), precision (**Pr**), recall (**Re**) and f1-score (**F1**).

3.3 Experimental Results

A total of 15 teams participated in the sharing of tasks, nine teams submitted the results of the operation in the final. For TOCFL training set, only 5 teams submitted the results of the operation. For the HSK test set, 9 teams have submitted the results of the operation. We have submitted three runs of results for both test sets. Table 2 shows the false positive rate. Table 3, Table 4 and Table 5 show the formal run results in detection-level, identification-level, and position-level respectively.

As shown in Table 2, the accuracy of the following two levels is reduced due to the high false positives. The results of Run1 and Run2 shows that the performance of word vectors trained by word2vec are better than that by fastText, since the fastText model makes the distance between similar words smaller. For example, the meaning of "trading" (贸易) is close to the "transaction" (交易) in Chinese, and word2vec can reflect this relationship. However, in the fastText, "trading" (贸易) is even more closer to "trade laws" (贸易法), which makes word vector by fastText cannot accurately reflect the sentence characteristics. Similarly, by comparing the results of Run1 and Run2, we can find that the classification performance of LSTM is better than CNN. Although CNN considers the local characteristics of the sentence, which makes it easy to high degree of similarity between the two sentences, LSTM can consider the relationship between the contexts of the sentence, which is particularly important in Chinese. Therefore, LSTM can capture the logical relationship between the sentences, e.g. *cause* and *contrast* relationship, etc.

Since the number of sentence in different label (correct and incorrect) is unbalanced, which will impact the result in all detection-, identification- and position-level. Hence, the wrong sentences are the majority in testing date. If all the sentences in the testing set are classified as wrong, the learning model will get high accuracy, precision, recall and f1-score, and even a higher false positive rate.

4 Conclusion and Future work

Since the grammar rules in Chinese are formal and strict, it is hard for foreign students to master Chinese. A computer-assisted learning tool which can automatically detect and correct Chinese grammatical errors is necessary for those foreign students. In this paper, neural network models, such as convolutional neural network (CNN) and long-short term memory (LSTM), were introduced for the task of Chinese

Results	Detection-Level							
	TOCFL				HSK			
	Acc	Pr	Re	F1	Acc	Pr	Re	F1
Run1	0.5420	0.5444	0.7014	0.6130	0.5191	0.5069	0.6026	0.5506
Run2	0.5026	0.5167	0.5918	0.5517	0.4949	0.4886	0.7113	0.5793
Run3	0.4847	0.503	0.3195	0.3908	0.5058	0.4902	0.2724	0.3502
Average	0.5098	0.5214	0.5376	0.5185	0.5066	0.4952	0.5288	0.4934

Table 3: Performance evaluation in detection-level.

Results	Identification-Level							
	TOCFL				HSK			
	Acc	Pr	Re	F1	Acc	Pr	Re	F1
Run1	0.2211	0.1588	0.3196	0.2824	0.3485	0.2800	0.3879	0.3252
Run2	0.2322	0.1675	0.3136	0.2122	0.3092	0.2681	0.4565	0.3378
Run3	0.4023	0.2810	0.1359	0.2184	0.4306	0.2886	0.1448	0.1928
Average	0.2852	0.2024	0.2564	0.2377	0.3628	0.2789	0.3297	0.2853

Table 4: Performance evaluation in identification-level

Results	Position-Level							
	TOCFL				HSK			
	Acc	Pr	Re	F1	Acc	Pr	Re	F1
Run1	0.0886	0.0002	0.0002	0.0002	0.0654	0.0024	0.0062	0.0035
Run2	0.0991	0	0	null	0.0373	0.0022	0.007	0.0034
Run3	0.2797	0.0012	0.0005	0.0007	0.2701	0.001	0.0005	0.0007
Average	0.1558	0.0005	0.0005	0.0005	0.1243	0.0019	0.0046	0.0025

Table 5: Performance evaluation in position-level

Grammatical Error Diagnosis. For capturing both semantic and syntactic information, we proposed the use of single word embedding as input of CNN and LSTM, which is similar to character-level embedding in English. In system evaluation, the recall and f1-score of our submitted results Run1 of the TOCFL testing data ranked the fourth place in all submissions in detection-level.

By participating in this shared task for CGED, we have made a preliminary study in this area. The future work will focus on improving the accuracy of our models.

Acknowledgements

This work is supported by The Natural Science Foundation of Yunnan Province (Nos. 2013FB010).

References

Piotr Bojanowski, Edouard Grave, Armand Joulin, and Tomas Mikolov. 2016. Enriching Word Vectors with Subword Information. *arXiv*: 1607.04606v1 [cs.CL].

Christopher J. C. Burges. 1998. A tutorial on support vector machines for pattern recognition. *Data Mining and Knowledge Discovery*, 2(2):121-167

Po-Lin Chen, Shih-Hung Wu, Liang-Pu Chen, and Ping-Che Yang. 2015. Chinese Grammatical Error Diagnosis by Conditional Random Fields. In *Proceedings of The 2nd Workshop on Natural Language Processing Techniques for Educational Applications*, pp: 7–14.

Shuk-Man Cheng, Chi-Hsin Yu, and Hsin-Hsi Chen. 2014. Chinese Word Ordering Errors Detection and Correction for Non-Native Chinese Language Learners. In *Proceedings of The 25th International Conference on Computational Linguistics: Technical Papers*, pp: 279-289

Sepp Hochreiter, and Jürgen Schmidhuber. 1997. Long Short-Term Memory. *Neural Computation*, 9(8):1735–1780.

John Lafferty, Andrew McCallum, and Fernando Pereira. 2010. Conditional Random Fields: Probabilistic Models for Segmenting and Labeling Sequence Data. In *Proceedings of the Eighteenth International Conference on Machine Learning*, pp: 282-289

Bernhard E. LeCun, John Stewart Denker, Donnie Henderson, Richard E. Howard, Wayne E. Hubbard, and Lawrence D. Jackel. 1990. Handwritten digit recognition with a backpropagation network. *Advances in Neural Information Processing Systems*, pp: 396-404

Tomas Mikolov, Ilya Sutskever, Kai Chen, Greg S. Corrado, and Jeff Dean. 2013. Distributed representations of words and phrases and their compositionality. *Advances in neural information processing systems*, pp: 3111-3119.

Chung Hsien Wu, Chao Hong Liu, Matthew Harris, and Liang Chih Yu. 2010. Sentence Correction Incorporating Relative Position and Parse Template Language Models. *IEEE Transactions on Audio, Speech and Language Processing*, 18(6):1170–1181.

Ronald J. Williams, and David Zipser. A Learning Algorithm for Continually Running Fully Recurrent Neural Networks. 1989. *Neural Computation*,1(2):270-280

Shih-Hung Wu, and Hsien-You Hsieh. 2012. Sentence Parsing with Double Sequential Labeling in Traditional Chinese Parsing Task. In *Proceedings of the Second CIPS-SIGHAN Joint Conference on Chinese Language Processing*, pp: 222–230.

Liang-Chih Yu, Lung-Hao Lee, and Li-Ping Chang. 2014. Overview of Grammatical Error Diagnosis for Learning Chinese as a Foreign Language. In *Proceedings of the 1st Workshop on Natural Language Processing Techniques for Educational Applications*, pp:42–47.

Chi-Hsin Yu, and Hsin-Hsi Chen. 2012. Detecting Word Usage Errors in Chinese Sentences f-or Learning Chinese as a Foreign Language. In *Proceedings of The 24th International Conference on Computational Linguistics: Technical Papers*, pp:3003–3018.

Marcos Zampieri, and Liling Tan. 2014. Grammatical Error Detection with Limited Training Data: The Case of Chinese. In *Proceedings of the 1st Workshop on Natural Language Processing Techniques for Educational Applications*, pp: 69-74.

Author Index